# TOWARD A THEORY OF PEACE

# TOWARD A THEORY OF PEACE

The Role of Moral Beliefs

**Randall Caroline Watson Forsberg**

Edited and with an introduction by
Matthew Evangelista and
Neta C. Crawford

CORNELL GLOBAL PERSPECTIVES

MARIO EINAUDI CENTER FOR INTERNATIONAL STUDIES

CORNELL UNIVERSITY PRESS    ITHACA AND LONDON

First published 2019 by Cornell University Press

Library of Congress Cataloging-in-Publication Data

Names: Forsberg, Randall, author. | Evangelista, Matthew, 1958– editor. | Crawford,
    Neta, editor.
Title: Toward a theory of peace : the role of moral beliefs / Randall Caroline Watson
    Forsberg; edited and with an introduction by Matthew Evangelista and Neta
    C. Crawford.
Description: Ithaca: Cornell University Press, 2019. | "An edited version of the
    thesis by the same name submitted by Randall Caroline Watson Forsberg in
    May 1997 to the Department of Political Science at the Massachusetts Institute
    of Technology, where she was studying for her Ph. D."—Editors' note. | Includes
    bibliographical references and index.
Identifiers: LCCN 2019025199 (print) | LCCN 2019025200 (ebook) | ISBN
    9781501744358 (paperback) | ISBN 9781501744365 (pdf) | ISBN 9781501744372
    (epub)
Subjects: LCSH: Peace—Moral and ethical aspects. | War—Moral and ethical
    aspects. | Violence—Moral and ethical aspects.
Classification: LCC JZ5581 .F67 2019 (print) | LCC JZ5581 (ebook) | DDC
    172/.42—dc23
LC record available at https://Iccn.loc.gov/2019025199
LC ebook record available at https://Iccn.loc.gov/2019025200

# Contents

# Editors' Note

*Toward a Theory of Peace: The Role of Moral Beliefs* is an edited version of the thesis by the same name submitted by Randall Caroline Watson Forsberg in May 1997 to the Department of Political Science at the Massachusetts Institute of Technology, where she was studying for her PhD. The thesis was certified in June 1997 by Forsberg's thesis supervisor, Joshua Cohen, then professor of philosophy and political science, and accepted by Barry R. Posen, professor of political science and then chairman of the Graduate Program Committee. The current volume was copyedited, corrected, and reformatted for publication by Sandra J. Kisner, administrative assistant at the Judith Reppy Institute for Peace and Conflict Studies at Cornell University, under our oversight. It is published with permission from MIT.

We are grateful above all to Sandra for her meticulous work; to Hirokazu Miyazaki, former director of the Mario Einaudi Center for International Studies, for endorsing publication of this book in the Cornell Global Perspectives series and providing funding for the workshop associated with its release; to Dean Smith, director of Cornell University Press, and his staff for their support; to Jonathan Miller of the Einaudi Center for his editorial and production help, including with the online version of this book; to Jill Breithbart for the cover design; to Elaine Scott for administrative support at the Reppy Institute; to Judith Reppy for general wisdom, for editorial advice, and for preserving the archive of the Institute for Defense and Disarmament Studies, upon which we drew for our introductory essay; to Agnieszka Nimark for preparing the archive for deposit at Cornell University Library; and to Evan Earle, Cornell University Archivist, for welcoming the collection and making it available to the public.

Matthew Evangelista, Professor of Government,
Cornell University
Neta C. Crawford, Professor of Political Science,
Boston University

## Editors' Introduction: Randall Forsberg and the Path to Peace

For Randy Forsberg, information and argument were power—the power to open and change minds, the power to build a movement.[1] Randy is probably best known as a founder of the Nuclear Weapons Freeze Campaign, a movement that acknowledged Americans' fear of nuclear holocaust and articulated the hope that nuclear war could be averted in the 1980s. The Nuclear Freeze movement inspired one of the largest political demonstrations in US history, when up to a million participants rallied in Central Park, New York on 12 June 1982. This was part of a larger political movement that pushed Ronald Reagan's administration toward the negotiating table with the Soviet Union, where he collaborated with Mikhail Gorbachev to end the Cold War.[2] The June 12th demonstration was only surpassed in early 2003 when millions of Americans protested the imminent US attack on Iraq. Randy protested that war as well.

Randy epitomized the practice of Habermasian discourse ethics well before Jürgen Habermas theorized it.[3] She believed in evidence, the force of the better argument, the use of reason in the search for truth, and the essential constitutive role in democracy of the commitment to nonviolence. But these were more than theoretical commitments. In a life cut short by cancer at the age of 64, Randy pursued a range of interconnected activities in trying to bring about a world without war. She was an analyst of military data, engaging public speaker, prolific writer, director of a research institute, mentor to young researchers and aspiring activists, write-in candidate for the United States Senate, and university professor. In her scholarship and activism, Randy practiced a form of argumentation that engaged the other respectfully and always used her brilliance honestly, without deception, meeting the claims of the other with better arguments. Randy was persistent, precise, and clear. And she had a more than slight streak of perfectionism, which is, in part, why her carefully crafted dissertation took so long to complete and why she intended to revise it before turning it into a book (as she explains in her preface).

In 1997, Randy completed her manuscript, *Toward a Theory of Peace: The Role of Moral Beliefs* and submitted it as her dissertation, earning her PhD in Political Science from the Massachusetts Institute of Technology. *Toward a Theory of Peace* is an ambitious attempt to identify the conditions under which the institution of war could be brought to an end. It draws on an extensive program of research into the phenomenon that Randy called "socially sanctioned violence" and focuses on the role of moral beliefs. Aside from excerpts published in an anthology in 2005, just two years before Randy's death, the work has not been available until the publication of this book, although the year after her dissertation was finished Randy published a related, short pamphlet, *Abolishing War*, in the form of a dialogue with Elise Boulding, a sociologist and founder of the field of Peace and Conflict Studies.[4]

In our view, this volume marks an important contribution to the literature on social change and especially to the goal of eradicating the scourge of war. It should be of interest not only to scholars but also to activists and ordinary citizens concerned about mass violence, who should welcome this thoughtful, erudite, and well-grounded analysis. Randy viewed the dissertation as part of a larger project, where she would develop a "theory of the conditions under which world peace might be established and maintained."[5] Because Randy's theory of peace was so closely linked to her military analysis and disarmament activism, we devote much of this introduction to summarizing her career, before turning to an overview of the book. The larger theory of peace is implicit in the outline of Randy's career and the way Randy worked.

## Early Life and Career

Randall Caroline Watson was born in Huntsville, Alabama in July 1943, which at the time of her birth was rife with racism overlaid by a veneer of Southern charm epitomized by the stately mansions that can still be seen in the center of town. Early on, her father Douglass Watson, the well-known Shakespearian and television actor, taught Randy to memorize her speeches. Randy usually spoke without notes and clearly loved the English language. She was educated at Barnard College in New York City, where she majored in English. In her first job after graduating college in 1965, Randy taught English, and throughout her life she was a fierce editor. Randy was always careful to say what she meant and generally meant what she said.

Randy married Gunnar Forsberg in 1967 and moved to Sweden where she began working at the Stockholm International Peace Research Institute, SIPRI, founded by the Swedish government the year before. SIPRI's mandate was to contribute to "the understanding of the preconditions for a stable peace and for peaceful solutions of international conflicts."[6] In many respects that mandate became Randy's life's work. SIPRI tended to focus on data collection and specialized studies of particular topics related to armament and disarmament, and it soon began and continues today to publish an authoritative yearbook, tracking the trends in various military forces and spending. SIPRI's guiding principle seems to be that understanding the nature of the problem of armament and war in all its empirical detail is a precondition for doing something about it. That is a principle in which Randy also strongly believed.

Randy soon became an English language editor at SIPRI and then one of its key researchers. Although she worked on many projects there, two stand out—both as bodies of work of which she was particularly proud, and as representative of themes that she would pursue in her subsequent scholarship and activism.

In the early 1970s Randy prepared a multicountry study of military research and development, the first attempt to assess the overall size of the worldwide military R&D effort.[7] What were her main conclusions? She found that most of the spending on new weapons development was concentrated in some twenty advanced industrial countries, with the efforts of the United States and the Soviet Union dominating the rest. And even though those two countries were engaged in a costly *nuclear* arms race, the bulk of their spending on research and development—and on procurement as well—was focused on conventional, non-nuclear military forces. In studying the patterns of spending for military R&D and procurement, Randy began to recognize that most of the conventional forces of the United States and the Soviet Union were not oriented toward defense of their national territories, but toward military intervention in foreign countries—and that was their main use. The Soviet Union had launched ground invasions of members of its own alliance, the Warsaw Treaty Organization, in 1956 and 1968, and in December 1979 it invaded neighboring Afghanistan. The United States, with a powerful fleet of aircraft carrier battle groups and tens of thousands of marines, had launched major interventions in Korea and Vietnam, many smaller invasions in Latin America, and was poised to intervene in the Persian Gulf.

The second major project that Randy pursued at SIPRI was an inventory of the world's long-range, so-called strategic nuclear weapons, with the emphasis again on the nuclear superpowers, the United States and the Soviet Union. Randy's detailed assessment of the strategic nuclear balance became the world standard, and she continued to prepare the data for publication in the SIPRI yearbooks even after she returned to the United States. What were the main insights she drew from her analysis of the nuclear arms race? First, that it had both a quantitative and qualitative dimension, and second, that the qualitative advances in technology were making weapons more accurate and, when targeted against the weapons of the other side, potentially destabilizing in a crisis. Randy was far from alone in recognizing these features of the nuclear arms race, but she was uniquely thorough in establishing the empirical foundations for her analysis.

At this point, the mid-1970s, one might not have recognized Randy Forsberg as a peace activist. She seemed more like what is sometimes called, with a bit of a pejorative tone, a "bean counter," engaged in estimating the numbers, character-istics, and costs of weapons. There is no doubt, however, that Randy was already at this stage committed to the long-term goal of abolishing war, and she was beginning to develop a theory of social change that would underpin her efforts at achieving that goal.

Randy thought she could use more training and more credentials. In 1974 she returned to the United States and enrolled in the graduate program in Defense Studies in the Department of Political Science at the Massachusetts Institute of Technology. At the time it was the preeminent program for training people to go on to civilian careers in the US Defense Department. Randy's work as a peace activist began at the same time, and thereafter her activist and intellectual careers were closely intertwined. Her application to MIT captures the beginning of what became a forty year intellectual and activist journey: "In 1967. . . I took what I thought would be a temporary job at SIPRI. In half a year of typing manu-scripts, I was exposed to information on international relations and on the arms race which put an end to my previous tendency to avoid politics and ignore social problems."[8]

Randy's understanding of war was very much informed by her empirical research, while her prescription of what to do about it stemmed from an evolv-ing theory of social change which was, itself, influenced by her own experience as a scholar-activist. That theory of change finds its fullest exposition in this book, but her application to MIT shows that her views were already forming:

> I think that the use of physical force is a primitive and undesirable form of behavior, on the social as well as the individual level. I favor more equitable distribution of wealth, power and opportunity, both within and among nations, but I think that the use of violence in this context is also undesirable and unnecessary. I believe that constructive social change, including the rejection of the use of military force as a political tool and a greater generosity of the haves toward the have-nots, can be brought about by education, information and persuasion, over a very long time span.[9]

A couple of years after Randy started her graduate studies at MIT, Fred Kaplan, who later became a prominent journalist of military affairs for the *Boston Globe*, the *New York Times*, and then the online magazine *Slate*, enrolled in the PhD pro-gram. Kaplan once described the Defense Studies approach as "entirely analytical; we learned how to do the calculations of nuclear deterrence, force requirements, that sort of thing. It offered very little in the way of history or political analy-sis."[10] Nevertheless, Randy and Fred, who shared a critical orientation toward mainstream US military policy, both valued the training they received at MIT.

Randy would later recommend the program to student activists who wanted to pursue further study of military policy, including Brian Burgoon, Neta Crawford, Natalie Goldring, Laura Reed, and Taylor Seybolt (who later worked at SIPRI).

One of the more influential teachers in the MIT program was William Kaufmann, a consultant to the US Department of Defense. Kaufmann was the embodiment of US military policy. He was known to have been the main (anonymous) author of more than a decade of the annual reports of the Secretary of Defense, through both Democratic and Republican administrations. Kaufmann taught two key courses in the MIT program, one on conventional forces and one on nuclear forces.

Randy (and also Fred Kaplan) came to see the analytical separation between these two types of forces as a hindrance to understanding how US military policy actually worked. It was during this period of the second half of the 1970s that Randy developed a crucial insight into the dynamics of the arms race: that nuclear disarmament would be impossible without dramatic reductions in conventional forces, and in particular their use for long-range military intervention. Partly this insight reflected explicit US policy: In the (however unlikely) event of a possible Soviet military invasion of Europe, the United States vowed to use nuclear weapons to defend its allies in the North Atlantic Treaty Organization if conventional forces proved inadequate. But the United States did not limit consideration of use of nuclear weapons to Europe alone; it also retained the ability to escalate to nuclear use in the course of a conventional war in Asia or the Middle East, in part as a threat to keep other powers from trying to hinder US military action in those places, and in pursuit of a policy of "extended deterrence" in defense of allies.[11] Randy came to see that a campaign to limit or eliminate nuclear weapons would fail if it did not acknowledge how closely such weapons were intertwined with overall US military strategy.

## From Scholarship to Activism

Randy's critique of nuclear weapons and foreign military intervention brought together two major strands of the US peace movement in the wake of the Vietnam War: the nuclear disarmers and the anti-interventionists. In 1979, in a book called *The Price of Defense*, she sought to bring those strands together in a practical proposal for the reform of US military forces. The book was the product of collaborative work with colleagues in the Cambridge area, known as the Boston Study Group. In a manner that was typical of Randy's inclusive style, the Boston Study Group comprised a range of participants, including Philip Morrison, the Manhattan project physicist and MIT professor, and Paul Walker, a fellow MIT graduate, US Army veteran, and Harvard research scholar, who had worked at the US Arms Control and Disarmament Agency.[12] *The Price of Defense* reflected the training Randy had received in William Kaufmann's courses and could be read as an alternative to the annual report of the Secretary of Defense. It went carefully through each component of the US military system in order to propose major restructuring and reductions with the goal of creating a nonintervention-ary conventional force and a minimum nuclear deterrent.[13] The book's language was accessible, and its authors argued that its proposals were "not only safe, but actually safer than the present policy, even if there is no corresponding change in other countries."[14]

In some respects, the timing of the book could not have been better. The Vietnam War had finally ended just a few years earlier, and Americans were tired of foreign military adventures. Negotiations with the Soviet Union on strategic nuclear forces had been underway for about a decade, but they had not made much progress. There was considerable sentiment in favor of more dramatic reductions, as Jimmy Carter had promised in his successful campaign in the 1976 presidential elections. In another respect, however, the timing of the book's publication could not have been worse. Nineteen seventy nine was the year the Soviet Union invaded Afghanistan and the nuclear arms race took an upturn, as the United States proposed to deploy new nuclear weapons in Europe to counter a category of Soviet weapons that were not covered by the ongoing strategic arms talks. Carter lost the presidential election of 1980 in favor of Ronald Reagan, and instead of winding down the arms race, the United States embarked on a major acceleration of military spending and a more confrontational approach to the Soviet Union. The Boston Study Group project, nevertheless, had an important influence on how Randy envisioned a step-by-step approach to disarmament and it shaped her agenda for change in the coming years.[15]

In 1980, Randy took a leave of absence from MIT to focus on the Institute for Defense and Disarmament Studies (IDDS), a small think tank she founded in 1979. IDDS was located in two small rooms in a modest office building on Harvard Street in Brookline, Massachusetts, just a few blocks away from her apartment on Longwood Avenue. Randy's vision for IDDS was to "study the nature and purposes of military forces in order to identify obstacles to and opportunities for disarmament." Its projects would "develop new types of information and analysis which are critical to the success of efforts for arms control and disarmament."[16] The Institute's staff quickly grew, and so did the burden of managing the payroll and other expenses. But as hard as it was to keep a new institution afloat, the Institute embodied Randy's theory of change: create a popular movement around the goal of confining the military to defense, cultivate new interest in new approaches to defense and disarmament among experts and journalists, and develop new curricula to help people understand military policy and prepare them to make informed choices about it.

The Reagan administration's military programs, combined with its seemingly cavalier attitude about the consequences of nuclear war, provided an opportunity for reviving the peace movement. Randy had already been circulating among peace organizations a proposal known as "A Call to Halt the Nuclear Arms Race." It became the basis for the Nuclear Freeze campaign. This was another example of Randy's scholarship influencing her activism. From her work at SIPRI on the nuclear arms race, Randy knew that the most dynamic element of the competition was the development, testing, and deployment of new systems—activities that easily outpaced the slow course of negotiations. From her study of US military policy, she recognized that the most dangerous weapons were the ones intended to create a so-called war-fighting capability—nuclear weapons that would pose a credible threat of a nuclear first strike escalation during a conventional armed conflict, and would thus make it more likely that a conventional war could trigger a nuclear holocaust.

# The Nuclear Freeze

The bilateral US-Soviet Nuclear Freeze was an attractive intermediate goal. It was an alternative to the demand for complete and immediate nuclear disarmament, but more ambitious than a campaign to stop a particular new nuclear weapons system, such as the MX missile or the B-1 bomber.

Many of the ordinary people who came to support the Nuclear Freeze were mainly concerned about the nuclear threat, not the link between conventional and nuclear forces—and there were a lot of those people. At the height of the movement in the early 1980s, there were some 5000 local Freeze organizations, with tens of thousands of members. The Freeze initiative appeared on ballots in 25 states, winning in all but one, and in 59 out of 62 municipal referenda.[17] And, more importantly, people saw for themselves what they could do to promote an end to the arms race.

Randy set up a clearinghouse of information about the Freeze and antinuclear activism at the Institute and instructed Mark Niedergang, who was then the staff person for the Freeze campaign, not to tell activists seeking advice what they *should* do to promote the Freeze, but to help them discover for themselves what they *could* do. By providing a clearinghouse for information about Freeze activism all over the country, Randy thus nourished rather than guided the movement. The flexibility allowed activists to tailor their efforts to local conditions and also to keep their sense of agency and enthusiasm high. No one had to give up a preexisting agenda to join the effort, and the Freeze campaign thus grew from its roots in Massachusetts to a nationwide campaign with links to many older antinuclear organizations.

The Freeze took off politically in the early 1980s, not only as a ballot initiative but also as proposed legislation in the US Congress. The Freeze became a factor in the 1984 presidential campaign, with most of the Democratic presidential contenders, including the party's nominee, Walter Mondale, supporting it.[18]

Randy thought it a mistake to politicize the Freeze at such an early stage of the public campaign, to make it captive to Washington politics before a more substantial grassroots effort had developed. In retrospect, she seems to have been right. No sooner had the Freeze turned into a legislative proposal than certain politicians attacked it as an extreme position and sought to introduce more "moderate" and "responsible" alternatives. Several senators, including Albert Gore of Tennessee, endorsed the oxymoronic "build down" proposal. Instead of stopping nuclear production and deployment, as the Freeze required, the United States would build a new mobile, single-warhead missile system—the so-called Midgetman—that would ostensibly be more stabilizing. The problem was that the Reagan administration was happy to build the new system, as long as it could continue to build the destabilizing multiple-warhead MX missiles that it really wanted—and the "build down" proponents acquiesced to that deal. The efforts by Gore and others to invent a centrist position between the "extreme" of the Freeze proposal and the grandiose plans of the Reagan administration only made matters worse, as Randy had feared.

Many of the Freeze activists understandably felt a sense of urgency, and politicians were eager to capitalize on that. But Randy's emerging vision of successful social change was a long-term one. Such change required a more fundamental transformation in people's moral beliefs about war and weapons than could be carried out by a single campaign, even one as popular as the Freeze. The transformation had to be sufficiently robust not to be undermined by the usual machinations of opportunistic politicians.

## Long-Term Vision

An important component of Randy's disarmament strategy entailed efforts to engage not only the general public but also the community of experts on military affairs. She maintained good relations with mainstream defense intellectuals at Harvard and MIT and in Washington. In the case of the Nuclear Freeze, for example, it was not only a matter of mobilizing popular support. Randy also won over establishment figures, such as John Steinbruner of the Brookings

Institution, who endorsed the bilateral Freeze.[19] She was particularly pleased at the opportunity to present the case for the Freeze in the magazine *Scientific American* in November 1982.[20] With an international readership of specialists and laypeople, *Scientific American* maintained a tradition of presenting technical expositions of key issues related to the arms race, such as nuclear testing and antiballistic missile systems, often combined with innovative proposals for arms control. By inviting Randy to lay out the case for the Freeze, the editors were welcoming her into the ranks of such luminaries as Hans Bethe and Richard Garwin, and recognizing her credibility before both popular and expert audiences. In January 1983, arms control experts, politicians (including then members of Congress Al Gore and Ed Markey) and leaders of antinuclear organizations, attended a meeting at the American Academy of Arts and Sciences to discuss the Freeze proposal in technical, strategic and political terms.[21] Randy received further acknowledgment when she was granted a MacArthur Foundation "Genius" award in 1983; funds from the award, distributed over five years, allowed her to continue to expand IDDS.

Despite the popular success of the Freeze, Randy's scholarly analysis told her that nuclear disarmament would not be possible without dealing with conventional forces as well. In 1984 she published an article in the *World Policy Journal* called "The Freeze and Beyond: Confining the Military to Defense as a Route to Disarmament."[22] This was the most thorough statement to date of her understanding of how disarmament and an end to war could come about. At the same time, she was developing a theory of social change—the subject of this book—that informed her understanding of how the Freeze campaign and subsequent disarmament efforts should proceed. Randy wrote the first draft of what became the "Confining the Military to Defense" article in the summer of 1979, more than four years before the final version was published. The draft, much longer than the published version, is available in the IDDS archives at Cornell University, and it contains an important passage illuminating her thinking:

> [A] difficult aspect of disarmament is that it cannot be accomplished in a single stroke, like the US withdrawal from Vietnam or the ending of above-ground nuclear tests. In this respect, its closest precedent is not the recent victories of the peace movement, but the nineteenth-century abolition of slavery. The abolition of slavery was an equally profound social change, which ended an ancient, pernicious, widespread institution after more than a century of protest and opposition.[23]

There are two features of Randy's theory of social change which are worth highlighting, as they were evident already at this early stage: First, such change takes a long time; it is measured in centuries rather than years. Second, change must be pursued in a step-by-step approach, with each step accomplishing something valuable in itself and encouraging further action.

Contrary to what some of its critics on the left implied, the Freeze was never intended to be permanent. This was also a point of misunderstanding with the European Nuclear Disarmament (END) movement, which had emerged as a major force in the early 1980s. Many European activists favored the denuclearization of Western Europe, by unilateral means if necessary, and viewed the Freeze proposal as a barrier to that goal. Randy worked hard to maintain good relations with European peace activists, and it helped that one of the leaders of END, Mary Kaldor, was a fellow SIPRI veteran.[24] Randy's European contacts extended beyond the antinuclear movement into the community of experts working on issues of conventional-force restructuring and the theory of nonoffensive defense—approaches quite compatible with Randy's way of thinking.[25]

For Randy and its other supporters, the Freeze did not reflect a satisfaction with the status quo. It was a necessary first step toward reductions, and it was appealing in its simplicity. As Randy put it in her 1984 article, "Because people despair of ever achieving the ultimate goal of a disarmed peace, it would be extremely difficult to motivate widespread popular efforts for change without a set of powerfully attractive intermediate goals, each desirable in its own right."[26]

As a by-product of her work on the Freeze and her efforts to promote it, Randy helped develop an extensive network of national and international contacts. With strategic foresight and typical generosity, she devoted some of the resources of her Institute to provide a "public good"—a series of publications listing all of the known peace-related activist groups and educational programs in the United States and beyond so that activists and students could form networks and become more effective in the promotion of peace.[27]

## The Peace Movement and the End of the Cold War

Highlighting the long-term objectives of Randy's disarmament strategy is not to understate the influence of the Freeze campaign and other activist efforts. Consider the demonstration that attracted between 750 thousand and a million people to Central Park in June 1982 in support of the Freeze, where Randy gave one of her most moving and effective public speeches. A strong argument can be made that the antinuclear sentiment that brought people to such events produced an impact on public policy. It probably reinforced the antinuclear tendencies in Ronald Reagan himself. It likely made him more open to the initiatives that the reformist Soviet leader Mikhail Gorbachev offered in the area of nuclear disarmament just a few years later. As far as Gorbachev is concerned, we have good evidence that he was emboldened by the antinuclear movement in the United States and Western Europe to pursue the unilateral initiatives of restraint that captured the public imagination and convinced the NATO alliance to bring the Cold War to a peaceful end.[28]

Randy was especially active during the 1980s in promoting some of the ideas that the reformist Soviet leadership later came to champion. Take, for example, the unilateral reductions and defensive restructuring of Soviet conventional forces that Gorbachev announced at the United Nations in December 1988. They bear a strong family resemblance to Randy's proposal for "confining the military to defense" and the kindred work that she pursued with European colleagues. She had been promoting nonoffensive defense for years in her visits to the USSR and in her meetings with Soviet colleagues elsewhere, and the idea eventually found a sympathetic ear in Gorbachev and his civilian advisers on military affairs. And, as Randy predicted, the dramatic reduction in the conventional military threat from the East paved the way for reductions in the nuclear threat.[29]

The end of the East-West arms race suggested that Randy's scholarship over the course of two decades had produced the correct diagnosis of the problem and her activism helped to fill the prescription.

## Preparing for a World without War

Randy was never sanguine about the risk of war, even as she recognized a secular decline in violence over time. In the 1990s, despite the peaceful end of the Cold War, she was still concerned about the persistence of war as an institution. She responded in three ways that by now should sound familiar: 1) with data collection or "bean counting;" 2) with activism; and 3) with scholarship. Running her Institute on a shoestring budget, she and her staff of mainly student interns continued collecting data on weapons and negotiations, as she published the monthly *Arms Control Reporter* and compiled the World Weapon Database.

Randy also launched a major multinational research project, called the International Fighter Study, which resulted in 1994 in the book, *The Arms Production Dilemma*.[30] In some ways related to the earlier IDDS World Weapon Database project that had produced books on Soviet missiles and Soviet military aircraft,[31] this initiative betrayed broader ambitions. As Randy wrote in the forward to the 1994 volume, in the wake of the end of the Cold War arms race "the industrial nations' shared security interests have created an unprecedented opportunity to develop security policies based on cooperation instead of competition or confrontation." Yet she recognized "serious obstacles to East-West and North-South cooperation in military security matters," including the perceived need to maintain a military-industrial base in the event of deterioration of the international environment and the pressure on governments to continue military production in the interest of employment.[32] Randy anticipated that even if countries could maintain adequate force levels without manufacturing new weapons, they might continue to do so to promote arms exports. By recruiting national experts to assess the state of the military aircraft industry in the main arms-producing countries—Russia, the United States, Germany, Italy, the United Kingdom, and Sweden—Randy sought to provide the basis for realistic assessments of military requirements and to make the case that arms exports were not necessary for national defense during a period of unprecedented world peace. Moreover, given the likelihood that exporting arms to the remaining few conflict zones would only exacerbate the risk of war, she favored a moratorium on weapons exports, coupled with her by now familiar emphasis on "nonoffensive defense" and limits on offensive capabilities. As she concluded the study:

> The linked issues concerning reductions on forces and limits on production and trade may be more complex than the topics of other arms control agendas. But the stakes are much higher. Over a decade, several hundred billion dollars could be saved and new global and regional arms races could be prevented. The role of force in the international system could be transformed.[33]

As we know, history took a different course. In the wake of the terrorist attacks of September 2001, the United States launched two major wars, in Afghanistan and Iraq. The costs of those wars, documented in the Costs of War project (https://watson.brown.edu/costsofwar/), continue to mount beyond what anyone could have imagined for a world in which armed conflict between major military powers seems a thing of the past. Randy did not live long enough to lead a revived peace movement to oppose the excesses of wars launched in the name of counterterrorism. She did, however, along with Saul Mendlovitz and Jonathan Dean, develop a proposal called Global Action to Prevent War, an attempt to create a worldwide coalition to abolish war and armed conflict.[34] And in 2002, in her first and only effort to seek electoral office, she ran a write-in campaign against Massachusetts Senator John Kerry in protest against his refusal to oppose the George W. Bush administration's rush to war against Iraq on specious grounds. Without her name even on the ballot, she garnered over 22,000 votes.[35]

## Toward a Theory of Peace

*Toward a Theory of Peace* is divided into two parts, the first making an argument about how to achieve the abolition of war, which Randy theorizes as an instance of a larger class of human behavior, "socially sanctioned large group violence." Randy argues that there were only a few other historical practices that fit in that category: human sacrifice, ritual cannibalism, slavery, and lethal corporal punishment for violations of law or custom. The second part of the book, the analysis of socially sanctioned violence, delves into a vast secondary literature in psychology, anthropology, archeology, and history, among other disciplines. Contrary to theories that posit an innate human tendency toward aggression, she argues that most people manifest a moral revulsion against violence—a sentiment that social institutions reinforce. All of these practices, some in existence for hundreds or thousands of years, were eventually eradicated, albeit over long periods of time, as moral beliefs about them changed. Cannibalism, human sacrifice, and slavery became abhorrent and unthinkable. Randy observed that

> The key aspect of these precedents for the abolition of war is the character of the moral rejection of the practice that developed not before but *after* each was abandoned, and the role of that much deeper moral rejection in preventing a future recurrence. In every case, once a previously sanctioned form of violence was banned, people developed an abhorrence of the practice that was deeply internalized, virtually universally shared, and constantly reinforced by a myriad of cultural signals.[36]

These examples are both precedents for the abolition of forms of socially sanctioned violence and illustrations of the process by which war might end, through the institutionalization of moral beliefs. Thus, Randy shows that there is nothing inherent or inevitable about war as a social practice: it is possible to limit and eventually end war. By examining past instances of socially sanctioned violence—practices treated as normal and even beneficial at the time—Randy highlighted the role of changing moral beliefs in eventually stigmatizing those behaviors and rendering them unacceptable.

While Part II could arguably stand on its own as an important contribution to our understanding of socially sanctioned violence in human history, most readers are likely more interested in Part I, which contains Randy's analysis of ending war. Here Randy explains how she thinks norms change, how war as a form of socially sanctioned violence could end, and why, by comparison to other approaches, her approach is likely to be more effective in promoting the end of war.

There are really two interrelated claims in her argument about ending war. The first is that for war to end, predominant moral beliefs about the use of force must change so that the only form of socially sanctioned violence is for defense against aggression. She calls this a democratic commitment to nonviolence, which she shortens to defensive nonviolence.[37] The second claim is about the process of change in moral beliefs over the long run, which she describes as interactive, involving feedback loops.[38] These are rich, sophisticated arguments, and we can only highlight some of the main points in this introduction.

Randy's arguments about the content of the moral beliefs about socially sanctioned violence are innovative. For Randy, the key shift that would enable humans to abolish war would be the adoption of the view that the only justified and just use of deadly force is for self-defense. For international war to end, a democratic commitment to nonviolence must be held by a number of core states. The commitment to defense will then gradually spread across the globe.

One of the most interesting aspects of this discussion is how it links democracy and nonviolence. Specifically, Randy argues, democratic states have already internalized and institutionalized the commitment to nonviolence, except in self-defense. In a sense, Randy offers a new definition of democracy, one that emphasizes its core commitment. Randy argues, "democratic institutions have prompted, or paralleled, a growing rejection of violence as a means of achieving political or economic ends within and between nations."[39] Democracy and a commitment to nonviolence are thus mutually constitutive:

> [C]ommitment to nonviolence lies at the core of democratic institutions. . . . Commitment to nonviolence protects and preserves freedom of expression and other civil liberties by precluding intimidation or coercion by violence or the threat of violence. Within democracies, wherever nonviolence is not the rule . . . other democratic rights and freedoms are lost or severely compromised.[40]

By tracing the link between democratic norms and nonviolence, Randy shows how a commitment to nonviolence is essential for democratic institutions *and* international peace.

But not all states have to be democratic for the transition to peace to occur. With enough states committed to democracy, they can individually, or through an international institution such the United Nations, react to aggressive states, demonstrating that offensive war will not be tolerated. This is in line with Randy's view that the world need not be perfect for war to end. Randy theorized that the core of a moral rejection of war would come in accordance with what she called the "least-change" criterion. Start by limiting the legitimate use of military force to one purpose—defense against aggression. The iterative process would occur over a long "period of transition, in which many aspects of politics and moral belief undergo flux and change."[41] She assumed "that there is a continuous interaction, mutual modification among political institutions, economic organization, a culture's 'world view' (general values and assumptions about the nature of the world and the important features of human life) and moral views about violent behavior."[42]

There are certainly aspects of the dissertation that Randy would have further developed. These were explicit in other contexts and implicit in the way she conducted her work. For instance, although Randy does not emphasize it in this book, she was keenly aware of how war undermined democratic norms and institutions. Further, her dissertation was completed before the Responsibility to Protect doctrine was articulated and ultimately adopted by the United Nations. Indeed, she anticipates some of the impulses behind the Responsibility to Protect. In some respects, the doctrine—to the extent it anticipates the use of armed force to prevent genocide and mass atrocities—offers a challenge to Randy's proposal to "confine the military to defense." Had she lived, she would have set herself the task of surmounting such challenges, perhaps with a proposal to create a genuine UN military force to be used only in extreme cases when populations were threatened with mass violence.

Randy also comments on the democratic peace theory as it had developed through the 1990s, suggesting her agreement with Bruce Russett's emphasis on democratic norms of nonviolent dispute resolution as an explanation for the fact that states that recognize each other as democracies rarely come into armed conflict. She was not, however, able to react to the empirical trends in the decline of war that Joshua Goldstein and Steven Pinker, among others, have described.[43] Randy would have found much to argue with in Azar Gat's *War and Human Civilization*, and much of interest in the work of Andrew Linklater, who builds on the research of Norbert Elias, someone who also influenced Randy's thinking.[44] Also relevant to Randy's notion of confining the military to defense as step toward abolishing war is the argument made by Oona A. Hathaway and Scott J. Shapiro about the role of the 1928 Kellogg-Briand Pact in stigmatizing aggressive war.[45] Finally, Randy would have been interested to engage the work of Kwame Anthony Appiah on the role of moral beliefs. His 2010 book, *The Honor Code: How Moral Revolutions Happen*, resembles Randy's *Toward a Theory of Peace* in its focus on moral beliefs and in its use of historical examples—in his case, the demise of dueling in early 19th century England; the end of foot-binding of Chinese women at the beginning of the 20th century; the abolition of slavery in the British empire; and the still-incomplete campaign against mistreatment of women in contemporary Pakistan.[46] Randy's emphasis on putting her scholarly efforts to the task of developing a strategy for the abolition of war distinguishes *Toward a Theory of Peace* from these other works, but engagement with them could have bolstered her own study. Nevertheless, this book is enormously rich as it stands.

Randy's activism and scholarship as the director of the Institute for Defense and Disarmament Studies also suggest how her work would have developed. It is likely that she would have, for example, further developed her theory of the process of belief change. Her own life's work suggests she thought both practical and normative arguments were important factors, along with the mobilization of social movements and the institutionalization of small steps along the way. This is not unlike the theory Neta Crawford developed in *Argument and Change in World Politics* when trying to understand the end of slavery and colonialism.[47] In fact, Crawford's participation in the antinuclear movement and by then two decades of working with Randy undoubtedly inspired the analysis in her own book. Where Randy and Crawford differ is in Crawford's more comprehensive discussion of the process of change. Both see an important role in changing normative/moral beliefs as a route to change and are attentive to long-term processes, which may play out over decades and centuries. Crawford, who paid attention to the substantive arguments of antislavery and anticolonial activists and their movement tactics, is more explicit about *how* normative beliefs and practices change. Change occurs through processes of persuasion, social mobilization, and the institutionalization of small gains, so that arguments that recur over the longue durée can begin at new starting points that take for granted the criticisms and alternative formulations that previous generations of activists gained through their work.

## Randy's Discourse-Ethical Approach

Randy believed in the power of a democratic mobilization that was the consequence of public deliberation. In her own work, that deliberation was informed by the knowledge produced by all of the data gathering, analysis, public education, and careful argumentation she pursued, and the work of IDDS was about arming the general public with information and convincing experts that there was an alternative to the way things had always been done. Indeed, much of Randy's approach to her work and the creation of a sustainable movement for peace embodies an explicit and implicit theory of argument, deliberation, persuasion, and social change that parallels the work on communicative action and the discourse-ethical approach to deliberation articulated by Jürgen Habermas, a member of the Frankfurt School of Critical Theory.

To greatly simplify, like Randy, Habermas is a theorist of democracy, and democracy is nonviolent. Specifically, Habermas argues that a society which seeks to solve social problems nonviolently depends on communication of a specific sort—characterized by a search for truth and consensus.[48] There are three aspects of Habermas's theories of communicative action, democratic deliberation, and discourse ethics that are relevant for understanding the underlying logic of Randy's approach to change. First, Habermas sought to understand how people could, ideally, come to consensus if we take the use of force off the table and require that people come to decisions through a process of communicative action. This is an ideal typical form of discourse-ethical deliberation. Second, Habermas was concerned to understand how it is that people become competent in the first place to participate in discourse-ethical deliberation. Only speakers with what he described as communicative competence would be able to fully participate in discourse-ethical deliberation and come to a reasoned consensus. And third, Habermas sought to explain how democracy came about and was deepened by the development of a public sphere, a space for citizens to engage in democratic deliberation outside government.

For Habermas, communicative competence is the ability of a speaker to fulfill the validity obligations of speech in communicative action: comprehensibility, truth, normative "rightness," and truthfulness.[49] Comprehensibility is the minimum condition, the ability to produce grammatically correct sentences. The speaker should also be saying what is true in a factual sense. Normative rightness is the idea that whatever normative claims the speaker makes are considered normatively valid by the community. This depends on a social consensus about deeper moral beliefs, such as thou shalt not kill. Finally, speakers must truthfully represent their beliefs and intentions. People engaged in an argument have to be able to back up their assertions with evidence, and when they are wrong about a fact or the logical conclusions they have drawn, they should admit it and change their position. Habermas suggests that while it is possible for some of us to lie, some of the time, a society where all lie cannot function because there is no basis for trust; communicative action presumes sincerity. The table below summarizes these claims and their relation to the content of speech.

Communicative Competence in Habermas

| VALIDITY CLAIM | CHARACTERISTIC | FUNCTION |
| --- | --- | --- |
| comprehensibility | understandable language | communicate |
| truth | verifiable propositional content | represents facts: accurately describes the world |
| normative rightness | normative | establish legitimacy |
| truthfulness | avowal | convey sincerity and intentions |

Randy cited Habermas's theory of communicative action in her dissertation, but more than that, she embodied it in her work. Discourse ethics takes force off the table; only the force of the better argument is allowed and force is only allowed in cases of self-defense. Randy's theory of getting to a world without war takes offensive force off the table. More than that, her form of analysis, argument, and political mobilization also exemplified discourse ethics. The work of the Institute and Randy's own work depended not on scaring people into agreement, or on glossing over details and dazzling audiences with incomprehensible data, but on convincing citizens, experts, and journalists with well-crafted arguments. Randy and the staff of the Institute for Defense and Disarmament Studies sought to increase and deepen public understanding about intervention, war, military forces, budgets, and industry so that it was possible for citizens to make informed choices about US foreign policy. In this effort, she made her work comprehensible and truthful, and she sought to hold her interlocutors in the military, arms control, and disarmament communities to a high standard of comprehensibility and truthfulness. She was careful to back up her claims with evidence, and to make sure others backed up their claims. Her work to educate the general public thus helped to constitute not only communicatively competent citizens but strengthened the public sphere.

Randy Forsberg's contributions to the cause of peace over her 40-year career were substantial. The Nuclear Freeze movement, even though it failed in its immediate goal of a bilateral halt to development, production, and deployment of new US and Soviet nuclear weapons, did influence the climate of public opinion and motivated officials in both countries to negotiate more seriously—ultimately leading to extensive nuclear reductions. Randy's work, in collaboration with European and Soviet specialists, on nonoffensive defense also contributed to the initiatives that Mikhail Gorbachev promoted to end the armed division of Europe. Despite these accomplishments, it is possible that Randy's most enduring legacy could be as a theorist of social change, who put forward in *Toward a Theory of Peace* a plausible case for abolishing war as the last remaining form of large-scale, socially sanctioned violence. When she died in October 2007, Randy had held the position as the first Anne and Bernard Spitzer Chair in Political Science at The City College of New York for barely a year. She aspired to continue the work she had carried out at the Institute for Defense and Disarmament Studies and to publish her dissertation and promote her theory of peace. The editors have prepared this book version of the dissertation in the hope that it will provide a posthumous contribution to the debate on the causes of war and how to prevent it.

Matthew Evangelista and Neta C. Crawford

# Preface

This essay is part of a larger project to produce a fully developed theory of the conditions under which world peace might be established and maintained.

To work on that project within the framework of a PhD dissertation, I have adopted a format which is somewhat unusual. In Part I of this essay, "Toward a Theory of Peace," I set out the main ideas of the general theory. Chapter 1 introduces the larger project and relates it to current political theory. Chapter 2 presents the main hypotheses. Then in Part II, "Socially Sanctioned Violence," comprising Chapters 3–6, I develop some of the main ideas set out in Chapter 2, leaving others for further study at a later time.

Part II presents theoretical and empirical evidence to support two of the main hypotheses put forward in Chapter 2: that a modest change in moral beliefs could catalyze the conditions needed to end war; and that a more profound change in moral beliefs, likely to follow the initial abolition, could prevent the future reinstitution of war. At the same time, Part II responds to three of the four main reasons to believe that war cannot be abolished. These are: human beings have innate aggressive instincts that trigger or foster war, and these instincts will always be with us; moral beliefs about ends that justify the use of armed force motivate war and, in the view of many, should do so; and even if world peace were achieved, it would not last indefinitely since eventually some severe stress would motivate those under stress to circumvent any global security system and go to war.

Part II looks at the roles of moral beliefs and innate impulses in causing and preventing various forms of socially sanctioned and nonsanctioned violence. It begins by reviewing the evidence that while innate aggressive impulses can lead to nonsanctioned violence in individuals and mobs, other motivations, particularly culturally determined moral beliefs, dominate innate aggressiveness in accounting for organized, socially sanctioned, large-group violence. It then shows that moral beliefs justifying sanctioned forms of violence tend to change over time, in tandem with changes in political and economic conditions, leading to the permanent abolition of previously sanctioned forms of violence; and it argues that in the same manner, the declining tolerance for war could lead to its abolition.

While Part II supports the main theoretical claims of Chapter 2 and responds to arguments against these claims, it does not complete the development of the material presented in Chapter 2. Several topics will require further attention. Most important, further development is needed on the relatively topical and politically oriented aspects of the theory, including the fourth main reason to believe that war cannot be abolished (the idea that insuperable political, economic, and cultural obstacles block the establishment of war-preventing institutions) and the claims concerning the prospects for attaining the degree of change in moral beliefs required to catalyze the initial abolition of war. The fully developed version of this material will explore the growing body of literature on the relationship between democracy and peace; it will look at the failure of past collective security arrangements to create a lasting peace; it will review the implications for the abolition of war of recent trends away from international war and toward civil and ethnic conflict; and it will discuss the relationship between historical trends and voluntary individual and government action in bringing about the conditions for the abolition of war. In covering these topics, it will provide a more thorough analysis of the relevant theoretical literature on ethics and public policy, ethical relativism, egalitarian social values, cultural evolution, and the causes of war and peace.

While the hypotheses presented in Chapter 2 exceed the scope of the subsequent development in Part II, the discussion of socially sanctioned violence in the latter pertains to all of the main hypotheses, including those on the spread of democracy and the initial abolition of war. At the same time, by giving a relatively complete statement of my theory of the conditions for the abolition of war, Chapter 2 shows that abolition is sufficiently plausible to give the study of socially sanctioned violence more than academic interest.

# Acknowledgments

I would like to thank the members of my thesis committee, Professors Joshua Cohen, Hayward Alker, and Kenneth Oye, for their exceptional support in the development of this work. Joshua Cohen and Hayward Alker, who have been on the committee from the outset, have read more versions than I care to enumerate; and at each juncture they provided useful comments on the ideas, the organization, and the sources. Their patience and confidence helped me keep working to articulate ideas which were extremely fuzzy at the outset. All three members of the committee read the last two drafts and made comments which had an important, constructive impact on the final outcome.

The thoughtfulness, support, and time they gave during a fairly arduous process made this project possible.

# Abstract

This essay concerns the theory of the conditions under which war might end. Chapter 1 introduces the topic. Chapter 2 presents the hypotheses that a modest change in moral beliefs could catalyze the conditions needed to end war; and that a more profound change in moral beliefs, likely to follow the initial abolition, could prevent the future reinstitution of war. Chapters 3–6 give theoretical and empirical evidence to support these hypotheses, and address three factors that are widely believed to preclude the abolition of war: innate aggressiveness, moral beliefs about ends that justify the use of armed force, and the tendency of political institutions, including peace enforcement institutions, to collapse under stress.

Chapters 3–6 focus on the relative weight of learned moral beliefs and innate aggressive impulses in causing and preventing various forms of socially sanctioned and nonsanctioned violence. These chapters present extensive evidence from various branches of psychology to show that while innate aggressive impulses can lead to nonsanctioned individual and mob violence, culturally determined moral beliefs dominate innate aggressiveness in accounting for organized, socially sanctioned, large-group violence. Then, surveying various forms of socially sanctioned violence, they show that the moral beliefs which support such practices tend to change over time, leading to the permanent abolition of previously sanctioned forms of violence. The inference is drawn that in the same manner, the declining tolerance for war could lead to its abolition.

Previously morally sanctioned and institutionalized but now abolished forms of large-group violence include ritual cannibalism, human sacrifice, slavery, and gruesome forms of corporal punishment. The case of ritual cannibalism is reviewed in depth and other cases are reviewed more briefly to assess the importance and variability of moral belief in the conduct of socially sanctioned forms of violence, and to illuminate the historical precedents for the potential abolition of war.

The essay concludes with a discussion of the implications of the rise and demise of successive forms of socially sanctioned large-group violence for anthropological theories of cultural evolution and state formation.

# TOWARD A THEORY OF PEACE

Part I

# TOWARD A THEORY OF PEACE

# THE IDEA OF A THEORY OF PEACE

## 1.1 Introduction

Reviewing a new book on the history of war by John Keegan, Sir Michael Howard (1993) endorsed the idea that today "for the sophisticated, hedonistic democracies of the West, a prolonged campaign, on however minor a scale, in which their fighting forces are likely to suffer serious losses has become almost unthinkable." Howard nonetheless dismissed Keegan's view that perhaps war itself is becoming unthinkable, no longer in the same continuum with politics: "The British pacifist Sir Norman Angell said much the same in 1909, and the Peace Pledge Union was repeating it in the 1930s. But I have an awful feeling that this is where I came in."

The question of whether war could become unthinkable has been posed again and again throughout this century—and not only, as Howard suggests, by pacifists. Before and during World War I, many groups tried to head off a new round of great power warfare. In 1896 internationally minded businessmen rekindled the Olympic games as a nonlethal form of competition that could serve as a surrogate for war.[1] In 1899, diplomats met in the Hague in an effort to prevent war by agreeing to refer disputes to international mediation or arbitration.[2] When World War I broke out, leaders of the women's suffrage movement in the United States and Europe began to work for peace as integral to the achievement of dignity and equality for all human beings.[3] The horrors of World War I prompted renewed governmental efforts to prevent war—the League of Nations and the first international disarmament negotiations.[4] In the interwar period, prominent public figures like Bertrand Russell[5] and Albert Schweitzer[6] denounced war, and Mohandas Gandhi developed a huge following in India for his teaching of nonviolent resistance to oppression. At the close of World War II, the founding of the United Nations represented a new governmental effort to end war, though one with limited great power support.[7] Since 1945, successive US and European popular protests—the ban the bomb movement of the mid-1950s to early 1960s, the anti-Vietnam protest of the late 1960s and early 1970s, and the antinuclear movement of the 1980s—have all shared the goal of moving toward peace.

What is remarkable about these successive peace efforts is that they have failed to create a sustained movement to end war. No other social change goal has been so widely supported over so long a period, only to vanish from public view at regular intervals, leaving little sense of progress from one surge of concern to the next.

Along with erratic public support, the idea of ending war has received uneven intellectual attention. Peace proposals abound,[8] and in the United States, peace studies also abound: there are over 100 colleges with programs of study leading to a major, a minor, or a concentration in peace studies.[9] There are sizable bodies of literature on various aspects of peace, such as arms control, confidence building, and nonviolent conflict resolution. There are also programs of study and bodies of literature based on the premise that war is likely to be with us indefinitely. This view characterizes not only most strategic studies, security studies, and war studies, but also much of the theory and teaching of international relations.

Missing from this wealth of material is a significant body of literature on the theory of peace.[10] Theoretical writing on peace should differ from peace proposals in offering substantial, well-documented explanations of the reasons to believe that some courses of action, or lines of international development, are more likely than others to lead to an enduring peace. It should differ from the literature on arms control and nonviolent conflict resolution in offering some account of the incidence of war. It should differ from war studies in trying not merely to clarify the causes of particular wars or groups of wars, but also to generalize across all wars and identify the features that distinguish cultures, areas, and time periods prone to peace from those prone to war. And it should differ from much international relations theory in attempting to identify and account for cyclical and secular trends in patterns of war and peace.

In this essay, I venture into the little-studied domain of the theory of peace, that is, the theory of the conditions under which war might end. The topic is controversial even before any claim is made because so many people are convinced that war cannot end. The position I adopt on the feasibility of the abolition of war is tentative. I start with the assumption that there may exist achievable conditions under which war could end; and I try to identify such conditions and a set of steps or trends that could lead to their creation in the future. My purpose is not, in the first instance, to argue that the abolition of war is feasible. I address a slightly different question: If we grant that it is worthwhile to investigate whether it may be possible for war to end, then what are the conditions under which the abolition of war would be most likely to happen, and what are the factors that have a bearing on whether those conditions are likely to be achieved?

There is an important difference between arguing that the abolition of war is feasible and investigating the conditions under which war might end. The first approach invites a simple "yes" or "no" response, whereas the second encourages the reader who finds the argument weak to engage in the search, improve upon the answer, refine it, dispute it at specific points, and, more generally, think seriously about the topic.

Is there any reason to construct a theory of something that has not happened and that, if it did happen, would be a one-time transition, a singularity in human history? I believe that this essay shows that such an undertaking is both meaningful and useful. But there are also precedents in other fields: theories of economic equilibrium, justice, or democracy. All of these theoretical discussions involve models of conditions that have not been achieved and may never be achieved, yet whose exploration and definition are intellectually and practically rewarding.

It must be acknowledged, however, that there is an important difference between a theory of peace and, say, theories of justice or of economic equilibrium: the latter offer analytical tools that can be adapted to various environments and value systems, whereas the theory of peace focuses, at least in the first instance, on a specific, well-defined goal. In that respect, the closest parallels for a theory of peace may be found not in philosophy or social science, but in public policy fields like public health or education. Like efforts to eradicate contagious disease or teach good health habits, or promote universal literacy or family planning, the abolition of war seems likely to involve changes in individual attitudes and behavior on a scale that is daunting. Experience in medicine and education has shown, however, that such tasks can be facilitated by the creation of conditions which, once established, generate self-perpetuating and ever-widening feedback loops.

Attempting to answer the question "Under what conditions might a stable global peace be established?" or, in other words, "Under what conditions might war cease to be a recurrent feature of human life?" requires a more comprehensive, rigorous study of the central issues of war and peace than do efforts to address narrower questions, such as "What conclusions about the future of war and peace can we draw from recent trends?" or "What conditions are conducive to the nonviolent resolution of border conflicts?" or "Why do some ethnic conflicts lead to violence, while others do not?" The difference between these two kinds of question parallels the difference between attempts to characterize partial and general equilibria in a complex system. The problem with partial equilibria is that they can easily be disrupted—shown to be invalid or uninteresting with respect to the general case—as a result of factors that lie outside their deliberately restricted fields of vision. The only way to provide an appropriate sense of proportion and perspective when studying parts of a large, complex system is to model the system as a whole. This does not preclude or invalidate the study of subsystems. On the contrary, it is generally accepted that the most fruitful course of inquiry is to alternate between the definition and elaboration of the overall model and detailed research on the parts.

For too long, the general question of the conditions for peace has languished, leaving the field of war and peace studies to narrower issues—in part, no doubt, due to the ridicule of those, like Michael Howard, who regard the permanence of war as an article of faith. It is possible that sustained, thoughtful study will show that there are good reasons to believe that war cannot end. But in no other area of scholarly research is the answer to such a first-order question treated as a starting assumption rather than a central issue for study and debate.

In some ways, constructing a theory of the conditions for ending war is like joining a duel: Recognizing the dominant view that war will never end, this essay attempts to articulate imaginable conditions under which war might end, and plausible paths—sequences of events reaching out from the present into the future—along which these conditions could be realized. If readers deem my arguments cogent and persuasive, they need not conclude that war definitely will end, nor that it will end in a fashion or for reasons identified here—only that under certain circumstances, it could conceivably end. If this is the case, then the topic clearly deserves far more attention than it has received hitherto.

## 1.2 Defining the End of War

Under what circumstances would it be reasonable to say that war had ended? This question raises issues about the *threshold* above which no violence should occur, the *duration* of unbroken peace, and its *quality of stability*, that is, its resilience or fragility. Since eliminating every individual act of violence is not possible and since war covers a continuum of violence that runs down to modest levels, it might be argued that at lower levels of violence (killing on the scale that has occurred over a period of decades in, say, Northern Ireland), war cannot be expected to end. The idea that war might end is, of course, different from the idea that all violence might end. It is possible to imagine a world without war in which murder, violent crimes, riots, and perhaps even politically motivated terrorism all continued. In order to say that war had ended, what would be the threshold above which no violence would occur?

The distinction between war and lesser acts of group violence rests on four aspects of each: war is *socially sanctioned*, *organized*, *premeditated*, and *relatively large in scale*, whereas lesser acts of group violence are not socially sanctioned to the same degree, and they tend to be smaller in scale, briefer in duration, and, generally, relatively unorganized and spontaneous. Interpreting "socially sanctioned" in a stringent, highly restrictive manner, one standard for judging that war had ended would be that all recognized governments had explicitly rejected war as an instrument of national policy and over an extended period of time (decades or more) had used exclusively nonmilitary means of resolving conflicts. A more demanding measure of the abolition of war, and the standard adopted here, includes not only the renunciation of war by governments in word and deed, but also the end of large-scale, sustained, premeditated violence by "rogue states" and substate actors. The idea that "break outs" and violent revolutions, civil wars, and secessions might cease altogether may seem particularly implausible, and I will return to this issue shortly. First, however, it is useful to consider briefly the related issues of the *duration* of a lasting peace and its *resilience*, that is, its quality of stability or potential reversibility.

For how long would war have not to have occurred in order for us to judge that war had been abolished? Over the course of the past 500 years, there have been several intervals of 50 years or more between great power wars. Thus, a peace of that length, even a worldwide peace, would not necessarily signify that war had ended. A convincing lower bound might lie somewhere between one and two centuries. Even after 200 years, it might be argued, war could conceivably recur some day. If it did, historians looking back might call the interval an unusually long peace, rather than an instance of the abolition of war.

Are there any conditions under which most observers might feel confident that peace, once established, would endure indefinitely? Several modern changes in what are now perceived as basic human rights—for example, the abolition of slavery, the enfranchisement of women, and the end of colonialism—exemplify the phenomenon of *unidirectional social change*, that is, political change which cannot be reversed, or can be reversed only under circumstances that lie far outside the range of contemporary experience. In all of the examples just cited, the changes in belief and practice represented aspects of a larger social change: society's recognition of a greater degree of dignity and worth of the individual than had previously been perceived or publicly acknowledged. These precedents and others suggest that once a certain degree of individual dignity and inviolability has been widely recognized, that recognition is extraordinarily difficult if not impossible to undo or reverse.

Some readers are likely to argue that ending war is not like ending slavery or colonialism, nor like enfranchising women or any other social change, because going to war may be necessary for the survival of a society or nation: that is, any nation which, for any reason, is faced with a choice between war and extirpation is likely to choose war, regardless of how long a global peace had endured.

To some extent this argument begs the question, because it ignores the fact that apart from war itself, there are few if any sources of impending extirpation of whole societies which war might successfully ward off. Setting aside that point, there is reason to believe that the image we have today of war as a potential means of survival could be replaced by an image of war as a disorganized, barbaric form of behavior, which lies beyond the pale of acceptable means to any end—just as today slavery lies beyond the pale of acceptable policy options, regardless of the stakes. Today we cannot conceive of "just slavery," in which the ends justify the means: in future the norm might be that there is no "just war," that the phrase represents nothing more than an oxymoron. Such a norm could provide a solid basis for believing that once abolished, war will never recur.

Precedents for social change of the magnitude and sweep of ending war are provided by human experience with the abolition of two other, long defunct but forms of socially sanctioned group violence: ritual cannibalism and human sacrifice. At the times and in the societies where these practices were common, ritual cannibalism and human sacrifice were each believed to be essential for the survival of the society concerned. Human sacrifice was intended to placate gods that could otherwise wreak havoc on crops or human life. Similarly, ritual forms of cannibalism were associated with the preservation and renewal of life across generations, and the warding off of evil spirits intruding from other tribes, which could weaken or destroy life forces in one's own tribe. What changed when these practices ended was neither the human capacity for destructiveness, nor the human tendency to justify socially sanctioned violence by assigning it life-or-death import, but the world views that legitimated forms of violence that would otherwise have been unthinkable.

A comparable change in overarching beliefs and perceptions about what is possible, necessary, and desirable in human life could conceivably lead to recognition of the fact that except when conducted in defense against attacks by others, war is motivated by goals like the desire for wealth or political power, not by the needs of sheer survival.

An interactive process of change in values and institutions relating to war, which, over a period of decades, increasingly restricted the legitimate use of force to defense, could conceivably lead, ultimately, to a situation in which large-scale, premeditated, organized violence was extremely rare, quickly ended by national or international action, and widely viewed as unacceptable, aberrant behavior that was expected to remain rare, limited in scale and duration, and controllable.

This situation, analogous to the current, extremely limited worldwide practice of human sacrifice and slavery, would be one in which we could say that war had been abolished.

In endeavoring to convey this degree of finality, I have tried to avoid using the phrase "the conditions for abolishing war," which suggests that the topic might be the conditions under which people might strive to abolish war. Although the dictionary meaning of "abolish" is to do away with or bring to an end,[11] the word carries connotations like those of "prohibit": it suggests a change in law which may or may not mirror a lasting change in practice. This is particularly true for "abolition," for which Webster's definition includes "2. the state of being abolished; annulment; abrogation: the abolition of unjust laws; the abolition of unfair taxes. 3. the legal prohibition and ending of slavery, esp. of Negro slavery in the US." Webster's synonyms for "abolition" include "nullification," "invalidation," and "revocation."

Even in nonlegal contexts, "abolish" and "abolition" imply, though they are not restricted to, a clear demarcation in time—one day a practice exists, the next it has been abolished—while the end of war, should it occur, seems likely to be a protracted and messy process, with a gray area that involves a good deal of back and forth before war has, in fact, come to an end. The notion that war could be abolished by a well-defined decision or action at a certain moment is implausible. It suggests that like the failed prohibition against alcohol, war might be outlawed without having ended.

"Abolition" does have a nonlegal, nonagency meaning emphasizing non-time marked denotation of a practice's ceasing to exist. If war came to an end by gradual fits and starts, then once it had ended, regardless of how it ended, we could say that war "had been abolished" and talk about its "abolition." In that case, referring to the "abolition" of war would be more time and agency neutral than discussing its "eradication" or "nullification," which carry stronger overtones of deliberate, time-specific human action. With respect to war, the word "cessation" is not a good substitute for "abolition" because the former often refers to a temporary ending, as expressed in the phrase "cease fire." The noun and verb "end"—as in "the conditions under which war might end" or "the end of war" or "human sacrifice ended millennia ago"—convey an appropriate image of an activity's stopping or ceasing to exist permanently after having existed for a long time, but some constructions using "end" are awkward. The noun "demise" is also useful in being time and agency neutral and unambiguous with respect to the finality of the ending. In dealing with the problem of expression, I use the nouns "end," "demise," and "abolition" as fully synonymous, and the verbs "come to an end," "end," "cease to exist," and "abolish" in the same way.

## 1.3 Standards for the Theory of Peace

Since little effort has been made to develop a formal theory of peace, there are no recognized guidelines for the content or forms of argument appropriate to such a theory. In this section, I propose several standards which I endeavor to meet in the following chapters.

First, contributions to the theory of peace should distinguish between the achievement of peace and the maintenance of peace: that is, they should distinguish between the conditions under which a global peace might initially be achieved, given the realities of today's world, and the conditions under which peace, once achieved, might be maintained indefinitely.[12] The account of the means of achieving peace should include a scenario of developments that could conceivably lead to a world without war. The key requirement here is identifying a path to peace that remains plausible even when one takes fully into account the many factors that make today's world prone to war.

The account of how peace, once established, might be maintained indefinitely should address the issue of unpredictable future stresses that could arise sooner or later and overwhelm national or international peace enforcement institutions.

Second, for both the achievement and the maintenance of peace, theoretical studies should give a sense of the relative importance of voluntary individual or government action, on the one hand, and, on the other, long-term social or economic trends that are relatively intractable to policy-driven intervention. In other words, theoretical contributions should endeavor to answer the question "Is peace likely to be achieved as the product of inexorable global trends (for example, the growing density of the worldwide web of financial and communication links), or as the result of conscious choice and deliberate action on the parts of nations, subnational groups, or individuals—and how might these two kinds of agency relate to one another?"

Third, hypotheses concerning the conditions for peace should strive to meet a "least-change" criterion. Many conditions may be conducive to peace—for example, the eradication of hunger, poverty, unemployment, and underemployment; the establishment of a minimum standard of education and health care within and between countries; or the legal acceptance and routine practice by most or all nations of an agreed code of basic human rights and civil liberties. Without denying the importance of these and other related goals both in themselves and as conditions conducive to peace, the theory of peace should have as its source of rigor the aim of specifying the minimum set of conditions that must be met for peace to be established and to endure. One school of thought might argue, for example, that all of the conditions mentioned above are not merely conducive to peace but necessary prerequisites to it, while another might defend a more modest set of requirements: the theoretical contributions will be judged not by the length of the list of conditions they propose, but by the case each makes for one set of conditions rather than another, as the conditions necessary and sufficient for the achievement and maintenance of peace. In this assessment, Occam's razor will apply: that is, between cases that are equally persuasive, the one that argues for the most readily achievable conditions—generally speaking, the shortest list of conditions of equal difficulty of achievement—must be judged the best. That argument will prevail until there is a more persuasive argument, or an equally persuasive argument for a more readily achievable list of conditions.

Finally, theoretical studies of the means of achieving and preserving peace should address factors widely believed to pose insurmountable obstacles to peace, arguing that they are illusory; or that their assumed role in preventing the end of war is illusory; or that they are real and do play a role in preventing the end of war, but that the hypothesized means of achieving or maintaining peace would circumvent or eliminate them.

Chief among the factors widely believed to preclude the abolition of war are the following:

- The innate aggressiveness of individuals, which can lead to or permit acts of violence against others.
- The tendency to ethnocentrism, which dehumanizes "others" and makes them acceptable victims of violent attack.
- Various motives for violence such as the instinct for self-preservation, tendency to self-aggrandizement, or situations of injustice or oppression.
- Vested interests in militarism or war, which block or undermine efforts at institutional reform and at strengthening tolerance and restraint.
- The condition of anarchy among nations, which leaves them without a superordinate means of peace enforcement (that is, the global equivalent of a national police force or national guard) to deter war and to end it with minimal loss of life if it starts.
- Fear of tyranny as the most likely alternative to anarchy, and unwillingness to accept any risk of tyranny as the price of peace. (Many observers believe that solving the problem of anarchy by establishing a world government with a monopoly on armed force would open the door to world tyranny.)
- The tendency of political institutions to collapse under pressure.

These oft-cited obstacles to a lasting world peace can be grouped into four main arguments which contributions to the theory of peace must rebut:

1. Human beings have innate instincts that trigger or foster war, and these instincts will always be with us.

2. Moral beliefs about ends that justify the use of armed force motivate individuals to participate in war; and such beliefs will also persist and, in the view of many, should do so.

3. Insuperable political, cultural, and economic hurdles block the establishment of international institutions for peacekeeping and peace enforcement, which might otherwise channel war-triggering impulses and beliefs into nonviolent forms of expression and nonviolent forms of conflict resolution.

4. Even if world peace were achieved under favorable initial conditions, peace could not be expected to last forever since sooner or later there would arise environmental, political, or economic stresses sufficiently severe to motivate those under stress to circumvent any global security system and go to war.

Of these four arguments, the first two—concerning the role of innate impulses and moral beliefs in motivating war—involve problems for both the achievement and the maintenance of peace. The third, on obstacles to the creation of effective peace enforcement institutions, concerns mainly the means by which world peace might initially be achieved, while the fourth, on the frailty of political institutions under stress, concerns the means by which peace, once achieved, might be maintained indefinitely.

# CONDITIONS FOR THE ABOLITION OF WAR

## 2.1 Introduction

Most studies of the underlying causes of war and peace focus on political institutions, economic conditions, culture, or genes. This study argues that alongside these factors, moral beliefs play an important role in perpetuating war and could play a key role in ending it.

Moral beliefs are a neglected dimension of political behavior. They are the "spirit in the machine" of much concerted human action: they motivate the creation of political institutions and ensure that institutions work as intended. In matters of war and peace, beliefs about "just" (or socially acceptable) and "unjust" (or unacceptable) uses of violence or armed force determine the course of events. The point is not that moral beliefs operate independently of institutions or culture, but that they help shape institutions and culture. For institutionalized forms of group violence such as war, moral beliefs resemble the gates of a walled town: they can grant admission to or shut out whole worlds of behavior, in which institutions and culture, transmitted from one generation to the next, channel impulses, needs, and desires into socially accepted forms of action.

Outside anthropology, the social sciences tend to treat moral beliefs as a constant rather than a variable—a constant which, though not necessarily uniform across populations nor well understood, remains substantially unchanged across cultures and over the course of human history. It is true that for many moral values—for example, marital fidelity, honesty, loyalty, and not stealing or killing—diverse cultures have much in common. In the realm of institutionalized violence, however, moral values differ from one culture to the next and change over time.

Because moral beliefs change slowly, over centuries or millennia, we often view the changes as differences in custom rather than changes in morality. Moreover, we tend to be ethnocentric, viewing the values of our own culture and time as normal, and the values of other cultures and times as peculiar. But close study shows that in virtually all cultures, what most people would consider basic moral values regarding violence do change. One important recent change in beliefs about acceptable forms of violence is documented by Michel Foucault in *Discipline and Punish: The Birth of the Prison* (1979), which looks at the decline of corporal punishment and rise of incarceration as the accepted means of punishing violations of the law. Over a period of several centuries, extremely painful forms of physical punishment, including torture and dismemberment, have been replaced almost entirely with incarceration in prison, that is, the largely mental form of punishment caused by the deprivation of privacy and of freedom of action. Over the same period, norms about acceptable forms of violence in families and communities have changed from permitting to forbidding acts in which husbands strike wives, parents and teachers hit children, and dishonor occasions deadly duels.

Most briefly put, my hypothesis is that war could be abolished if, in an analogous development, one of several competing contemporary views of "just war" became the norm: this is the view that there is no just use of armed force except defense, strictly and narrowly defined. According to this view, there is no just use of force among nations except when one nation violates the norm and attacks another, in which case the victimized nation and other nations are justified in resorting to the minimum use of force needed to stop the attack and repel the attacker's forces. Within nations, given this same view, the use of deadly force is never justified except as a means of defense against attack. Specifically, it is not acceptable for either subnational groups or the international community to use violent coups d'etat, armed revolt, guerrilla warfare, or armed intervention against an existing government to rectify injustices or to establish basic human rights or civil liberties. The one exception, which can be strictly defensive, is armed intervention by the international community with the limited purpose of ending genocidal bloodbaths in civil or ethnic conflicts.

The view that defense is the only acceptable reason for the use of deadly force is already the norm for interactions among individuals in most nations. In countries with well-developed democratic institutions, there are no circumstances which legally or morally justify the use of deadly force by one person on another, with the single exception of the employment of physical violence or armed force to defend oneself (or help defend another person) if physically attacked by someone who is violating this standard. I call this view "democratic commitment to nonviolence" or "commitment to nonviolence except for defense, narrowly defined," which I shorten to "commitment to defensive nonviolence."[1]

The standard of defensive nonviolence resembles the pacifist standard of absolute nonviolence in incorporating unqualified rejection of the use of violence by some individuals against others as a means of achieving political, economic, or moral ends. Defensive nonviolence differs from pacifist nonviolence, however, in permitting one narrowly defined exception to the rule that individuals must never resort to deadly force, that is, the minimum use of deadly force needed to end the threat or use of deadly force by others.

In section 2.2, I expand on the thesis that commitment to defensive nonviolence could bring about the abolition of war. In doing so, I draw several key distinctions. First, I distinguish between general conditions which could lead to the end of war and the *least-change* conditions, on which I focus. Most readers will agree that while sweeping, utopian political and economic change might lead to the end of war, such change is of little interest. What is at issue is not the most comprehensive but the most modest change in current world conditions that could conceivably lead to the end of war.

Second, in identifying the least-change conditions for ending war, I distinguish between the conditions needed *to bring about the initial transition* to the abolition of war, and the conditions needed *to preserve peace indefinitely*, once war has been abolished. I argue that solid commitment to defensive nonviolence in part of the international community could catalyze the changes needed to bring about the initial transition to the abolition of war, but that what is needed to preserve peace indefinitely is a more profound moral rejection of war, which is likely to develop only after the initial abolition.

In discussing the conditions needed to bring about the initial abolition of war, I differentiate between the conditions needed to stop *international* war and those needed to end *internal* civil or subnational war. To catalyze the abolition of international war, I argue, it is likely to be essential for moral commitment to defensive nonviolence to be reflected in an international security regime able and willing to enforce this standard.[2] In the case of internal warfare, the key factor is the development of a norm sufficiently powerful and widespread to marginalize the holdouts. Because commitment to nonviolence is weakened by the observation or experience of war, and by national policies which arrogate a right to use force as a means to ends other than defense, the development of the degree of individual commitment to defensive nonviolence needed to end internal wars would be facilitated by steps to end international war.

Next, section 2.2 turns to the prospects for achieving the *degree* of commitment to defensive nonviolence needed to catalyze the transition to the abolition of international war. I argue that the modern shift to individual-centered political organization, which underlies and infuses democratic institutions, makes the near-term future achievement of the needed degree of commitment to defensive nonviolence possible and even likely. Even though "the democracies" have engaged in many acts of self-interested military intervention, they have maintained the standard of defensive nonviolence in interactions among themselves; and as democratic institutions spread to more and more nations, this standard will characterize their foreign policies more and more fully.

The asymmetrical character of commitment to defensive nonviolence (that is, fighting fire with water, not with fire) enhances the prospects for a near-future transition because it is compatible with the establishment of an international peace enforcement capability that can deter international war without raising the specter of a tyrannical, all-powerful world government.

In the last part of section 2.2, I summarize my hypotheses on the relationship between moral beliefs and other factors in accounting for the perpetuation and potential demise of war.

Section 2.3 compares and contrasts my hypotheses with those of other approaches to peace. First, I identify a number of complementary approaches, which would strengthen commitment to defensive nonviolence, but which focus on government institutions and political culture, rather than on the character of moral belief about war, as the key instruments of change. While agreeing that institutional and cultural change are central components of any change in norms, I argue that lack of clarity and consensus about the nature of the moral change to be achieved vitiates efforts to create supportive institutional and cultural change.

Then I discuss three competing approaches to peace, which differ substantially from the approach presented here. These are: (1) the view that commitment to complete nonviolence (pacifism) is a better catalyst and the needed means to ending war; (2) the view that the conditions for the abolition of war include the existence of political freedom and economic equity (or, the fulfillment of basic human needs) throughout the world; and (3) the view that war cannot be abolished, only held at bay more or less successfully (that is, made infrequent and brief and small in scale when it does occur) by military power balancing. In response, I argue as follows:

**Commitment to complete nonviolence**: Preponderant individual commitment to complete nonviolence cannot be achieved before the initial transition to the abolition of war, but it is likely to develop after that transition, when it will become central to the long-term maintenance of peace.

**Minimum standards of freedom and justice**: While conducive to the abolition of war, greater freedom and justice than exist today are not necessary for the abolition of war, that is, not required as part of the "least-change" conditions for the initial abolition of war. Furthermore, since concepts of adequate freedom and justice are constantly evolving, and since peace is conducive the achievement of greater freedom and justice, it more useful and practicable to treat peace as a condition for freedom and justice than to treat freedom and justice as conditions for peace.

**Power balancing:** The idea of deterring war through power balancing was a product of a particular phase in world history (the last five centuries), in which expansionist, imperialist "great powers" competed for the control of territory, resources, and international trade. The phenomenal rise in per capita income during the past century, and the replacement of economic competition based on the physical control of natural resources (on land and while in transit over water) with competition based on the superior technological transformation of natural resources, has made war-based means of striving for political power and economic wealth economically obsolete and counterproductive. The susceptibility of war to being abolished has grown as a direct function of the decline in the utility of war as a means to power and wealth.

## 2.2  Main Hypothesis

### "Least-change" Conditions for the Abolition of War

Because moral beliefs and political behavior tend to change in interactive ways, with feedback loops in both directions, moral beliefs are likely to take one form during *the initial transition* to the abolition of war, and a substantially different form in *the later process of maintaining peace* for the indefinite future. In this section, I discuss each of these phases in turn.

#### MORAL BELIEFS CAPABLE OF CATALYZING
#### THE INITIAL ABOLITION OF WAR

The time between the continued practice of war and its complete cessation will inevitably be a period of transition, in which many aspects of politics and moral belief undergo flux and change. During such a time, various combinations of political and economic conditions could conceivably lead to the abolition of war. In this essay, I make a case for a limited, well-specified set of changes as the "least-change" conditions capable of leading to the abolition of war. I argue that a modest shift in norms (that is, predominant moral beliefs) in some nations could lead to changes in government policy in those nations, and later to changes in belief and policy in other nations, sufficient to bring about the abolition of war. In other words, I argue that a modest change in moral beliefs in some nations could serve as a catalyst, jump-starting the transition to abolition and minimizing the larger political and economic changes needed to complete the process.

The least change needed to catalyze the transition to the abolition of war would be for one of several contemporary views of just war to become the norm in a number of nations: this is the view that there is no just use of deadly force except defense (of oneself or others) against the use (or threat of use) of deadly force initiated by those who are not (yet) committed to this standard.

For defensive nonviolence to be the norm would mean that in the relevant nations, this moral standard receives not mere lip service, but robust support, manifested in actions as well as words. Specifically, the following conditions would have to be met:

- In the committed nations, most people refuse to use or condone the use of deadly force to achieve political or economic ends, such as opposing oppression or injustice at home or pursuing economic interests abroad.
- The governments of those nations publicly espouse defensive nonviolence as the foundation of their security policies, and practice this standard by maintaining armed forces that are trained and equipped solely for defense (of their own nation or others) against external attack, and for humanitarian intervention to stop genocide.
- The committed nations undertake to enforce the standard of defensive nonviolence—that is, to deter and halt military aggression and genocide— and to foster the global spread of the view that such actions are wrong by establishing joint means of rapid intervention to prevent or end such acts among themselves and, when most other nations have joined them, throughout the world.

The catalytic role of the initial commitment by some nations to defensive nonviolence would be twofold. First, the example set by the participating nations would be likely to foster the global spread of democratic values and institutions, including commitment to defensive nonviolence. People in other nations, seeing that defensive nonviolence is not only morally attractive, but also politically respected and viable as a government policy, would be likely to give this position more weight in their own thinking. Second, the joint practice of defensive nonviolence by a group of nations would be likely to reduce the number and scale of occurrences of international aggression, civil war, and genocidal ethnic conflict; and the declining incidence of war, in turn, would make adoption of a policy aimed at ending war seem less utopian and more useful than it seems to most people today. Eventually, when commitment to defensive nonviolence became the norm in most (if not all) nations, war would end in the sense defined in Chapter 1: it would be rare, small in scale, and quickly ended through international action.

**The degree of commitment needed for the initial abolition of *international* war:** The degree of commitment to defensive nonviolence needed to catalyze the transition to the abolition of war cannot be predicted with precision, but some sense of the value can be given.

For commitment to defensive nonviolence to be meaningful as a condition for ending war, the number of countries in which this value is the norm must be fewer than all countries. The reason is that if every country were fully, explicitly committed and prepared never to use armed force except to the minimum extent needed to defend against its use by others—and, with respect to civil wars, if every individual and subnational group within every country were, similarly, committed to employ only nonviolent means of resisting oppression and injustice—then we could be sure that war would never occur. But identifying this situation as meeting the conditions required for the abolition of war would amount to little more than a tautology: that is, if every person and political organization in the world were absolutely committed never to go to war, then war would cease to occur.

In other words, for the conditions set out above to be significant, there would have to be some nations, some subnational groups, and some individuals *not* committed never to use violence or armed force as a means to political or economic ends. Thus, the question of the extent to which the relevant conditions must be met can be phrased in relative terms, for example, "What proportion of committed to uncommitted nations, and what degree of commitment among the committed, would have to be reached in order to lead to the abolition of war within the reasonably near future?"

If, for the moment, we limit this question to the degree of commitment to defensive nonviolence needed to end international war, then the answer might be that the establishment of such a commitment among the handful of great powers—perhaps the United States alone, perhaps the United States joined by one or more of Russia, China, Britain, France, Germany, and Japan—would be sufficient. These nations alone, without the assistance of any other nations, currently have, or could field, sufficient military power to stop and reverse international military aggression by any other nation, or by any of their own number (except possibly the United States), anywhere in the world.

Another possible answer is that commitment to defensive nonviolence by any substantial group of nations—say, any 20 nations from among the 50 most populous nations—might be sufficient to lead to the end of international war because the example these nations set and the rhetoric they used to explain and support their policy would be contagious: sooner or later, enough nations with enough military power to make deterrence effective would join them. These two examples suggest a more general rule: What is needed to make war very rare and very brief and small in scale when it does occur is the espousal of democratic commitment to nonviolence by enough nations to reach a specific (but not yet identified) threshold of *relative* military power—that is, the ratio of the combined military power of nations supporting this commitment to that of nations not supporting—sufficient to deter acts of aggression by the nonsupporters.

Yet another possibility might be that international war would end only when all nations except a handful of rogue states were committed not to use armed force: fewer than, say, ten holdouts might be a sufficiently small number for the international community to be able to monitor the problem nations closely and keep their aggressiveness in check. This suggests another possible rule: the holdouts must be few enough in number not to overload the capacity for attention and rapid response on the part of the international community.

These two rules can be combined in a more general response to the question:

The minimum quality and quantity of democratic commitment to nonviolence needed to end war is the level at which the supporters, when combined, will deploy enough military power to be able to put a quick end to acts of aggression by holdouts (regardless of whether the latter act singly, simultaneously, or in concert); will have shown their willingness and ability to take quick, effective action to stop aggression; and, thus, will be able to deter virtually all acts of international aggression.

The charter of the United Nations gives the UN Security Council the right and duty to oppose international aggression; but the charter has been interpreted and applied by the five permanent members of the Security Council (Britain, China, France, Russia, and the United States) and the ten rotating members in such a way that hitherto, the United Nations has not functioned as an impartial international peace enforcement organization. In other words, the nations represented in the Security Council have not demonstrated the willingness or ability to consistently take quick, effective, joint action to stop and reverse international aggression. In principle, this lack could be remedied within the existing terms of the UN charter, with or without various proposed measures of UN reform. Alternatively, it could be remedied by a more ad hoc arrangement: a new, possibly explicitly temporary collective defense alliance comprising all and only countries committed to limit the use of force to defense, narrowly defined.

In sum, an optimistic response is that the establishment of the standard of defensive nonviolence among a few nations might suffice to persuade others of the same view, until eventually the committed nations would predominate in the international community. A conservative response is that the commitment to defensive nonviolence will suffice only when the supporting nations, in combination, are able and willing to put a quick end to acts of international aggression by holdouts perpetrated anywhere in the world. It would not be surprising if the actual threshold lay somewhere between these two extremes, perhaps at the point where the committed nations, acting together, command sufficient military power to successfully defend against and deter international aggression against any of their number.

**The degree of commitment needed for the initial abolition of *civil* war:** It is not obvious that the conditions specified for the abolition of international war will lead to the abolition of wars within nations and wars that may spill over national boundaries but involve no more than one national government: civil wars over governance, wars of secession, and wars over territorial affiliation or political control among subnational groups identified by ethnicity, religion, language, or some other aspect of regional populations. Wars of this kind tend to be smaller in scale than international wars, that is, they typically involve fewer military and civilian casualties and smaller numbers of combatants per unit time. (The recent bloodshed in Rwanda is the exception that proves the rule.) At the same time, internal wars tend to be protracted, continuing intermittently for decades rather than the months or (formerly) years of a typical international war. Equally important, internal wars are generally fought by subnational groups, at least on one side, and, thus, are not susceptible to prevention by agreements solely among governments—that is, agreements among a relatively small number of well-defined parties, whose policies and actions are subject to international scrutiny and to some degree limited by agreed international rules of order. Instead of lying mainly in the hands of governments, the prevention of internal wars lies mainly in the hands of the individuals who comprise the subnational groups that fight such wars.[3]

To what extent would the individuals that potentially make up warring subnational groups have to become committed to nonviolent means of resistance and protest in order for internal wars to end? And what conditions might bring about needed degree of commitment?

The degree of individual commitment to defensive nonviolence needed to end internal wars must be substantial, representing well over half the population. The reason is that even though the likelihood of armed revolution or guerrilla warfare grows with the intensity and scale of dissent, relatively small-scale dissent by individuals not committed to nonviolence can fuel a civil war.

On the matter of how democratic commitment to nonviolence might take root among the great preponderance of individuals in regions of conflict, I propose three possible paths. One route involves a trickle-down effect of the commitment by the international community to renounce the use of armed force as an instrument of policy. What might trickle down are the principle that violence should never be used except for defense, and the sense that this principle is taken seriously by the vast majority of people and their leaders. In a second possible route, individual commitment to defensive nonviolence might grow as a product of the spread of democratic institutions, which facilitate nonviolent change and inculcate commitment to nonviolent processes of group decisionmaking.

Third, *individual* commitment to nonviolence might grow as a function of the long-term global trends that make both international cooperation and the spread of democratic institutions increasingly common: that is, growing global interaction and interdependence in finance, trade, the environment, communications, and so on. In this case, however, the causality is likely to be indirect: that is, the growth of individual commitment to defensive nonviolence brought about by global changes in communications and economic activities would be likely to foster both the global spread of democratic institutions and, more particularly, the spread of commitment to defensive nonviolence *on the part of governments.*

Whatever the precise combination of factors responsible for growth in individual commitment to defensive nonviolence, it is unlikely that any major new institution involving the use of force—apart from the international peace enforcement military capability discussed earlier—will play a significant role. The existing institutions of representative government and law enforcement (police, courts, prison, and so on) generally suffice not only to prevent the outbreak of war, but to reinforce individual commitment to defensive nonviolence (that is, commitment neither to conduct armed violations of the law, nor to take the law into one's own hands, with violent action).

In fact, the key issue is whether the needed degree of commitment not to use violence in internal wars is likely to be a cause or a product of the establishment of democratic institutions.[4] Does there need to be some minimum standard of human rights and civil liberties—the absence of violently repressive governments and of anarchic, failed governments—before civil wars and ethnic wars will end? Clearly, the presence of democratic institutions (along with economic equity or the fulfillment of basic human needs) is conducive to commitment of defensive nonviolence; and in a world where all states maintained a high standard of participatory democracy (currently found only in a few democracies), we should expect a near-universal commitment to defensive nonviolence. The question, then, concerns the relative independence and order of precedence in the interactive spread of democratic institutions and commitment to defensive nonviolence.

I contend that the number of nations which currently have democratic institutions (or even the much smaller number reached by, say, 1945)[5] and the extent of participatory democracy in those nations have surpassed the threshold needed to create a global ethos and expectation of individual worth and dignity; and that given this ethos, individual commitment to defensive nonviolence is likely to spread and deepen more rapidly than will democratic institutions and participatory practice. The main evidence for this claim involves the history of actual transitions to self-government and democratic institutions over the period since World War II. In the great majority of cases, authoritarian, repressive governments (both foreign and domestic) have been replaced by more representative, liberal governments through a process of nonviolent opposition, protest, and change. Moreover, in virtually all parts of the world where democratic institutions had not previously existed, acts of nonviolent resistance against oppression and injustice, undertaken more or less spontaneously by ordinary individuals, have played a critical role in the ouster of repressive governments. Fine examples of this have occurred in earlier decades in India and Iran, and in the past decade in the Philippines, the Baltic states, Eastern Europe, and Latin America.[6] Moreover, in 1996–1997 nonviolent public demonstrations in South Korea, Serbia, and Burma have repeatedly challenged repressive governments, and, in Serbia, won the concessions to justice and freedom which they sought.

## MORAL BELIEFS CAPABLE OF MAINTAINING PEACE INDEFINITELY

Because of the interactive nature of moral beliefs and political practice, there is likely to be a further evolutionary change in moral norms regarding war once war has ended: a shift from the view that war is sometimes a necessary evil to the view that it is an unthinkably barbaric practice which lies beyond the pale of civilized behavior. This development would parallel the changes that have taken place in the past when previously sanctioned forms of group violence have ended. The most important precedents—institutionalized forms of violence or violation which were practiced routinely in all parts of the world for hundreds or thousands of years—are ritual cannibalism, ritual human sacrifice, slavery, and mutilating or lethal corporal punishment for violations of law or custom. In all of these cases, practices that had once been morally condoned and politically acceptable or even required became first repugnant, then illegal, and, eventually, unthinkable.

The key aspect of these precedents for the abolition of war is the character of the moral rejection of the practice that developed not before but *after* each was abandoned, and the role of that much deeper moral rejection in preventing a future recurrence. In every case, once a previously sanctioned form of violence was banned, people developed an abhorrence of the practice that was deeply internalized, virtually universally shared, and constantly reinforced by a myriad of cultural signals. As a result, in later crises of the kind once thought to justify the abolished practice, the practice was no longer considered an option for dealing with the problem: instead, it had become irrelevant as a means of coping with any problem.

This degree of moral rejection of war—its transformation into an unthinkable barbarity which, like slavery, torture, and human sacrifice, is an absolute evil that can never be justified as the lesser among evils—is a condition that would be likely to develop over a period of decades after war had initially been abolished, mainly as a function of the nonoccurrence of war; and it is a condition which, once achieved, would be likely to preserve peace throughout the longer-term future, regardless of the crises and pressures that might arise.

## Prospects for Achieving the Catalytic Threshold of Commitment: Democracy and Defensive Nonviolence

### DEFENSIVE NONVIOLENCE AND INDIVIDUAL-CENTERED POLITICS

A change in beliefs about "just war" of the kind needed to end war represents one plausible outcome—and quite possibly the most likely outcome—of global political and economic trends which have been under way for several centuries and seem likely to continue for the foreseeable future. At the heart of these trends, flowing from them if not causing them, is a fundamental change in attitudes toward the individual. Premodern complex societies (for example, Greece, Rome, China, and India) all had hierarchical social orders in which the individual's worth varied with social standing. In contrast, to a degree not matched since the time of the some of the simplest societies, modern society attributes equal worth to each individual. Though far from complete in any society, this "leveling" of the social worth of all human beings has fostered or paralleled the development of democratic institutions. At the same time, democratic institutions have prompted, or paralleled, a growing rejection of violence as a means of achieving political or economic ends within and between nations.[7]

Though little recognized, the renunciation of violence as a means to any ends except defense is as much a cornerstone of democratic institutions as its widely recognized counterpart, freedom of expression. Commitment to nonviolence protects and preserves freedom of expression and other civil liberties by precluding intimidation or coercion by violence or the threat of violence. Within democracies, wherever nonviolence is not the rule—for example, in subnational regions controlled by organizations like the Mafia or the Ku Klux Klan—other democratic rights and freedoms are lost or severely compromised.

Commitment to nonviolence lies at the core of democratic institutions, where it can be seen most clearly if the means of political decisionmaking are contrasted with those of predemocratic societies. In the empires, kingdoms, and principalities that preceded contemporary republican forms of government, national decisionmaking authority was vested in individuals or small elites who were believed to be qualified by criteria recognized as arbitrary—genes or wealth—rather than by talent, training, or any other quality relevant to the job; and whose authority was routinely guaranteed by superior military power. In other words, the winning combatant in armed contests for the crown was routinely recognized as the legitimate holder. Similarly, clearly incompetent, weak-minded heirs to the throne were generally kept in place despite their limitations, on the grounds that the relevant factor for authority was the inherited mantle, not competence.

With the rise of democratic institutions and republican forms of government in the 16th–18th centuries, the highest decisionmaking authority was no longer entrusted to arbitrary forms of succession, nor to superior wealth which could buy superior military power. Instead, the ultimate national decisionmaking authority of the executive and legislative bodies began to rest on two nonviolent sources: the opinions of the entire populace, expressed through the mechanism of "one man, one vote"; and nonviolent, largely verbal means of persuasion, including negotiation, bargaining, and trade. The essential shift in this transition was from arbitrary authority backed up by military power to authority derived from the opinions of the ruled, backed up by the nonviolent means of persuasion incorporated in democratic procedure, due process, and civil liberties (particularly freedom of expression).

Near-universally supported as the standard for the behavior of individuals within democratic nations, defensive nonviolence is also widely supported, albeit less well-understood, as a moral position on international war. This position represents a special version of the classical "just war" view: war is just so long as the ends are just and the means are proportionate to the ends. First articulated by St. Augustine of Hippo around 400 AD (during the break up of the Roman Empire), just war reasoning has predominated among political leaders ever since. Over the last two centuries, however, the idea of "peace through law" has begun to replace just war thinking. The idea is to apply in international affairs the domestic standard that enforcing the law (specifically, enforcing the nonuse of deadly force) is the only just use of deadly force. This standard is far more restrictive than the traditional just war guidelines; in fact, it is closer to the pacifist rule that there are no just uses of violence or deadly force. For if every nation, every subnational group, and every political leader refused to use armed force except in self-defense (or to help defend others from armed attack), then armed force would never be used.

The great potential of democratic commitment to nonviolence to serve as a bridge to a world without war lies in the fact that this commitment is well understood and strongly supported as a norm in domestic affairs in most nations. As a moral concept, democratic commitment to nonviolence has incomparably greater public support in all parts of the world than either pacifism or the just war view. And wide experience in domestic affairs regarding the practical application and interpretation of commitment to nonviolence except for defense offers innumerable examples and precedents which would facilitate the interpretation and application of this principle in the conduct of international affairs.

## DECENTRALIZED INTERNATIONAL GOVERNANCE

Many people may doubt that the espousal of democratic commitment to nonviolence in international affairs, alone, will lead to the abolition of war. The reason is that even if democratic institutions continue to spread, atavistic nations bent on conquest and empire may continue to exist, or to arise, and threaten aggression, or conduct aggression, against their neighbors. The only way to prevent this, the argument goes, is to create a world government with a monopoly on armed force; but this cannot be done without risking intolerable tyranny. In other words, the conditions required to maintain a lasting peace would jeopardize freedom, and, freedom deserves to come first both in its own right and as a condition for genuine peace (not tyranny masquerading as peace).[8]

In this context, the anarchic state of the international system poses a serious dilemma of political organization. On the one hand, upholding and strengthening norms does seem to require legal systems which not merely codify but enforce the norms. On the other hand, without any system of checks and balances on the use of power, it does not seem wise to give the United Nations power analogous to that of a national government; that is, exclusive control of the military means of enforcing peace worldwide. This could lead to tyranny in either of two forms: the tyranny of the majority, or a condominium among the great powers.

Fortunately, the principle of commitment to nonviolence except for defense offers a way to supplant anarchy with law and law enforcement while avoiding the danger of creating a despotic world government.[9] This third choice involves creating an international regime in which some nations jointly undertake to limit the use of their own armed forces strictly and narrowly to defense of themselves and defense of each other against external attack. Such a regime—a federation based on no other interests, obligations, or powers except a shared commitment to end nondefensive uses of force—would serve as a substitute or "dress rehearsal" for the effective functioning of the UN as a guarantor of security in the manner originally planned. The process of creating the regime would resemble the process of negotiating arms control agreements: nations would voluntarily, out of perceived self-interest, undertake to forego the use of armed force beyond national borders, except when defending one's own or a partner's borders, in exchange for a reciprocal commitment by other nations. The participating nations would undertake to come to each other's aid if attacked, and take other helpful arms control and foreign policy initiatives to promote participation in the regime and to maximize its effectiveness.

If the formation of a defense-oriented international security regime prompted a rapid, strong, and fairly even spread of commitment to defensive nonviolence around the world, that might trigger support for a more ambitious program of demilitarization, confidence building, nonviolent conflict resolution, and multilateral peacekeeping and peace enforcement—a program which would vest in the United Nations (or a subgroup of participating governments) a weak form of world government. The UN (or the subgroup) would then offer effective means of war prevention. It would not, however (at least, not initially), require or provide guarantees of human rights or human welfare, beyond freedom from war.

If the international spread of democratic commitment to nonviolence were more erratic, however—delayed in many parts of the world for decades or longer—then the development of a defensively oriented security regime of the kind outlined above might not play a major role in the demise of war. Instead, war might end in a more haphazard, drawn-out process, as a function of various nations' independent policies which limit the use of force to defense in their own conduct of international affairs. In this case, it can be argued, effective international peace enforcement institutions are not a necessary condition for peace, only a highly conducive condition.[10]

## The Relationship between Moral Belief and Other Factors in Accounting for the Rise and Demise of War

In making a strong claim for moral beliefs as a determinant of war, I do not mean to suggest that such beliefs exist in a vacuum, detached from the institutions that teach and implement them, or from the choices and life experiences of the individuals who hold them. On the contrary, predominant moral beliefs represent nothing more than an abstraction from their manifestation in institutions, in culture, in the ideas that people are likely to articulate, and in actual behavior.

What, then, is the causal relationship that I postulate between norms, on the one hand, and political institutions, economic organization, and other aspects of culture, on the other? What determines the path along which the normal curve moves over time? Are moral beliefs only a mediating factor between some other "first cause" and the existence or nonexistence of a socially sanctioned form of violence such as war?

For the purposes of this essay, I assume that there is a relationship of continuous interaction and mutual modification among political institutions, economic organization, a culture's "world view" (general values and assumptions about the nature of the world and the important features of human life), and moral views about violent behavior. Perhaps one of these factors—the economic, the political, the moral, or the world view—or some other factor, such as technology, tends to play a leading role in bringing about social change, while the others tend to follow. The leading factor may well differ from one era to the next, or from one society or part of the world to another.

More formally, the causal chain which accounts for the rise and demise of institutionalized, socially sanctioned forms of group violence, including war, is, I hypothesize, as follows:

1. A crisis (economic, political, or existential) leads to the practice of a form of group violence that had not previously occurred.
2. For one reason or another, the practice becomes embedded in a larger system of moral beliefs—that is, beliefs justifying the practice; and these beliefs, rather than the initial crisis conditions, subsequently become the main motivation for perpetuating the practice.
3. Because culturally transmitted, predominant moral beliefs are "sticky" (tending to persist until deflected), the practice may continue long after the conditions that originally gave rise to it cease to exist.
4. Eventually, however, the development of new circumstances leads to a weakening of the moral view according to which the practice was justified.
5. The combination of changed circumstances and changed beliefs lead to the abolition of the practice.
6. The ratchet effect involved in the banning of a previously sanctioned form of group violence, and the natural deepening of moral opposition once a practice has ceased make its recurrence virtually impossible.[11]

Postulating an evolutionary, interactive character between predominant moral beliefs and the cultural and political environment, I do not argue that moral beliefs play the *leading* role in the rise or demise of various forms of socially sanctioned group violence.[12] I support more limited claims for the role of moral beliefs in permitting or preventing socially sanctioned forms of violence: First, for violent forms of social action generally, moral beliefs serve as a gate which can be wide, facilitating violence, or narrow, deflecting stress toward nonviolent expression. Second, moral beliefs represent an important independent variable in the interplay of ideas, institutions, and political and economic conditions that perpetuate a sanctioned practice of violence. Third, under current international conditions, a modest change in moral beliefs about war in some nations could catalyze the further political and economic changes needed to bring about the initial cessation of war. Finally, the moral abhorrence of war that can be expected to develop once the practice has ended is likely to be the single most important factor in the long-term preservation of peace.

## 2.3 Comparison With Other Approaches

As noted earlier, the theory of peace presented here differs from certain other ideas about peace mainly in identifying a condition which, if achieved, could reasonably be expected to preserve peace indefinitely: that is, the emergence of a universal moral revulsion or abhorrence toward war.

The question of the conditions under which the abolition of war, once achieved, might last indefinitely has not generally been studied separately from the question of the conditions under which war might initially cease to occur. Even the transition to the initial abolition of war is rare as a subject of study compared with a much broader version of the topic: that is, the conditions under which the incidence of war might decline. The latter question—how to make the world more peaceful without ending war altogether—has received a great deal of attention.

Generally speaking, ideas about the achievement of peace focus on voluntary individual or government actions which, in their authors' views, would improve the prospects for peace. In some cases the author may believe that the relevant actions would achieve their goal by fostering the growth of certain moral beliefs; but relatively few authors identify war-condoning or war-preventing moral beliefs as lying at the heart of the matter. In many cases, however, the stress on specific actions (for example, UN reform or national military budget cutting), rather than on general moral principles, represents a way to operationally distinguish between two quite different policies which, given the cooption of the word "defense," might otherwise appear to be based on identical moral beliefs.

### Complementary Approaches Focusing on Institutional Change

For the most part, other proposals for strengthening peace complement the approach outlined here, rather than competing or conflicting with it. They involve strengthening conflict-prevention and conflict-resolution institutions, along with related developments in culture and formal education of a kind likely to strengthen democratic commitment to nonviolence.

Complementary approaches differ from the approach presented here mainly in how they identify the fulcrum of change. Their authors tend to assume that moral beliefs are too malleable—too subject to self-interested interpretation—to provide a reliable foundation for peace, and that only carefully constructed institutions can reliably translate good intentions into consistent results. My approach, too, calls for carefully constructed educational, policy, and peace enforcement institutions to reinforce and operationalize moral values in complex situations. It differs from the others mainly in underscoring the need for explicit, morally defined limits on the legitimate uses of armed force as the foundation for institutions that are likely to be effective in preventing (or ending) war.

There are three main approaches to peace, which tend to overlap with each other and with the views put forward here, but have important differences in emphasis. They are: arms control and disarmament; the establishment of a genuine, supranational world government or, on a more modest scale, the strengthening of the United Nations' collective security institutions and peace enforcement capabilities; and the establishment or strengthening of other, dedicated means of nonviolent conflict resolution.

Certain subsets of these general approaches deserve special mention. Early armament-oriented approaches involved proposals for general and complete disarmament. Notable among these were the proposals debated in the interwar disarmament negotiations among the major European powers, the United States, Russia, and Japan;[13] the disarmament plan included in Clark and Sohn's proposal for world peace through world law (1966); and the McCloy-Zorin agreement negotiated by the US and Soviet ambassadors to the United Nations during the summer of 1961.[14] After the early 1960s, the idea of general and complete disarmament was considered unrealistic, and attention focused instead on partial arms limitation and arms reduction measures ("arms control" agreements).[15] A new approach introduced in the 1980s stressed qualitative (as well as quantitative) changes in armed forces, which would build confidence between potential military opponents by reducing the risks of surprise attack, preemptive offensives, and mobilization for large-scale aggression. In addition to recently agreed measures for on-site inspection of stored equipment, observation of maneuvers, and data exchanges, more far-reaching proposed confidence building measures involve structural reconfiguration of armed forces to defensively oriented means of defense. Prominent among the theorists of defensive defense are Lutz Unterseher (Studiengruppe 1984), Wilhelm Nolte (Nolte and Nolte 1984), Bjørn Møller (1987–), Dietrich Fischer (1982), and Egbert Boeker (Barnaby and Boeker 1982).[16] Following the collapse of the Soviet Union and the Warsaw Pact, and the gradual integration of the states of eastern central Europe into West European institutions, a number of analysts incorporated defensive defense concepts in a broader approach called "cooperative security."[17] Under this approach, potential military opponents would cooperate in developing confidence-building security policies. A cooperative approach could be applied globally to processes and concepts of security involving some or all of the military great powers (the United States, Britain, France, Germany, Russia, and China); or it could be applied regionally among the key players in major regional conflicts (for example, Israel, Iraq, Iran, Saudi Arabia, Syria, and Egypt), or between countries with border disputes (for example, India and Pakistan).

Among the means of nonviolent conflict resolution, some involve early warning;[18] others focus on institutions and techniques for effective nonviolent conflict resolution through negotiation and mediation;[19] and one emphasizes organized, systematic civilian resistance as an alternative to armed revolt or armed defense.[20]

The approaches that involve the creation of some form of world government have a history dating back for centuries.[21] In this century, support for better international governance has broadened to include interest in international law and international norms as factors that can help prevent armed conflict.[22] Like arms control and disarmament measures, and proposals for confidence-building defenses, most ideas on ways to strengthen the peace-fostering roles of the United Nations and international law are fully compatible with my approach: indeed, practical changes in all of these areas would be desirable and, in some cases, required to implement my approach. Again, my approach differs from these others in arguing that no combination of peace-fostering measures is likely to lead to a peace that is global and lasting unless those measures aim to limit the use of armed force to defense, narrowly defined, and to end other uses of armed force, designed to support, protect, or advance "national interests."

As noted earlier, the dissolution of the Soviet Union and the former Yugoslavia have focused attention on the need for a stronger body of law on secession, which lies at the boundary between domestic and international law and between civil and international war.[23] Another related area involves collective security arrangements of a partial rather than universal nature: many of those who believe that an effective world security system lies far off and may never be possible support more limited collective security arrangements—such as NATO, the Organization for Security and Cooperation in Europe, or the Western European Union— as a viable alternative means of strengthening peace for the foreseeable future. Such arrangements represent adaptations of Karl Deutsch's "pluralistic security communities"—that is, groups of nations which share enough common values to join together to prevent war among themselves and protect each other against war with other nations.[24]

All of these institutionally based paths to a more peaceful world are compatible with the morally centered conditions for the achievement and maintenance of peace that I describe; all of them would help strengthen commitment to nonviolence; and some combination of them would probably be required to operationalize (that is, to express and enforce) the predominant commitment to defensive nonviolence that I identify as key to peace. Similarly, most of the changes in popular culture and children's education that have been proposed to strengthen commitment to nonviolence would not merely complement the moral changes needed to end war, but help bring them about.

## Competing Approaches

There are areas of significant difference between the ideas put forward here and three other, competing approaches to peace. Two of these might be described as lying to the left of mine politically: one identifies commitment to nonviolence with no exception for defense as the most effective path to peace, or the only path with moral integrity; the other identifies minimum conditions of political freedom (that is, civil liberties and human rights) or economic justice, or both, as prerequisites for peace. A third competing approach, which lies to the right of mine politically, is the "power-balancing" view that the closest the world can come to a complete and lasting peace is to keep war at bay through military deterrence and military balances of power.

### UNQUALIFIED COMMITMENT TO NONVIOLENCE

Those committed to nonviolence without exception for defense tend to believe that condoning any use of violence, including defense narrowly defined, is immoral and, even more important, represents a slippery slope that will lead to the perpetuation of war. Instead of drawing a moral line between defense and aggression, they draw a line between violence (regardless of the ostensible purpose) and nonviolence.[25]

This is certainly a morally consistent view, and one which is arguably more internally coherent and powerful than the view that I advance, that democratic commitment to nonviolence offers a more readily achievable route to the complete rejection of war which is needed for a permanent peace. Clearly, commitment to absolute nonviolence is not merely conducive to the development of the view that war is unthinkable, but represents a far larger step toward that view than does qualified commitment to nonviolence. The problem I see with this approach is that commitment to total nonviolence requires a leap of faith that lies well beyond the reach of most people, whereas commitment to defensive nonviolence is already the predominant view of most people. In today's world (as distinct from a future world with little or no warfare), the great majority of people are likely to oppose any approach to peace that excludes the right to and means of self-defense. Moreover, it is feasible—and possibly essential for peace in the longer term—for most individuals to be able to make reasonable judgments about whether or not given uses of force are defensive, and even whether a given use of deadly force was limited to the minimum required for defense.

By refusing to publicly support defensive uses of military force and to draw a sharp distinction between defense of a nation's sovereignty and territorial integrity on the one hand, and aggression or intervention to advance national interests on the other, those whose who advocate total nonviolence leave the practical business of defining the norms that are applied in public policy to those who support the use of force to advance national interests—and who deliberately blur the distinction between defensive and self-interested uses of force to win public support.

There is, however, one pragmatic point that may favor those who support complete nonviolence in the industrial countries, though not necessarily in Third World areas where opposition groups are fighting for freedom or justice. Because of its ambiguity—absolutely rejecting war for "us" but not for "them"— this approach may be emotionally and politically the path of least resistance to a world without war. Ironically, trends in US military strategy and geopolitical thinking, which emphasize the use of aircraft and missiles to conquer less technologically advanced Third World armies with no loss of US lives, illustrate the enormous appeal of a world in which the rich and powerful live in a "zone of peace," while other parts of the world continue to suffer from war.[26]

The United States is continuing to maintain large, powerful, very costly military forces that underscore the US ability to protect itself, its friends, and its interests even though the Clinton administration and congressional leaders agree that there is today no imminent threat of major war involving the United States or the Western world,[27] and no other threat that is worth putting US soldiers "in harm's way," as it is euphemistically phrased. The consensus on the lack of any cause worth dying for (or, in the view of proponents of nonviolence, worth killing for), for the first time since 1939, is indicative of positive changes in the international system and in attitudes toward war. In large part, it reflects the fact that since the end of the Vietnam War, US public opinion and US government policy have moved much closer to democratic commitment to nonviolence than they were earlier, even though current government policy statements continue to maintain the right to use force "to protect vital national interests." Thus, in the long run, it is possible that unwillingness to risk dying, rather than principled opposition to killing, will make nonviolence the norm.

## POLITICAL FREEDOM AND ECONOMIC JUSTICE

As suggested above, many people in the industrial nations combine unqualified commitment to nonviolence for themselves and their own countries with support for or acceptance of the use of armed force by Third World groups to rectify injustices in their nations and regions. This moral position does not fundamentally differ from that of politically conservative adherents of the just war view: for both, the morality of the means (the use of deadly force) depends on one's assessment of the justice of the ends. The problem with this position is that acceptance of certain wars as just by people who otherwise are committed to total nonviolence obstructs and undermines the development of the more deeply rooted norm of nonviolence that is needed to make war unthinkable.

The earlier section on the abolition of internal (civil) wars raised a question about whether such wars were likely to end in areas where democratic institutions have not been established. In that section, I argued that over the last 50 years, there have been many cases in which the transition to democratic governance was accomplished largely or entirely by means of nonviolent protest and resistance. Thus, it cannot be argued that war cannot end unless and until democratic institutions have been established in all countries. It can be argued that the more countries that have established democratic institutions, the less likely will be both civil wars and international wars of aggression. From the viewpoint of the "least change" conditions for the abolition of war, a reasonable case can be made that democratic institutions now exist in a sufficient proportion of the world's nations, and in adequate quality in those nations, that war could conceivably be abolished prior to any further spread of democracy. At the same time, it must be stressed that the abolition of war should not be seen as depriving those who seek political freedoms and equality before the law of a useful means to those goals. On the contrary, to the extent that repressive regimes respond with violence and brutality to nonviolent protests supporting social change, they lose legitimacy and authority at home and abroad, setting the stage for their own demise. Thus, rather than identify peace as unrelated to or counterproductive for the spread of freedom, we can assume that the abolition of war is likely to foster the spread of democratic values and institutions.

Similarly absent from my list of conditions for peace is any economic factor, such as the establishment of a minimum standard of living around the world, the elimination of the most egregious disparities in wealth and opportunity within or among nations, or even further guarantees than exist today of equality of opportunity. The argument here parallels that regarding the need for democratic institutions as a prerequisite to peace: the establishment of a minimum standard of living and the narrowing of the gap between rich and poor are both likely to be conducive to peace, but neither is a necessary precondition to peace. Just as is the case for freedom, an argument can be made that defining justice as a condition for peace is putting the cart before the horse: war and threats of war are, in the first instance, an instrument of the rich and powerful, who can use their wealth and power to secure various advantages in any open military contest. The abolition of war is likely to promote economic welfare and equity. Regarding the distribution of wealth, ruling out the use of force by the mighty to preserve or extend their advantages would improve conditions for narrowing the income gap between the rich and poor nations. Regarding the fulfillment of basic human needs, it is widely recognized that disarmament can promote development, by freeing up resources, removing obstacles to international aid, and changing domestic economic priorities.

In many cases, the view that peace cannot be achieved without prior conditions of political democracy or economic justice may be more an expression of concern with freedom and justice than a considered view on the conditions for peace. Thus, the same view might be more accurately phrased in one of the following formulations: (1) Global deficiencies in democracy and justice are more pressing and merit more urgent attention than do problems of war and peace, which are less acute; (2) Working for peace should not be misinterpreted as accepting the status quo in regard to oppression and injustice; (3) Rich nations (or, domestically, middle-class yuppies) may have the luxury of addressing the intractable issues of war and peace; poor nations and poor people have to focus on problems of economic survival; or, finally, (4) Just because I am a rich yuppie and have the luxury of taking a principled position on the intractable and (given the low likelihood of my action having any serious political impact) theoretical issues of war and peace, that does not mean that I do not give a high priority to the concrete, urgent economic and political problems of those who are not as well off as I am, at home and abroad.

The idea that peace might be more readily achievable than freedom or justice and could facilitate and strengthen efforts for freedom and justice seems to offend the sensibility of many liberal and progressive activists, as though time and effort put into political efforts to end war (or intellectual efforts to think through how to end war) necessarily steal time and effort from trying to help the less fortunate in our own societies and in the world. But if, on reflection, one concludes that ending war can be achieved more quickly and easily than ending oppression and injustice, and that ending war would greatly help efforts to end oppression and injustice, this resolves the sense of competing priorities.

In cases where there is no effort to make a serious assessment of the prospects of achieving peace, freedom, or justice to the degree needed to bring about the others, but merely a casual statement such as "If you want peace, work for justice," I infer that the real content of the claim is something like "Working for justice is a higher priority for me than working for peace; and besides, I believe that insofar as justice is achieved, the prospects for peace will be increased." The claim that justice is conducive to peace is consistent with the idea that principled commitment to nonviolence is an important factor, but not the only factor which affects the prospects for peace. The fact that the speaker gives justice a higher priority than peace is the expression of a personal preference, not a theoretical idea about the relationship between the two.

The leading intellectual proponent of the view that peace cannot exist without justice is Johan Galtung, who introduced the concept of "structural violence" into peace research in the 1960s.[28] The core meaning of the concept is that people are subjected to forms of physical "violence" (starvation, malnutrition, disease) and other severe deprivations comparable to the losses suffered in war not only as a result of acts of war, but also as a result of the ostensibly "nonviolent" structure and workings of capitalist socioeconomic systems. Later generations of peace researchers have incorporated the concept into their work using the shorthand phrases "positive" peace and "negative" peace: positive peace is peace with justice and freedom (and, more recently, appropriate treatment of the natural environment); negative peace is the mere absence of war.

The Galtungian school does not explicitly claim that justice is a precondition for the abolition of war. Instead it argues that peace without justice is not genuine peace, nor likely to be a lasting peace. Many university-based "peace studies" (or "peace and justice" studies) programs are based on this view, which has encouraged students to learn about poverty and inequality but has not been particularly fruitful as a source of ideas, research, or public debate on the conditions for ending war.

### POWER BALANCING

Analysts and politicians of the "power-balancing" school of thought believe that war cannot be abolished, only kept at bay.[29] They argue that the most reliable, effective means of keeping war at bay is the deterrent effect of the threat of punishment for aggression by means of retaliation with conventional or even nuclear military forces. They believe that military alliances and military power balancing strengthen deterrence by increasing the forces available for retaliation and bringing the political legitimacy of multilateral support to deterrent threats—and, perhaps, by bringing the discipline and predictability required by military alliances into the turbulent course of international affairs. They assume that it is dangerous to disarm, because this will weaken deterrence and increase the risk of war. For the same reason, they tend to put a higher priority on maintaining the internal coherence of power blocs than on goals conducive to the abolition of war, such as limiting weapon deployments and military actions as narrowly as possible to defense, or supporting the growth of egalitarian, participatory international political institutions.

The main reasons advanced by the power-balancing school for the view that war cannot be ended are the key obstacles to war addressed in this essay: innate human aggressiveness, powerful incentives to go to war, the lack of a world government to prevent war (and the potential for tyranny inherent in the creation of a world government), and the frailty of political institutions in general, and peacekeeping and peace enforcement institutions in particular, when placed under great stress.

In brief, my comments on these obstacles are as follows: the nature of innate aggressiveness is not such as to preclude the abolition of war; like domestic violence, the tendency to go to war can be restrained by appropriate socialization, even when powerful incentives for war appear to be present; limiting the use of armed force to defense offers avenues for creating a nontyrannical peace enforcement system; and a deeply internalized moral commitment to nonviolence can make peace enforcement institutions work even when placed under stress. These arguments are developed more fully in Part II of this essay.

## Conclusions

Like advocates of complete nonviolence, experts of the power-balancing school often support arms control and the strengthening international security institutions.[30] At the same time, like adherents of power balancing, nonviolent activists usually describe their goal as "reducing the risk of war" rather than "ending war." As a result, the public is left uncertain as to the real differences in the peace-related goals and means supported by these schools of thought. The shared value that pierces the public's confusion is an interest in making a warlike world more peaceful. This lowest common denominator of the most prominent schools of thought has an unfortunate impact: it leaves the public with the view that available public policy choices cannot do more than affect the risk of war in the short term; none will actually increase or decrease the (presumably very dim) prospects of ending war altogether in the longer term.

By failing to develop a theory of how war might end and a set of political and security strategies to achieve that goal, advocates of complete nonviolence, along with advocates of power balancing, have limited public debate to the question of how to reduce the risk of war and the costs of preparing for war in a world where war is inevitable. Typically, the difference between those two schools on this question boils down to whether to rely on more or less armed force for the purposes of deterrence and warfighting. In any such dispute, middle-of-the-road publics generally take the view that "it's better to be safe than sorry": thus, they agree to spend more rather than less to buy more rather than less armed force. This creates a self-fulfilling prophecy, since maintaining more than enough force to minimize the risk of war in the short term precludes confidence-building limits that would deter war in the short term while moving gradually toward the conditions needed to end war over the longer term.

Part II

# SOCIALLY SANCTIONED VIOLENCE

# THE ROLES OF INNATE IMPULSES AND LEARNED MORAL BELIEFS IN INDIVIDUAL AND GROUP VIOLENCE

## 3.1 Introduction

Chapter 2 describes conditions of commitment to defensive nonviolence under which war might initially end, and related conditions of abhorrence of war under which, once ended, war could be permanently abolished. This chapter and those that follow attempt to make a convincing case that war is susceptible to being permanently abolished. The evidence and arguments adduced address three of the four obstacles to the abolition of war raised in Chapter 1: the view that human beings have innate aggressive instincts that trigger or foster war; the view that moral beliefs which warrant and motivate war persist; and the view that even if peace were initially achieved, pressures would arise sooner or later that would lead to war. The first two of these obstacles pertain to the feasibility of the initial abolition of war, as well as the feasibility of the long-term maintenance of peace; the third concerns only the long-term maintenance of peace. I defer to later study further elaboration of other aspects of the conditions under which peace might initially be achieved, including a response to the fourth obstacle to peace cited in Chapter 1, the view that insuperable obstacles block the establishment of effective international institutions for peacekeeping and peace enforcement.

The material in Chapters 3–6 supports the hypotheses about the achievement and maintenance of peace with the argument that war is one among many forms of socially sanctioned group violence, and is subject to rules of individual motivation and social organization that apply to all forms of socially sanctioned group violence:[1]

- **The role of innate aggressiveness in causing violence:** Some individual acts of violence ("crimes of passion") and some group acts of violence (mob rioting) are motivated by aggressive impulses (feelings of hostility and desire to hurt); but even such acts include an important component of rational choice. To the extent that acts of violence are motivated by innate impulses rather than rational choice, they represent a loss of control. In sane adults, aggressive impulses do not represent a spontaneous instinct or drive; they are always *reactions* to a source of provocation and they subside when the provocation is removed. There is no form of innate aggressive energy in human beings which arises spontaneously and accumulates until it is expressed in one form or another. From the viewpoint of the society or nation, institutionalized, socially sanctioned forms of group violence are always the product of deliberate choice based on calculations of risk, cost, and benefit. From the viewpoint of the individual, active participation in (and to some degree, even passive noninterference with) socially sanctioned group violence represents not the loss of control indicated when the motive for an act is an aggressive impulse, but rather the exercise of deliberate, highly organized choice and compliance.

- **The role of moral beliefs in preventing nonsanctioned violence and permitting sanctioned violence:** In every culture, learning to control the expression of feelings and impulses is a central part of childhood development. Among other things, learning to "sublimate" aggressive and sexual impulses, that is, to redirect or rechannel the former away from acts of violence and the latter away from sexual acts, is central to ego formation and to the development of a healthy, mature adult. The developmental process creates a baseline inhibition (a habit or predisposition) against violent behavior and an ability to choose whether or not to commit acts of violence—both of which are control functions whose operation involves specific areas of the brain. I hypothesize that the universal childhood process of learning to sublimate aggressive impulses creates an internalized moral presumption in adults that all forms of violence are wrong; and that society superimposes on this underlying presumption a set of exceptions to the general rule, along with reasons and contexts for the exceptions. The exceptions are morally explained, socially sanctioned forms of individual and group violence. The main role of learned moral beliefs in socially sanctioned group violence is to lower the barrier to violence which all individuals internalize as a fundamental moral premise.

- **Changes in moral beliefs about and practices of socially sanctioned forms of group violence:** From time to time in various cultures, new forms of socially sanctioned group violence appear or existing forms of socially sanctioned group violence disappear. Changes in practice are associated with corresponding changes in socially taught moral beliefs about acceptable and unacceptable forms of violence. In some cases, the rationale for a given form of sanctioned violence seems to fade, giving way to the presumption that it is *not* an acceptable form of behavior: in such cases, spontaneous changes in moral belief appear to be the main cause of the demise of a previously sanctioned practice. In other cases, changes in political, social, or economic organization and related changes in world view seem to lead to the rise or demise of a given practice of socially sanctioned violence and to the condoning moral beliefs associated with it.

- **The role of moral beliefs in preventing a recurrence of previously sanctioned forms of group violence:** Forms of violence which were once socially sanctioned but then abolished never recur in the societies that previously practiced them. The reasons for this stem from changes in consciousness, world view, and moral belief, not from the absence of conditions similar to those in which the violence was previously sanctioned. I hypothesize that there is a loss of innocence or consciousness-raising process which occurs when the moral rationale for a practice to which there is an underlying aversion is stripped away: once a given practice is perceived as an absolute evil (not a necessary or justifiable evil, nor, potentially, the lesser among evils), this perception cannot be erased; future efforts to restore the practice on the grounds that it is an acceptable or necessary evil fall on deaf ears.

When applied to war, these general rules regarding the roles of innate impulses and learned moral beliefs in the conduct and prevention of socially sanctioned forms of group violence suggest the following specific conclusions: War is not the product of an innate aggressive "drive," nor of innate aggressive impulses, nor is it a inevitable part of the human condition. It is a product of culturally shaped moral beliefs about this form of violence, introduced at a certain juncture in human history. Generally speaking, such beliefs tend to change, both by fading and by being eroded when changing political and economic circumstances reduce the perceived utility of a given form of violence. There is reason to believe that both fading and erosion are weakening the moral beliefs that make war socially acceptable and motivate individual participation in war. Moreover, the history of other forms of socially sanctioned violence suggests that if war is initially abolished, a more profound abhorrence of the practice is likely to develop, which will prevent its future recurrence.

The remainder of this introduction expands on the obstacles to the abolition of war which are addressed in Part II; it introduces the types of evidence supporting the views outlined above; and it outlines the organization of the evidence in this and the succeeding chapters.

## Skepticism about the Abolition of War

Skepticism about the feasibility of the permanent abolition of war is usually based on ideas about innate human aggressiveness, stress-induced violence, or the weakness of peace enforcement institutions. Some argue that since human beings have innate aggressive tendencies, it is foolish to expect human societies to stop committing acts of aggression, permanently and completely. Even if some nations ceased to make war for one reason or another, innate aggressiveness would generate "rogue" states, with aggressive political leaders who will try to use armed force to advance their national interests, and easily aroused followers willing to implement such decisions.

Another widespread view is that, unlike the actions of individuals, the actions of nation-states are not constrained (or only very loosely constrained) by moral considerations. Nations, the argument goes, are likely to take any action which their leaders perceive to be in the national interest; and if war is likely to promote national interests, nations will make war. This argument may seem a bit overdrawn, but a more modest version of the claim is quite compelling: nations which experience severe stress (economic, environmental, political, etc.) may resort to war in an effort to avoid losses, make compensating gains, or strengthen national cohesion. In other words, regardless of potential future changes in institutions and norms, in times of great stress, nations may turn to war as a remedy of last resort.

Finally, many political analysts argue that in theory, war might be abolished if there were a global counterpart to national governments—that is, a world government with a monopoly on armed force—but in practice, such a government would pose an unacceptable risk of world dictatorship, and for this reason its creation is both undesirable and unlikely. This means that even in the best case, international peacekeeping institutions are likely to be too weak to prevent war or quickly end up backsliding (that is, the reintroduction of war after it had stopped) by rogue states, aggressive leaders, or nations under stress.

Each of these doubts about the feasibility of the abolition of war has considerable *prima facie* plausibility; and the combination of the three might seem to seal the fate of abolition. The hypotheses presented in Chapter 2 about the role of moral beliefs in perpetuating and preventing war were developed, however, with the goal of putting these doubts to rest. Thus, in this and the succeeding chapters, as I elaborate on the role of moral beliefs in matters of war and peace, the material is organized and focused so as to provide a direct, full response to each concern.

## Evidence for the Key Role of Moral Beliefs in Institutionalized Forms of Group Violence

Diverse kinds of evidence support the view that despite innate human aggressiveness, powerful moral opposition to war, once achieved, would prevail even in situations of extreme stress and in the absence of an all-powerful world government. History and anthropology offer precedents for the permanent demise of socially sanctioned forms of group violence and violation that were once widely practiced and, at the time, considered vital to the well-being of society—practices whose abolition was comparable to that of war in character, magnitude, and scope. In those earlier cases, the *initial ending* of each practice seems to have been due to changes in circumstances and in world view and moral beliefs, while the later *global reach and permanence* of each ban appears to have been the product of an increasingly deeply rooted, universal, self-perpetuating moral belief that the practice could not be justified under any circumstances. The historical and anthropological evidence for the role of moral beliefs in the practice and subsequent abolition of previously sanctioned forms of institutionalized violence is discussed in Chapters 4 and 5. Chapter 4 surveys a number of forms of violence that were once widely practiced and socially sanctioned but later abolished; and it discusses the role of moral beliefs in the rise and demise of those practices. Chapter 5 presents a detailed case study of the practice of socially sanctioned group violence which is most remote from modern experience—and therefore most powerful in illustrating the importance of learned moral beliefs in accounting for sanctioned violence—that is, ritual cannibalism.

A separate but related body of evidence concerning the relationship between moral beliefs and violent behavior, reviewed in this chapter, lies in an area that cuts across psychology, psychoanalytic theory, social psychology, neurobiology, and criminology. Experimental, clinical, survey, and statistical research and theoretical studies in these fields suggest a model of how biological features of aggression, early childhood development, and culturally shaped, normatively loaded ideas about violence interact to permit or prevent violent behavior by groups and by individuals. The remainder of this introductory section presents the main conclusions drawn from these studies, which are discussed in more detail in subsequent sections.

Recent psychobiological and neurological research has revealed a great deal about the innate, physiologically based tendency of human beings, *when provoked*, to exhibit physical signs of angry arousal and to experience hostile affect, and, sometimes, aggressive impulses (that is, impulses toward violence or other harmful behavior) toward the source of the provocation. Every recent study underscores, however, that there is *no* evidence that aggressive impulses necessarily lead to violence, and *no* evidence for the existence of a physiologically based form of aggressive "energy" that can build up inside people until it is released, like an electrical charge or water behind a dam. On the contrary, recent research indicates that violent actions by mentally and physically healthy, mature human adults—whether conducted alone, in small groups, in large groups, or on behalf of society as a whole—are *always* the product of voluntary choice and of culturally shaped cost-risk-benefit assessment by the perpetrator(s).

Under special circumstances, pathological states of human physiology may cause the subject to manifest forms of verbal or physical violence which are virtually involuntary: these states include brain lesions (created, for example, by accidents or tumors); abnormal brain conditions associated with severe retardation; and abnormal chemical or hormonal balances associated with psychosis and other severe mental illness. These conditions tend to dampen or eliminate the operation of areas of the brain and neural pathways which control the expression of affect, modulate or regulate behavior, and inhibit or "control" (prevent, or determine the direction, form, and intensity of) acts of violence. Intoxication by alcohol and other drugs, and withdrawal from intoxication, can have similar effects, particularly those associated with irritation and uncontrolled or ill-controlled movement. In healthy, sober adults, *learned ideas* about acceptable forms of behavior, *learned habits* or patterns of behavior, and *learned expectations* about social rewards and punishments determine the form in which individuals express spontaneous impulses, including but not limited to anger and aggressive impulses.

Advances in the study of the brain, developmental psychology, and psychoanalytic theory all indicate that learning to control or "sublimate" the expression of all kinds of feelings and impulses, including aggressive impulses, is a central aspect of the normal childhood sequence of growth and development. Sublimation permits planned, organized behavior by allowing the individual not to childishly "act out" intense emotions, urges, or impulses, but instead to channel feelings into socially acceptable and socially productive action. As indicated above, for an adult to lose or fail to develop the ability to control the violent expression of hostile feelings is a sign of serious mental illness, retardation, brain damage, or severe chemical imbalance. The forms of behavior in which adults do express emotions and impulses are influenced by internalized cultural norms, some of which are learned in early childhood, others acquired later in life. Social norms tend to set particularly strong, clear limits in the realms of violence and sex, where the inability of individuals to control behavior could immediately affect the prospects for group survival by increasing the birth rate or the death rate.

Institutionalized, socially sanctioned forms of group violence (including war), even more than individual acts of violence, are determined not by biologically based aggressive impulses but by cognitively controlled decision making processes. The need for community and the importance of the community in the life of the individual motivate the perpetrators of institutionalized violence. Individuals carry out prescribed acts of violence because they need a social context for identity, they need social acceptance and approval, and they want to avoid opprobrium and punishment; and because they have internalized normatively loaded, culturally shaped beliefs about the violent practice as an acceptable means for the community to secure a valued goal.

The claim that learned, culturally determined beliefs play a more important role than innate aggressive impulses in perpetuating war as a social institution, and that different beliefs could end war, is a special case of a more general claim: culturally determined moral beliefs about acceptable and unacceptable forms of violence play a far more important role than innate aggressive impulses in the rise, conduct, and demise of *all forms* of institutionalized, socially sanctioned group violence.

The next section of this chapter discusses in more detail the relationship between innate aggressive impulses and violent behavior in the individual. The third section addresses the shared and differing features of individual and group violence, socially sanctioned and socially banned forms of violence, and impulsive and institutionalized violence.

## 3.2 Sources and Features of Violence by Individuals

Is there an innate aggressive drive or instinct in human beings? If so, does it play an important role in the causes of war? And does it preclude the abolition of war? These questions can be answered today with far more authority and clarity than they could three decades ago, when two popular books—Konrad Lorenz's *On Aggression* (1967) and Robert Ardrey's *The Territorial Imperative* (1967)— claimed that war is the product of an innate tendency to aggression embedded in the limbic system that humans inherited from prehuman species. The publication of these books and pressing public policy issues concerning war and crime led many psychologists and sociologists to undertake experimental, survey, statistical, and epidemiological studies in an effort to identify the innate (biological) and learned (social) sources of violent behavior. Over the same period, burgeoning research on neurology, biochemistry, mental illness, and brain damage provided far more fine-tuned means than had previously been available for investigating the biological etiology and somatic features of violent behavior in humans and other animals.

Despite their disparate vocabularies and contexts, studies across a wide range of disciplines[2] show a substantial degree of consensus on the nature of the innate propensity to violence in human beings, and the impact of social learning factors on the tendency to perform violent acts. The overarching conclusion is that acts of violence by mature, mentally and physically healthy, sober adults do not reflect an innate aggressive drive or instinct in the human species, which imposes an involuntary or semivoluntary compulsion on individuals (acting singly or in groups) to conduct violent acts. Instead, violence on the part of healthy adults is the product of a deliberate, fully voluntary, cognitively controlled decision making process in which individuals weigh (even if poorly and briefly) the potential outcomes of the action, including harm to the victim, social approval or disapproval, legality, punishment, and other potential costs, risks, and benefits. In other words, to the extent that acts of violence by individuals are biologically driven, they are caused by abnormal, pathological conditions; normal biological conditions and development in humans create adults who are routinely able to inhibit violent action even when they experience intense stress or intense aggressive affect.

The following sections develop this perspective and its ramifications for the conduct and abolition of war. First, I look at the biological, social, and developmental psychological factors which in the overwhelming majority of individuals developmentally elicit a tendency to inhibit violence which prevails throughout the lifespan. In a small minority of individuals, on the order of five percent, the interaction of these factors leave violence-inhibiting neurological structures, patterns of behavior, and personality preferences undeveloped. In those individuals, biological, psychological, and conceptual factors will tend to facilitate or encourage violence throughout the lifespan. This section shows that rather than an innate aggressive drive, the innate features of aggression in individuals are: (1) a capacity for violent behavior, particularly in response to provocation; (2) innate somatic reactions to (or components of) the arousal of feelings of hostility or anger; and (3) physiological structures that in most individuals inhibit the expression of hostility or anger in violent behavior.

In the second section, I look at the later social influences which contribute to voluntary choices to commit violence among both the minority who are predisposed to violence and the majority who predisposed to nonviolence.

## Physiologically Based Aspects of Aggressive Impulses and Violent Behavior by Individuals

Over the past 30 years, there has been an explosion of research on aggression by biologists, psychologists, and anthropologists on aggression, following the "ethological" accounts put forward by Lorenz and Ardrey. Pointing to examples of aggressiveness and territorial defense in the animal kingdom, Lorenz and Ardrey argued that the human species inherited both tendencies. Subsequent research showed that the activities among animals called "territorial defense" actually involve two other forms of behavior: intermale aggression, and differences in aggressive behavior on familiar and unfamiliar ground [Moyer (1976); see further below]. This clarification did not, however, put to rest the idea that human beings have an innate tendency toward aggression. On the contrary, studies of the "psychobiology" of aggression have identified various physiological systems in humans which are regularly associated with anger (or irritation) and violence. These include neural brain localities, endocrine and hormonal levels, and manifestations of arousal or excitability. Research on mentally ill and brain-damaged patients and on populations of violent criminals indicates that certain brain lesions and excesses or deficits of certain chemicals are associated with unprovoked acts of violence.[3]

As Lorenz suggested, human physiology does include systems derived from those in prehuman animals—specifically, neurological structures and states of blood chemistry—which are associated with the onset or the cessation or inhibition of hostile, aggressive affect and (when it occurs) related violent behavior. Lorenz and Ardrey were wrong, however, in reading into animal behavior an innate tendency to proactive aggression against others of the same species, except for male contests for sexual predominance in some species. The contexts and forms of violent attacks and aggressive posturing among nonhuman mammals are limited to four specific kinds:

| Type of aggressive behavior | Induced by |
| --- | --- |
| 1. Predatory | 1. Appearance of natural prey |
| 2. Fear-induced | 2. Threat, distress calls of young (perceiving threat) |
| 3. Irritable | 3. Pain, frustration, deprivation |
| 4. Intermale | 4. Male of the same species[4] |

Of the four, only predatory aggression—that is, hunting other animals for food—involves unprovoked "offensive" attacks, designed to kill or disable a living creature. This form of aggression has a direct counterpart in human behavior, which is hunting or fishing for food.

The other three forms of violence, particularly as exhibited among nonhuman primates, are specifically reactive and defensive in nature. Fear-induced violence is generally the result of being at the receiving end of predatory aggression, or being fearful of this. Exposure to a potentially dangerous foe produces a "fight or flight" reaction, in which flight is always attempted first (except among mothers protecting their young), and fighting for survival is a last resort. Irritable aggression is a violent reaction to a source of irritation, which is most often pain, but can also be the frustration associated with a failure of an expected response or the withdrawal of an expected pleasure.

At first glance, intermale aggression seems to be closest to the standard image of aggressive behavior in human beings: among primates, intermale aggression involves hostility and aggressive displays by two males of the same species, who are competing for sexual access to female partners. But primate intermale aggression differs from human war in all key respects:

- With rare exceptions, primate intermale aggression is limited to aggressive *posturing* and causes no physical harm to either party.
- In situations where the two males are part of the same group (or becoming part of the same group), the function of the aggressive posturing is to establish the dominance order in the group *without deadly violence*. A surprising recent finding is that the dominance rank does not provide tangible benefits, such as access to more, better, or earlier food or sexual activity (unless the group is facing extinction). Instead, the function of the dominance order, along with that of the aggressive posturing, is to prevent uncertainty and resulting potentially deadly violence within the group.
- In situations where the two males are not part of the same group, the male which is on familiar territory will dominate the interaction, because his entire energy is dedicated to the confrontation, while the male which is on unfamiliar territory will be preoccupied with an "incompatible" behavior, which is the caution, exploration, and readiness to flee that always predominates on unfamiliar territory.

Among nonhuman animals and, as far as can be detected physiologically, among humans, the aggressive reaction to a provocation (a predatory threat, an irritant, a competing male) ceases as soon as the provocation is removed: there is no residual aggressive energy to be discharged. Similarly, there is no accumulation or build-up of aggressive energy prior to the provocation (or, in the case of hunting for food, prior to the observation of a suitable prey).

Each of the four main types of aggressiveness in nonhuman animals is associated with specific somatic changes and intense activity in specific areas of the brain and neural network; and no two clusters of somatic effects can occur simultaneously. Because of the mutually exclusive character of aggressive reactions with each other and with certain other clusters of somatic effects (for example, those associated with humor, sexual arousal, or hunger), each cluster is called an "incompatible response" to each of the others. If an incompatible response is induced, the prior somatic state will simply disappear.

The study of patients with brain damage has shown that the physiological sites and effects associated with various types of aggressiveness in humans resembles that in animals; but the similarity between humans and other animals in the somatic features of some forms of aggressive *affect* does not show that violent *behavior* is instinctive in human beings. On the contrary, one of the most important recent findings is that certain areas of the brain serve as "on-set" and "off-set" switches for aggressive behavior: the on-set switches turn on the somatic reactions and aggressive feelings associated with hostile responses to provocations; the off-set switches control the behavior that follows the arousal of hostility, inhibiting violence and other socially unacceptable actions. Experiments with animal (mainly mouse) brains, studies of human brain damage, and psychopharmacological studies all show that the on-set and off-set switches can be turned off or dampened by brain lesions and by drugs. Patients who suffer an accidental injury that creates a lesion in the off-set area exhibit abrupt outbursts of verbal abuse and physical violence (called "explosive violence"), which represent a dramatic change in behavior compared with their preinjury pattern. Alcohol and illegal narcotics generally decrease or block the function of the violence-inhibitors, and withdrawal from the effects of alcohol and other illegal and prescribed drugs can have a similar impact. Earlier in this century, many mentally ill patients who exhibited extreme violence had the aggression "on-set" area surgically removed, which made them exceptionally passive as well as nonviolent. Today, medications are prescribed for this purpose.

Physiologically induced episodic (repeated) violence which lies entirely beyond the voluntary control of the individual occurs only in the presence of certain pathological conditions: brain lesions in parts of the brain that regulate behavior; and abnormalities in body chemistry associated with some severe mental illnesses or with the use of intoxicants and other drugs which interfere with the operation of those parts of the brain (simulating brain lesion). In other words, the propensity of the overwhelming majority of individuals, who do not suffer from pathological neurological or neurochemical conditions and have not consumed alcohol or other drugs, is not to express aggressive impulses in violent behavior.

The normal condition of nonviolence is a product not only of brain structures that regulate or inhibit violence, but also of the interactive development of the brain, behavior, perception, and personality in early childhood. Generally speaking, pathological physiological conditions impede and degrade developmental learning of the kind that helps prevent violent behavior. This learning includes the acquisition of language, the development of motor skills, and the development of a sense of mastery over the external environment. In other words, there are interactive social-biological feedback loops which tend to reinforce and strengthen the operation of the brain areas that inhibit violence in the course of the early childhood development of normally endowed individuals, or to weaken the operation of those areas in individuals with abnormalities in regulatory systems or chemistry or with severe mental retardation. The opposite can also occur, however: appropriate nurturing and training can assist those with abnormalities to develop more normally, while neglect, violence, verbal abuse, and lack of physical activity can weaken autonomic regulation. Given these findings, it is not surprising that among lifetime career criminals with repeated violent offenses, the rates of brain malformation, psychosis, other severe mental illness, and mental retardation are several fold greater than they are in the population at large.

Finally, there is a well-documented correlation between the level of serum testosterone (and steroid hormones more generally) in the blood and violent behavior. In some way, hormones are believed to contribute to the extraordinarily skewed incidence of crime in general and violent crime in particular among males, who account for 90 percent of violent crime, and especially males between the ages of 14 and 18, who account for about half of all violent crime by males. (These statistics hold across many cultures, in which the absolute rates of violent crime differ widely.) The statistics of violent crime suggest that there are two main populations who engage in serious violence, with different motives and propensities. The first is a very small fraction of the population who participate in violent acts throughout their lives, from early childhood to past 50 and who are responsible for the bulk of "stranger violence" (assault and homicide) associated with armed robbery and thrill-seeking violence. The second is a proportionately much larger group of teenage youths, who due to high testosterone levels or other features of adolescence, have aggressive impulses that are more easily aroused and more readily translated into violent action than is the case for the population at large. The same youths tend to drink or do drugs, further lowering their self-awareness and their neural inhibitors against violence; they participate in gangs and in other competitive small-group behavior, in which violence is admired, instigated, and encouraged; and they are responsible for the bulk of "friend and acquaintance" violence, typically committed when the perpetrator (and, often, the victim) is intoxicated and engaged in roughhousing or other forms of competitive and often illegal activity.[5]

As suggested by the existence of behavior-regulating neurological structures and functions, which serve to inhibit the expression of aggressive affect in violent action, there is no innate human aggressive "drive," which, on its own, generates violent behavior. No physiological evidence at all has been found for the existence of an aggressive form of energy, which is capable of building up inside of individuals (or groups) and which must then be released in one form of action or another. Study after study explicitly rejects the "hydraulic" theory of aggression suggested by Freud, when he postulated the existence of an aggressive drive.[6] The physiologically based tendency to aggression in (normally developed) humans is entirely reactive and basically defensive in nature. (This comment applies to acts of violence toward other humans: hunting and fishing for food are obviously proactive forms of aggression.) For this reason, the use of the term "aggression" (for the deed) or "aggressiveness" (for the capability, intent, or propensity to harm), with its connotation of unprovoked attack or intrusion, is misleading. What human beings have inherited from prehuman species is not a tendency to launch unprovoked attacks on others of their own species, but a tendency to use violence as a last resort to defend against attacks by others and to end protracted pain or frustration caused by external factors.

## The Impact of Social Learning on Predispositions to and Choices of Violent Behavior by Individuals

Increasingly, studies of the sources of tendencies to violent or nonviolent behavior on the part of individual humans have identified a process involving the interactions of three main factors: (1) biology, specifically, neurological and neurochemical structures and states which tend to permit or inhibit violence; (2) social learning, in which parents, teachers, peers, other members of the community, television, and other media directly or indirectly teach or induce the child to conduct or not conduct violent acts in general and in specific situations; and (3) the psychological blending of biological predispositions and social influences in personality, habits of behavior, motivation, affect, and ideas about acceptable and unacceptable forms of behavior in the realm of violence and aggression. This view, sometimes called the "bio-psycho-social" model of the sources of aggression, was increasingly common during the 1970s and 1980s; and it predominates in the major scholarly studies published since 1990.[7] The following discussion focuses on two types of social learning with substantially different effects on the tendency to violent behavior: first, the interaction between the child and its parents during the first five years of life, which tends to finalize the development of physiological and psychological aspects of the *disposition* of individuals to perform or not to perform violent acts in certain situations; and second, the impact of other, later social influences—such as teachers, peers, and television—on *voluntary choices* to perform or not to perform violent acts in various situations, made both by those who are disposed to violence behavior and by those who are not so disposed.

## PARENTING AND EARLY CHILDHOOD DEVELOPMENT OF THE INTERNALIZED ABILITY TO INHIBIT VIOLENT BEHAVIOR

As noted earlier, lifelong tendencies toward violent or nonviolent behavior tend to be set during the first five years of life, by an interaction between the physiological endowment of the individual and social learning.[8] Children with a normal biological endowment and adequate parenting learn not to conduct violent acts and develop the ability to maintain control under enormous stress. In contrast, children with either problematic biological features or inadequate parenting fail to develop the ability to control violence and translate aggressive affect into nonviolent (mainly verbal) forms of behavior. "By the time even very young children present in clinics, a self-perpetuating cycle of acting out, punishment, and rejection resulting in more acting out has been firmly established" (Landy and Peters 1992, p 17). (The remainder of this part gives extensive excerpts from Landy and Peters 1992.)

Both parents and children bring innate endowments to their interaction. For parents, these include "their own experiences of being parented . . . and sense of control of circumstances" (p 17). In addition "the degree of social support and life stressors will impact significantly on the amount of energy and the emotional availability of the caregivers and may have an enormous impact" (p 17).

The infant brings a number of individual characteristics into the early relationship, such as the degree of predictability, responsiveness, irritability, hypersensitivity, and the like. "For the child who develops an aggressive conduct disorder, it is likely that a 'goodness of fit' with the principal caregivers does not exist and the infant begins to experience traumatic dyssynchronies at a very early age that start to produce significant aberrant social, biochemical, neurological, and emotional development. To protect himself or herself from the pain of these early interactions the infant may 'close himself to stimuli, thereby inhibiting the generation of information necessary for continued growth'" (pp 17–18).

Early experience with the primary caregiver affects the development of affect regulation, that is, the child's ability to "redirect, control, modulate, modify and bring about adaptive functioning in emotionally arousing situations" (p 3). In the first 3 months of life, the developmental goal in the sphere of affect regulation is "obtaining physiological homeostatis or self-regulation" (p 4) which allows the infant to "maintain a state of equilibrium in the face of internal and external stimulation" (p 4). Between 3 and 12 months, "the infant develops cognitive capacities that allow for an understanding of the relationship between actions and consequences and the formation of mental representations or memories of people and events" (p 6). Between 9 and 12 months, the key change is the

development of a relationship with the primary caregiver which serves to organize affect, cognition, and behavior. As patterns of interaction with the primary
caregiver "are internalized their emotional quality and synchrony will have
a significant impact on the child's style of affect regulation and ultimately on
their [sic] capacity to reduce the expression of aggressive behavior under stress"
(p 6). At first, the capacity for "object constancy" is fragile: it takes the infant
many months to remember and utilize the memory of attachment figures in
times of stress and frustration.

Between 12 and 24 months, "children become capable of displaying and label-
ing a full range of human emotions, including sympathy, jealousy, and other
more subtle affective experiences. They develop an increasing awareness of self
as an autonomous agent and, most important, change from a style of affect
regulation that is primarily sensorimotor to one that relies on representational
capacities. These growing symbolic capacities, which include language and pre-
tend play, are vital in the further development of the ability to monitor, modify,
and modulate behavior and emotional expression. Play and language . . . are
used increasingly to modulate tension and anxiety throughout the second and
third years of life. Similarly, representations of pleasant experiences, objects, and
attachment figures become stable and begin to sustain the child during times
of stress and separation from primary caregivers. Children become able to use
negotiation and to inhibit behavior in response to limits. . . . Finally, prosocial
behavior and empathetic response to distress of others [may occur] as early as
18 months" (p 7).

Between 24 and 36 months, "affect becomes much more integrated with
thoughts and cognition. As language and play become more elaborate. . ., children
become increasingly able to describe and control . . . anger" through language and
play. "Well modulated children can talk about internal states and feelings, which
facilitates control over nonverbal emotional expression and enhances regulation
of the emotions themselves" (p 8).

Between 36 months and 60 months, children "begin to internalize standards
and rules and to identify with the caregivers who have provided them with external limits for aggressive behavior and have modeled and encouraged capacities to
modulate it. The development of conscience enables children to delay immediate impulses . . . and frees them from primary reliance on external controls and
standards. . . . " The capacity for empathetic response and an understanding of
the viewpoint of others increases. "As part of this capacity, children are able to
understand their own part in bringing about consequences. A sense of personal
responsibility, a 'wish to please' as well as the desire to succeed become important
in social adjustment and academic achievement. . . . " (p 9).

Young children acquire the capacities discussed above "through a combination of biological maturation" and "sensitively attuned, appropriately timed interactions with caregivers" (p 9).

## SOCIALIZATION TO PERMIT OR INHIBIT VIOLENT BEHAVIOR IN OLDER CHILDREN, TEENAGERS, AND YOUNG ADULTS

Normally developed children who do not exhibit exceptionally aggressive behavior by the age of 5 can develop a tendency to commit violence at a later age as a result of various social influences.[9] During the still-formative late childhood and teenage years, substantial influence can be exerted by parents and other adults at school and in the community; by peers; and by television and other mass media. In each of these environments, the tendency to violent behavior can be increased by several mechanisms:

- Observing violent behavior on the part of others;
- Being subjected to violence, particularly in the form of punishment by parents;
- Being explicitly told or implicitly informed that violent behavior is admirable or desirable in itself (for example, because it demonstrates toughness or machismo), or acceptable as a means to other ends (such as obtaining money or objects through robbery, or exhibiting power or status); and
- Experiencing pressure, inducement, instigation, or encouragement to violent behavior from third parties.

The first two of these influences, observing violent behavior and being subjected to violence, particularly violent punishments, may also occur in early childhood; but their impact in later years, like that of the latter two influences, lies mainly in prompting the formation of ideas and "behavioral scripts" about what is just, fair, morally right, or socially acceptable or desirable, and about how to enhance feelings of power, control, dominance, or status. This contrasts with the effect of observed and experienced violence and violent punishment in very small children, who directly associate such trauma with lack of protection and support from, and the interpretation of rejection and abandonment by, the primary caregiver—and, thus, people in general. Where the older child and teenager *emulate violence by others*, the very young child *responds to his or her fear and sense of failure with disruptive behavior*, which elicits reactions from adults that confirm the child's negative expectations, in a self-reinforcing vicious cycle.

For older children and teenagers, the social influences which may teach that violence is appropriate, acceptable, or desirable in certain situations can take a myriad of forms. Family, school, films, videos, music lyrics, and television can each contribute, for example, to the view that men are more violent than women, or that male violence is good when the capability for winning a physical fight is associated with the leadership qualities of determination, courage, and decisiveness (the Schwarzenegger model of a male hero), or that male violence against women is an inevitable part of life (as in some rap lyrics).

If responsible adults at school or in the community overlook certain forms of violence (for example, fistfights) as an inevitable part of growing up, or encourage such violence, this may strengthen the belief that society is unlikely to punish spontaneous violence, or that there are no serious costs associated with violent behavior. Other examples of condoning social environments which exacerbate tendencies to violence are offered by cheering observers of barroom fights and enthusiastic bleacher crowds who applaud and urge on disruptive behavior by soccer "hooligans."

In some cases, "subcultures of violence"[10]—such as the communities centered on organized crime families, inner city gangs, or drug distribution networks—may socialize more generally for, rather than against, violence. They may foster general readiness to use serious or lethal violence in a wide variety of situations. In such cases, the mitigating impact on individual violence of the larger society's norms about unacceptable forms of violence may be largely or entirely eliminated.

## 3.3 Sources and Features of Violence by Groups

As attested by the numerous and diverse book-length surveys of aggression published in the last decade, the biological, psychological, and social origins of violent acts by individuals are so diverse, complex, and subtly interwoven that it is extremely difficult to integrate them in a coherent theoretical view. In fact, serious integrative efforts are just beginning to appear.

Recognizing this, we must expect the sources of violent practices by organized groups to be even more elusive. Aggressive behavior undertaken jointly and simultaneously by disorganized or fully decentralized groups—clusters, crowds, and mobs—resembles aggressive behavior by individuals, but with features exaggerated by the tendency of groups to polarize behavior. In contrast, the origins and features of violent practices undertaken by, or on behalf of, organized groups may, but need not, resemble violent acts by individuals. The following discussion begins with an attempt to provide a map of the universe of human-against-human violence, in which individual and group behavior can be situated and compared.

## The Domain of Human-on-Human Violence

When considering what perpetuates and might help end war, it is helpful to situate war in the larger field of human violence. Different branches of social science typically focus on different parts of this domain: for example, many anthropologists treat war as a scaled-up version of individual aggression (a human "bad" which reflects irrationality or a loss of control), while many political scientists treat war as rational, deliberately chosen means to well-defined ends—in Clausewitz's famous dictum, "an extension of politics by other means." In this study, I attempt to reconcile and integrate these and other views of war within the framework of a larger map of the universe of human-on-human violence.

Since the universe has a number of important dimensions, it cannot be fully represented graphically on a two- or three-dimensional chart; but it is, nonetheless, useful to imagine the domain of violent behavior as analogous to a topographical map of a multidimensional surface, in which different features predominate in different areas. All positions within the domain represent points along more or less continuous measures of particular dimensions of violent behavior. For the purposes of this essay, the important dimensions are as follows:

1. The *deliberateness* of the action, which ranges from unintended through impulsive to hasty to carefully planned.
2. The *independence* of the action, which ranges from proactive (unprovoked) to reactive (provoked).
3. The *angry, hostile affect* associated with it, which ranges from high to low.
4. The *legality* of the action, which ranges from illegal (criminal violence) through legally permitted (parents' spanking of children) to legally required (all individuals in a society paying taxes that support the implementation of the death penalty or the prosecution of a war).
5. The *scale* of the action, which ranges from individual through small group (tens or hundreds) to large group (thousands or more) to actions conducted by or on behalf of a society as a whole.
6. The *moral quality* of the action in the society in question, which ranges from condemned (as wrong or evil) through tolerated or permitted to highly prized. This quality must be assessed separately for the following major subsets of the actor's social universe: (1) the violent actor, (2) the actor's family or community, or other important reference group(s), (3) the society at large (encompassing the nation or state), and, finally, (4) the international community. The moral assessments of an action by different subsets of the actor's social universe—such as the family and the peer group, or the nation and the international community—may differ radically. The actor must then construct a moral framework in which the conflicting views are reconciled.

Various aspects of violent action tend to be correlated with one another, sometimes to an extent that makes them indistinguishable from one another. For example, any act of violence that is *legal* in a given society is necessarily *morally sanctioned* by that society. Acts of violence that are *deliberately planned* (rather than hasty or impulsive) are usually *proactive*, but they may be reactive. Similarly, *impulsive reactive* violence is nearly always associated with *anger*; but anger (specifically, an angry sense of injustice or an angry desire for retribution) is also likely to be involved in cases of *planned reactive* violence. (Palestinian acts of terrorism provide an example of the latter.) *Anger* is less likely to be involved (or, likely to be involved in a much more subtle, indirect fashion) in *carefully planned criminal* violence, such as murder as a means of acquiring wealth.

Three tables help clarify, formalize, and interrelate these distinctions. Table 3.1 distinguishes between proactive and reactive violence, and between forms of violence committed exclusively by humans and those committed by other animals as well. Table 3.2 gives an illustrative list of various forms of violence that distinguishes between large- and small-scale violence, and between legal and illegal forms of violence. Table 3.3 adds more fine-tuned distinctions regarding scale of the action and the degree of social approval for both legal and illegal forms.

While many permutations and combinations of the various dimensions of violent action are possible in theory and have real-life manifestations, three

**TABLE 3.1**   Shared and differing propensities to and contexts for violence among humans and other animals

---

I.  Genetically inherited propensities to and contexts for violence that are common to humans and other animals

   1a. Pro-active, inter-species: predatory violence (hunting and fishing)

   2a. Reactive (to threat), intra- and inter-species: defense of self, young, family, community

   2b. Reactive (to irritant), intra- and inter-species: violent expression of intense irritation, frustration, or anger caused by another

II. Learned, culturally variable propensities to and contexts for violence that are unique to humans

   1b. Pro-active intra-species: violence associated with taking food (or food-producing territory) needed for survival

   1c. Pro-active intra-species: violence as a means to other culturally-shaped goals, such as
- increasing wealth, power, territory, or access to natural resources;
- confirming or reinforcing individual or group identity or self-esteem; conveying status;
- exacting retribution or revenge; or
- establishing or re-establishing justice.

---

*Source:* Author's estimates.

*Notes:*

*Pro-active acts of violence* (set '1') involve situations in which the perpetrator's assault is unprovoked. Generally speaking, pro-active violence is planned, controlled, and instrumental.

*Reactive acts of violence* (set '2') involve reactions to an external threat or irritant. Reactive violence tends to be spontaneous, hasty or ill-considered, 'instinctive,' and driven by fear, irritation, anger, or rage.

**TABLE 3.2** List of forms of assault and killing illustrating differences in scale and legality

**Small scale: Individual (one-on-one) and small group violence**

*Illegal*
- Deliberate, thrill-seeking attack on stranger (e.g., drive-by shooting)
- Unintended part of planned crime (e.g., unplanned murder during a robbery)
- Deliberate component of planned crime (e.g., murder of spouse for insurance)
- Crime of passion: attack on an acquaintance or person known well (e.g., murder of a spouse during a fight)
- Product of mental illness, brain damage, or chemically-induced condition
- Police and prison guard brutality (e.g., beating imprisoned individuals) and police use of excessive force

*Legal*
- Sado-masochistic sexual activity between consenting adults
- Boxing
- Assaults in other contact sports (e.g., football, ice hockey, rugby)
- Spanking of children by parents and teachers
- Abortion
- Defense of self or others against assault or threat of assault or murder

**Large scale: Larger group violence, and violence conducted on behalf of society**

*Illegal*
- Gang-prompted violence by individuals and by groups
- Organized crime's threats and acts of violence as a means to coercion
- Political violence (e.g., terrorism, coups d'etat, assassination, union busting, intimidation of picket-line crossers)
- Mob violence against individuals or groups, including arson and lynching

*Legal* (when conducted by or on behalf of a society as a whole)
- War, including guerrilla warfare, civil war, international war
- Law enforcement: the death penalty; other forms of corporal punishment;
- Law enforcement: threats and acts of injury or death as means of capture and restraint of unarmed suspect

*Source:* Author's estimates.

**TABLE 3.3** Mapping the domain of human-on-human violence: illustrative list of forms of violence showing differences in scale, legality, and social approval

| | SCALE (NUMBER OF PERPETRATORS) | | | | |
|---|---|---|---|---|---|
| LEGALITY AND DEGREE OF SOCIAL APPROVAL IN THE PRACTIC-ING SOCIETY | INDIVIDUAL (ONE-ON-ONE) | SMALL GROUP (2-99) | LARGE GROUP (100–9,999) | LARGE FRACTION OF SOCIETY (10,000–10 MILLION) | SOCIETY AS A WHOLE, OR STATE ON BEHALF OF SOCIETY AS A WHOLE |
| | | (INCL. ETHNIC, RELIGIOUS, POLITICAL, CRIMINAL, AND OTHER SUBCULTURES) | | | |
| Required by law generally but not always approved by most | | | | • civil war (acts of, or on behalf of, original government) | • international war <br> • public execution for infidelity (Saudi Arabia) |

| | SCALE (NUMBER OF PERPETRATORS) | | | | |
|---|---|---|---|---|---|
| LEGALITY AND DEGREE OF SOCIAL APPROVAL IN THE PRACTICING SOCIETY | INDIVIDUAL (ONE-ON-ONE) | SMALL GROUP (2-99) | LARGE GROUP (100–9,999) | LARGE FRACTION OF SOCIETY (10,000–10 MILLION) | SOCIETY AS A WHOLE, OR STATE ON BEHALF OF SOCIETY AS A WHOLE |
| | | (INCL. ETHNIC, RELIGIOUS, POLITICAL, CRIMINAL, AND OTHER SUBCULTURES) | | | |
| Not required but legal and generally approved or tolerated | · spanking (pre-1960 USA) <br> · abortion (Europe) <br> · defense of self or other against attempted murder, assault, rape | | | | · police use and threats of use of deadly force against unarmed suspects <br> · female circumcision (Sudan) |
| Legal, approved by some, opposed by others | · spanking (post-1980 USA) <br> · boxing (USA) <br> · abortion (USA) | | | | · death penalty (USA) |
| Illegal but tolerated (little public outcry or legal opposition), and/or condoned by a subculture which serves as a reference group for the perpetrator(s) | · teenage and young adult fights <br> · child asexual and physical abuse <br> · - spousal sexual and physical abuse | · organized crime <br> · political violence; e.g., terrorism <br> · political violence; e.g., coups d'état <br> · violent ethnic customs (blood feuds, ritual mutilation, etc.) | | | · police brutality <br> · prison guard brutality |
| Illegal, socially condemned, and actively opposed by law enforcement institutions and popular culture | · assault <br> · rape <br> · murder <br> · boxing (Europe) <br> · armed robbery <br> · spanking (post-1980 Sweden) | · mob violence <br> · lynching | | · civil war (acts of those aginst government) | · dealth penalty (Europe) |

Source: Author's estimates.

contrastive combinations are particularly important for the study of socially sanctioned group violence:

First, there is virtually the opposite of socially sanctioned group violence: this is impulsive, angry individual violence which is illegal and morally condemned by the society at large, by the actor's reference groups, and usually by the actor. Violence caused by serious mental illness (schizophrenia) and by brain damage is frequently (if not always) placed in this cluster, although in some cases it is so impulsive as to be genuinely involuntary. In the normal range of behavior (absent serious mental illness and brain damage), much family and community violence (domestic abuse and barroom brawls) tends to be hasty and ill-considered. Alcohol and other drugs contribute to impulsive or ill-considered, illegal violence because such drugs lower the individual's normal, learned inhibitions against socially unacceptable behavior.

Second, criminal violence, which is illegal and morally condemned by the society at large, tends to be condoned by the actor(s) and by the actor(s)' important reference groups. Such action is likely to be planned and deliberate, not impulsive, particularly if conducted by a group, such as an organized crime family or a gang. Deliberate, planned murder and assault belong in this category, whether conducted by an individual or by a group.

Finally, socially sanctioned, institutionalized violence is legal and morally condoned by the society at large and generally (though not always) by the actor(s) and the actor(s)' reference groups.

As suggested by these descriptions, the relative weights of innate affect and learned moral belief in motivating violent action differ greatly in different forms of violence. The uncontrolled expression of innate aggressiveness is probably the dominant factor in unprovoked, highly impulsive individual violence, as well as in the escalation of affect and action during mob violence. At the other end of the spectrum, learned moral beliefs about just uses of violence play a dominant role in motivating forms of socially sanctioned violence which are legally permitted (like parents' spanking of their children) or legally required (the individual's direct or indirect participation in society's exercise of war or infliction of the death penalty).

## 3.4 Motives for Participation in Institutionalized Group Violence

In all societies, deliberate acts of life-threatening violence by a single individual toward another are considered morally wrong and illegal, unless they occur under well-defined conditions for which exceptions have been specified. Sometimes fatal acts of violence are unpremeditated. Similarly, people in small groups or mobs may engage in ill-controlled violence, such as trampling others to death in a panic, or in impulsive violence, such as throwing stones, breaking glass or structures, or starting fires in a riot. Crimes of passion and other acts of impulsive or ill-controlled individual violence and small group or mob violence are the forms of violence for which the perpetrator's motivation draws most heavily on innate aggressive impulses and least on rational cost-benefit calculations, or culturally shaped ideas about just, appropriate, or necessary uses of violence.

In contrast, socially sanctioned forms of violence, and, in particular, institutionalized forms of large-group violence, are rooted entirely in learned ideas about just, appropriate, or necessary uses of violence and cognitively based cost-benefit calculations, that is, by the same kinds of factors that influence and motivate other forms of social and political behavior. In all societies, people come to believe that violence is wrong except in culturally condoned circumstances as a result of essentially the same processes.

Human beings are born with a capacity for violence and other forms of intentionally hurtful behavior, which is part of the repertoire of means of self-protection. The small child's tendency to express or "act out" aggressive impulses in violent behavior is, however, tamed during the developmental process of learning to sublimate (control the form of expression of) feelings and impulses. This aspect of the normal process of childhood socialization, which occurs in every culture, is central to the development of the ego, the perception of being in control of oneself and one's life, the ability to plan and organize behavior, and the ability to have emotion-laden interactions and relationships with other human beings.

The universal childhood process of learning to sublimate hostile affect and aggressive impulses (among other feelings and impulses) creates a baseline degree of routine inhibition against violence, along with a deeply internalized belief that inflicting physical harm or pain on others is wrong. In other words, this aspect of socialization leaves the child at 5–10 years of age with the ability to choose to commit violent acts that hurt others, but with the belief that doing so is morally wrong and with the ability to choose not to commit violent acts even when under stress or experiencing intense hostility.[11]

Overlapping with the early process of learning to control the expression of affect and impulses, and continuing into the later childhood and the teenage years, virtually every culture teaches that there are certain exceptions to the general rule that violence is not an acceptable form of behavior. Normatively loaded beliefs about situations in which it is tolerable, admirable, or even socially required for individuals to use violence as a means to a greater good or as the lesser among evils are superimposed on the baseline inhibition against violence and belief that violence is wrong. Generally speaking, institutionalized forms of group violence are legitimated and perpetuated by powerful incentives for individuals to participate in (or passively tolerate) the practice, and powerful disincentives for active resistance to it. The incentives and disincentives—various social rewards and punishments—are powerful largely because the practice is associated with a world view and system of moral beliefs which are routinely used to explain or justify the organization of society and the main goals of society. In a sense, institutionalized forms of violence constitute a symbolic representation of society: to reject, condemn, and refuse to participate in those forms of violence is to reject the society, or at a minimum to demand a wholesale rethinking of society's values and of the rationale for its forms of organization and activity.[12]

Following the early and later aspects of socialization, some individuals may commit impulsive acts of lethal violence, but such acts tend to be relatively rare (say, one per thousand of population), and even then, predominantly by individuals whose failed or poor process of childhood socialization led to the development of a psychopathic personality. The overwhelming majority of individuals who participate in organized, socially sanctioned group violence would never, on their own, commit an act of premeditated, planned lethal violence; their violent actions as members of a group are induced entirely by their culturally shaped moral beliefs and their need for community. For this reason, the forms and the frequency or intensity of socially sanctioned group violence vary with culture and within given cultures, over time.

This model does not account for the origin of institutionalized, socially sanctioned forms of violence, only for the participation of individuals in such practices and, in that sense, the perpetuation of the practices. Chapter 4 gives a speculative view of the social origins of institutionalized forms of violence.

# SOCIALLY SANCTIONED GROUP VIOLENCE
Features, Examples, and Sources

## 4.1 Introduction

In discussing socially sanctioned violence, it is useful to begin with a brief recapitulation of certain points from Chapter 3. There I observe that there are two key differences between the forms of individual and group violence which are illegal and morally wrong in a given society, and the forms which, though considered wrong in the abstract, are legal and morally condoned in specified contexts because they are viewed as the lesser among evils or "necessary" (that is, useful) evils. These differences concern the proportion of a society implicated in a given practice of violence, and the role of learned norms in motivating the individual's participation in the action.

In virtually all societies, violent acts which go against social norms—especially potentially lethal types of violence—are conducted by a very small minority of the population; in contrast, socially sanctioned forms of group violence are performed, actively supported, or at least tolerated by the great majority of people.

The difference in participation is mirrored in differences in motivation: Individual and small group forms of violence which go against norms are conducted *in spite of or in defiance of social norms.* Such counter-norm violence is likely to occur as a product of: (1) emotionally or physically induced lowering of learned inhibitions against violence in a situation where the perpetrator is provoked (crimes of passion); (2) a psychopathic personality developed during childhood as a result of physical or social problems or deficiencies; or (3) the longer- or shorter-term adoption of the norms of a subculture of violence, such as those fostered by youth gangs, the drug subculture, or organized crime.

In contrast, individual participation in socially sanctioned forms of group violence is conducted *in compliance with social norms*. The motivation for violent acts of this kind lies in feelings and ideas that are very nearly the opposite of those associated with acts of socially banned violence. In acts of socially sanctioned group violence, the individual maintains control of his or her actions, including the deliberate conduct of violence, in order to meet society's expectations. Each person takes part either as an active participant or as a noninterfering observer out of a combination of mutually reinforcing motives: obedience to authority, desire for social approval and acceptance, fear of social disapproval and punishment, and the internalization of the socially taught moral views that support the action. In this respect, the motivation for participating in socially sanctioned violence is identical to the motivation for engaging in the entire range of socially accepted, nondestructive behavior which predominates in any viable society.

In addition, two other factors typically facilitate participation in socially sanctioned forms of group violence and may also play a role in the conduct of some forms of socially condemned violence: these are the routinization of the activity, which obliterates the individual's sense of initiative and responsibility; and the cultural dehumanization of the intended victim in a variety of ways before, during, and after the violence. The impact of both factors is to reduce sympathetic or empathic feelings for the victim, and the feelings of guilt and remorse normally associated with the action.

**Examples of socially sanctioned group violence**: The following sections of this chapter review some widely practiced forms of socially sanctioned group violence, with a view to illustrating the special motivations and social organization that characterize this form of behavior. This brief survey has several purposes:

First, it underscores that war is by no means unique as a sanctioned form of violence practiced around the world for centuries or millennia. The existence of other widespread forms of institutionalized violence may not seem supportive of the thesis that war is amenable to abolition; but the fact that virtually all of the other practices have died out does lend support to the thesis.

The second purpose is to derive from the now-abandoned forms of socially sanctioned group violence a means of artificially distancing ourselves from the practice of war. Televised news makes war appear to be an unending and omnipresent aspect of the human condition. But when we look back at earlier, now-abandoned practices of socially sanctioned violence, we are reminded that at the time when they were legitimate, they, too, seemed to be a lamentably unavoidable part of the human condition. This suggests a useful analogy: Contrasting modern views with contemporaneous views of now-abandoned practices suggests a way to think about war as if it had been—and, thus, could be—abolished. The general idea is to focus not on the rationales currently associated with war, but on the features that war shares with now-abolished forms of violence: the inhumanity, the barbarity, the indiscriminate arrogation by society of the right to destruction of individual lives. When we think back to earlier forms of violence, the rationales that legitimized them at the time fade into the background; what remains in the foreground is the monstrosity of the behavior. If we think about war from a parallel future vantage point, as though looking back at an activity that had been abolished, we would dissociate the barbarism of this instrument of power from the ends to which it is put. In other words, our moral assessment of the ends—whether achievable by other means, or abandoned along with war—would no longer have a bearing on our moral assessment of the means.

Third, surveying the justifying contexts and reasons for earlier practices of socially sanctioned violence helps to clarify the relationship between utility and morality in this realm of human behavior. In the case of older forms of socially sanctioned violence, an argument was made that on balance, despite the harm to the victim (if harm was acknowledged), society was better off with the practice than without; but in each case, this moral assessment was a function of a more general set of values embedded the society's culture and world view. This suggests that a form of violence which is condoned in one society may not be condoned in another not because the link between cause (the violent practice) and effect (the social good) is no longer believed to be valid, but because the effect which is valued in the first society has become irrelevant, or a matter of indifference, or a social bad in the second.

Finally, the review of now-abandoned practices suggests a useful metaphorical handle on the role of moral beliefs in the conduct of war. Generally speaking (across time and culture), learned moral beliefs reinforce the developmentally acquired, internalized ability not to express hostility in the form of violent action: socially taught, articulated moral beliefs strengthen the inarticulate acquired barrier to (or control over) violent behavior. When a given form of violence is socially sanctioned, however, social norms lower the conscious part of the internal barrier to violence. As long as the practice is legitimate, the role of moral beliefs is not only (and perhaps not mainly) to motivate the action, but to permit it, that is, to help overcome inarticulate, internalized inhibitions against violence. Once a practice is banned, moral beliefs spring back to their more usual position of reinforcing the individual's self-control and inhibitions against violence.

**Defining socially sanctioned group violence**: In surveying socially sanctioned forms of violence, I have used a broad definition of "violence." The definition is not so broad as to include Johan Galtung's "structural violence": that is, harms that are inflicted on individuals by virtue of an inequitable form of social organization, such as starvation, poverty, illiteracy, disease, high infant mortality, indignity, and lack of any influence on public policy.[1] The exclusion of these forms of harm does not indicate that they are less harmful than active violence; in many cases, the opposite is certainly true. But the purpose here is to identify common features and sources of active forms of violence, and there is reason to believe that the features and sources of structural violence may diverge substantially.

With respect to physical violence, I have used a very broad definition, including three main variants:

**Intentionally caused (or permitted) physical hurt, physical injury, or death**: Activities of this kind are assault, rape, and homicide, and include massive and particularly brutal forms of such acts, such as torture, genocide, or war.

**The systematic, coercive deprivation of individual freedom of action with the threat of physical harm or death**: Practices in this area are slavery and lesser but still severe forms of involuntary servitude, including most of those where the victim is called a serf, villein, bondman, or indentured servant.

**Physical violation of the bodies of the dead**: The main actions in this area involve various forms of cannibalism, and the use of human body parts as materials for worked goods, such as skulls for bowls, bones for needles or necklaces, skin for fabric, etc.

The inclusion of the second and third areas—slavery and the violation of dead bodies—stretches the definition of "violence" slightly; but in all three areas, the practice involves active, physically aggressive acts against the body of another human being. Moral objections to activities in the three areas have shared features, and the rationalizing moral justifications for activities in the three areas overlap substantially in form and content. Thus, the moral positioning of socially sanctioned "violence" taken in the narrowest sense (the first area) is clarified by including in the set of surveyed socially sanctioned practices those in which the violence is threatened (the second area) or symbolic (the third).

Given this broad approach to "violence," I define institutionalized socially sanctioned forms of group violence, including war, as practices which have the following features in common:

Each involves the deliberate infliction, or the coercive threat of infliction, of bodily harm or physical violation on some humans by others.

Each is condoned by society as a whole and generally involves either action by individuals who represent the society as a whole, or publicly visible, legal action conducted by a large fraction of the population, with the support (or, at a minimum, noninterfering tolerance) of the rest.

In each case, members of the society generally view the activity itself as morally wrong (bad, unethical, abhorrent) outside the specific context in which it is socially approved or required.

The society explains and justifies the activity in specified context as a means to a greater good, or the lesser among evils.

There are five forms of socially sanctioned group violence which share these characteristics and which have been practiced in virtually all parts of the world (that is, practiced extensively on every continent) over centuries or millennia. They are:

1. Ritual cannibalism
2. Ritual human sacrifice
3. Slavery
4. Physical punishment for violating law or custom (including execution, flogging, burning, drawing and quartering, branding, and the cutting off of body parts; and the violent treatment of suspected lawbreakers, including interrogation with torture and trial by ordeal)
5. War

In addition to these widely practiced forms of institutionalized violence, there are many other practices of socially sanctioned violence which have been less widely practiced. Most tend to be found only in certain parts of the world. Some were socially sanctioned but involved individual rather than group practices: that is, they were conducted not by or on behalf of society as a whole, but by individuals on an ad hoc basis, often out of sight of the community, or by a cultural subgroup. In many cases, practices of this kind may have been tolerated by the society, but not strongly approved; and the moral justification may have rested more heavily on individual philosophy than public morality.

**Organization of the chapter:** In the next section of the chapter, I give a cursory overview of some practices of violence that were socially sanctioned but not widely practiced. These activities give a sense of the range and nature of the violent acts comprised by the abstract category of "socially sanctioned, institutionalized violence" and the importance of variable, culturally derived world views and moral beliefs, in accounting for these practices.

In the following section, I survey in somewhat more detail three of the practices which, like war, were independently developed and practiced in many different cultures in all parts of the world: corporal punishment for violations of law or custom, human sacrifice, and slavery. The fourth such practice, ritual cannibalism, is reviewed in more detail in Chapter 5.

The subsequent sections of the chapter uses these diverse examples as the basis for a speculative consideration of the processes which led to the start of various processes, and the process which led to their demise. The chapter concludes with a discussion of the relationship between efficacy and morality in the practice and abolition of various forms of socially sanctioned violence.

## 4.2 Some Socially Sanctioned Forms of Physical Violence and Violation

The varieties of human hurtfulness are mind-boggling. If we were able to identify all of them, the list of violent practices which were socially approved in one part of the world or another for some period of time would probably run to hundreds of activities, or perhaps thousands, depending on how fine-tuned the typology, and how small the group credited with "social approval." In identifying some of the myriad contexts and forms of violence, this brief survey makes no claim to offer a representative sample. The purpose here is merely to insure that the reader does not restrict the scope of socially sanctioned violence to the five most widely practiced forms, which are the focus throughout most of this essay, four of which often or always involve lethal violence.

What leads to the extraordinary variety in the forms of socially sanctioned violence is not so much the specific physical impact of an action on a (generally live) human body (though that, too, can be greatly varied), but the context and meaning of the action. Thus, this list groups the forms of socially sanctioned violence by the context rather than the physical form of the action.

**Political violence:** Torture of prisoners conducted by individuals who represent a society (or a prevailing religion) has already been mentioned as a form of legal punishment. Torture has also been common as a means of interrogation or a means of persuading a victim to "confess" to something or to do something he or she would not do otherwise. Terrorist attacks and political assassination are other forms of political violence which are sanctioned in some quarters.

**Family and other community punishment:** The deliberate physical punishment of some people by others, outside of the framework of court-imposed punishment and at the discretion of the perpetrators, has been legal and socially condoned more often than not over the past 10,000 years. Violence by some members of families toward others—mainly by men toward their wives—has been sanctioned in many cultures for millennia. Dobash and Dobash (1979) document ancient practices in which wives were considered chattel, which husbands could treat as they liked, including killing. Whipping, ear boxing, and spanking of children at home and at school has a long tradition in the Western world and in some other cultures. Some professions involve organizations which have the right to inflict physical punishment on their members. This is particularly true of military service and warrior societies. In religious organizations, bodily humiliation, mutilation, or flagellation may be approved or required.

**Birth control:** Infanticide has been widely practiced as a form of birth control. In very early times and among cultures operating at the subsistence level, infanticide of newborn children of both sexes was used to keep the population constant. Subsequently and even today, population statistics show a disproportionately large number of boys as a result of the killing of newborn girls in countries where male offspring bring prestige or are valued as warriors or as sources of support for their parents in old age.

**Rituals relating to puberty, adulthood, and marriage**: Scarification, genital mutilation, and other ritual forms of cutting, mutilating, or distorting the natural shape of the body are common. Well-known examples include the binding of women's feet in China, elongated ears or necks in parts of Africa, and genital mutilation in various countries. (Related bodily but nonviolent symbols of men's control over women include the requirement for full body covering among Muslim women, and the orthodox Jewish practice of having women shave their heads and wear wigs, so that they will be unattractive to men other than their husbands.)

**Mortuary rituals (or lack thereof)**: In some simple societies, the bodies of the dead are treated in ways that people in most other cultures would consider a violation and degradation of the deceased. Shocking treatment includes not only the forms of ritual cannibalism discussed in Chapter 5, but also cases of double burials, in which bones are dug up after the flesh has decayed, and put through various secondary processes; and cases in which bodies are left in the open in or near a village to decay or be consumed.

**Trophies and soul appropriation**: Many of the cultures which practice ritual cannibalism or human sacrifice have other, related practices which involve some form of violation or degradation of the body (and, more to the point from their perspective, the soul) of others. Common practices are scalping, head-hunting, and head-shrinking. Less common are practices which involve the use of human bones as the raw material for tools, weapons, and utensils.

**Practices in medicine and related fields**: The histories of medicine, alchemy, magic, shamanism, sorcery, and voodoo are replete with examples of recipes and procedures that involve parts of human bodies, particularly but by no means exclusively blood, hair, nails, and ground bones. In addition, the practice of medicine has included more direct forms of physical "violence or violation," the most common of which are surgery, bloodletting, and enemas. In some cultures, seriously ill patients were killed or expected to commit suicide. In others, those considered physically undesirable were killed, including malformed children and women who had miscarriages.

**Sports and entertainment**: Despite the padded gloves, the objective of boxing is to physically hurt the loser and, if possible, beat him into losing consciousness. This is a milder version of blood sports conducted for entertainment, which include the fights to the death among Roman gladiators, playing a game like soccer with a human head in one South American tribe, and in medieval times the potentially lethal sport of jousting.

**Preserving honor and conflict resolution:** Many cultures have well-defined customs involving the use of violence, including lethal violence, as a means of preserving, restoring, or signaling honor, or responding to dishonor. These include blood feuds, a common form of "low-intensity" war among tribes and chiefdoms in all parts of the world. A variant of this custom appeared in renaissance Europe in the form of the duel to the death as a response to an insult, which lasted for several centuries. The readiness of the Japanese samurai to take their own or others' lives upon their masters' orders is legendary.

## 4.3 Human Sacrifice, Slavery, and Corporal Punishment

It is, perhaps, surprising that there are as many as five distinct practices of socially sanctioned group violence and violation which, as far as can be determined today, have arisen independently on every continent, and which in many cases have had substantially similar morally justifying frameworks. This convergence would be less surprising if the practices were universal, but that is not the case. None of the practices has existed at all stages of political and economic development; each is found predominately, though not exclusively, in cultures with a particular degree of scale and complexity. But only some cultures with the relevant degree of complexity and scale had a given practice: In other cultures with a similar political and economic structure, the practice was simply absent, or it was known to exist elsewhere but considered abhorrent and unthinkable.

The similarity yet diversity in actual practices of these common forms of socially sanctioned group violence is consistent with the "multilinear" view of cultural evolution developed in the 1950s by Julian Steward (1955), one of the preeminent American anthropologists of the century. The underlying concept is that human beings have certain tendencies or capacities, which are expressed in certain forms of social organization and social behavior, and which emerge in some cases but not others as a result of factors which may be too complex or subtle to identify. This perspective accounts for customs and patterns of behavior which develop independently around the world, and yet should not be viewed as necessarily embedded or preprogrammed in human nature. Human sacrifice, slavery, and corporal punishment for violating law or custom (along with ritual cannibalism, discussed in the next chapter) are such practices. Like them, I contend, war is common, yet not a feature of the human condition inextricably embedded in human nature; instead, like them, war is susceptible to being abolished. To support the case that these are, in fact, practices comparable to war, the following discussion underscores the features which they share with war: their prevalence as confirmed social institutions; their inhuman cruelty; the morally based rationales and affect, which recognize but excuse the cruelty involved; and the importance of the stakes perceived to be at issue in the societies concerned.

## Human Sacrifice

Broadly speaking, human sacrifice takes two main forms. The main meaning of the term refers to a religious ritual in which individuals are killed in order to communicate with or influence the behavior of a god or gods. In addition, the term is sometimes used to include death rituals in which family members, servants, and others are killed and buried with the head of a household or other highly placed individual, generally in order to accompany and continue to serve that individual after death. Even though this second practice differs substantially in goal and tenor, I have included it under the general rubric of human sacrifice for convenience, distinguishing between the two by calling the first "religious sacrifice" and the second "mortuary sacrifice."

The sacrifice of human victims occurs mainly in agricultural societies (that is, not in hunter-gatherer or industrial societies). The practice is situated at a particular juncture in political-social development, with respect to both the form of social organization and the length of the period during which the practice is prevalent. There is a far larger group of customs of "religious sacrifice" which do not involve human victims. Such customs predominate in the religious practices of both more and less developed societies. Among some simple bands and tribes which have a custom that can be considered a religious sacrifice (or analogous to religious sacrifice), the victim is the totem animal of the group. Among agricultural societies with a long history of religious sacrifice, early practices involving human victims typically gave way to animal sacrifices, then vegetable products (representing the harvest), and, finally, strictly symbolic offerings, for example, the wine and bread use in the Christian sacrament of the Eucharist.

The practice of human sacrifice by early agricultural societies existed in all parts of the world where large agricultural societies were found: in China and Japan;[2] in India and across the Indian subcontinent;[3] in the Middle East and throughout the circum-Mediterranean area from Carthage (Tunisia) to Greece and, in its earliest days, Rome;[4] in the Mayan, Aztec, and Inca empires of Central and South America;[5] and in parts of Africa and North America.[6]

In many cases, the purpose of human sacrifice was to persuade the gods responsible for fertility (of land, animals, or people) to provide bountiful crops, healthy babies, and productive livestock. Sometimes the sacrifice ritual had aspects associated with the fertility of the land. For example, the blood of the victim might be poured into the earth (Egypt), or the victim might be cut up and the body parts distributed around the ground (India).[7]

The most vivid examples of the killing of sacrificial human victims in a ritual that was a public occasion are those which survived into the modern period, such by the Aztecs in Mexico and the Khonds in India, and those for which detailed accounts or well preserved archaeological remains exist, such as for the Mayans and the Incas. The Aztecs and Mayans stabbed human victims who were laid across an altar, in rituals designed to maintain the order of time, the sun, and the seasons. The Khonds had a three-day ritual once or twice a year, at the end of which the victim was in some cases stupefied or dead; then the flesh was cut from the bone in small pieces, one for each household, which buried their piece in their plot. The victims, called Meriahs, were bought or raised for the purpose, kept in enclaves and fed and clothed until one or another was chosen to be sacrificed. Among the Khonds and the Aztecs, as well as other societies with this direct type of human sacrifice, the victim, once selected, was believed to take on the qualities of the god to which the sacrifice would be made. This made the victim a suitable means of communicating between man and god; and it generally made the victim holy, sacred, and powerful. Where victims were chosen from among the people, rather than taken from among captured prisoners of war or kidnapped from another tribe, they were sometimes honored and feted before the event, and given their choice of all of life's pleasures.

Even when the victim was a stranger and when the rite involved both celebration and great cruelty, a sense of evildoing might still pervade the proceedings. For example, the following words, uttered by the sacrificing priest, were recorded as opening part the Khond ritual:

> We obeyed the Goddess and assembled the people. Then the victim child wept, and reviled, and uttered curses. All the people rejoiced except those with whom the child had dwelt and the Jani. They were overwhelmed with grief; their sorrows prevailed entirely over their expectations of benefit, and they did not give either their minds or their faith to the Gods. . . . Oh Deity! why have you instituted this miserable heart-rending rite? The Earth Goddess told the Jani to reply to the victim: "Blame not us, blame your parents who sold you, what fault is ours? The Earth Goddess demanded a sacrifice; it is necessary for the world. If the tiger begins to rage, the snake to poison, fevers and every pain afflict the people, a sacrifice becomes necessary."[8]

In many other cases, the relationship between the religious sacrifice and the well-being of the community was indirect. Special sacrifices might be offered during natural catastrophes, such as drought, flood, or pestilence, to quell the presumed anger of the gods. The Carthaginians and extended settlements of Phoenicians around the Mediterranean had a long-lasting practice of sacrificing children by burning them on an altar during times of crisis, including losses in war as well as natural catastrophes. For example, in 310 BC, they conducted a massive sacrifice of 500 sons of nobleman, who were burned in a large pit, in an attempt to avert a defeat at Syracuse.[9] Most references to human sacrifice in the Old Testament are diatribes against the practice of sacrificing children to Molek or Baal; but some references suggest that at certain periods the Israelites considered Yahweh and Molek identical, and also took part in the ritual.[10]

More generally, sacrifice was a means of maintaining a good relationship with the gods, expressing various feelings typical of a subordinate, such as gratitude, humility, or repentance for wrongdoing. One source, surveying the region from Egypt to the Indus valley during the first two millennia BC, identifies "propitiatory, dedicatory and expiatory rites involving children and adults on special occasions" as having been practiced through the region.[11]

Another version of a generalized effort to maintain good relations with gods was the practice of "foundation sacrifice," that is, burying a child or adult under the foundation of a house or public building. This practice was common throughout Europe, the Middle East, and Asia from ancient times and persisted in many places, against social norms, into the middle ages and even the early modern period. In the British Isles, the Druids supported the practice, and sacrificial victims have been found at Stonehenge, suggesting an origin fully independent of the practice in the Middle East and Asia.

Finally, a common form of sacrifice, conducted as part of a public ritual, was the killing and burial of family members and servants who accompanied an important person to the grave. The monumental examples of this practice are well known: the group burials with Kings in the pyramids in Egypt, and the massive underground burials of ancient Chinese rulers, in which clay or wooden figures were later substituted for live or dead human bodies. Less well known practices were widespread, going back not just to the early city states, but to some of the oldest agricultural villages in southeast Europe (present day Yugoslavia, Turkey, Romania, and Bulgaria), where some graves include not just finery and utensils but wives or children. In some cases, the scale of sacrificial burials was massive. The ancient city-state of Ur has 16 tombs for royal burials dating from around 2300 BC. The number of retainers in these tombs varied from 12 to 80.[12] In Japan in 2 BC, the entire personal retinue of Prince Yamatohiko, brother of the Emperor, was buried alive, and "for several days they died not, but wept and wailed at night."[13] Just as animals were substituted for humans in religious sacrifices, clay and straw human figures and symbols for humans were substituted for humans in later burials in Egypt, China, and Japan.

The practice by which the widow of a dead man was expected to go to her death, called suttee after the Indian word "sati," is noted in historical records from many parts of the world. It seems to have been occurred persistently, however, over a period of one to two millennia, mainly in China and India, where it was extolled by the predominant religions (Shintoism and Hinduism, respectively). In the case of China, the values associated with the practice were honoring the dead and showing self-discipline. India, where the wife was expected to die on the funeral pyre or on a later memorial pyre, the dead husband was believed to go to a godlike afterlife which the wife could share. In India, suttee was legally banned by the British in 1829, and it is believed to have ended on any significant scale by around 1860.[14]

## Slavery and Related Conditions

**Slavery:** Slavery has been practiced more recently than any other common form of socially sanctioned violence except war and capital punishment. While slavery is not, in itself, a form of physical violence, it creates a situation in which the victim is perpetually threatened with violent assault, up to and including death, and in which many individuals regularly suffered physical abuses. Many if not most slaves in 19th century America were beaten and raped (or forced into sexual relations); many were permanently separated from their families when they were sold; and they remained permanently under a penalty of death for attempting to escape to be reunited with their families or for any other reason.

The most well known practices of slavery are the enslavement of blacks from Africa in the United States in the 18th and 19th centuries, and the practice of slavery in ancient Greece and Rome. Each of these cases is considered special and atypical, in part because the practices in modern America and in the classical world differed substantially. But slavery has been practiced in all parts of the world at one time or another, continuously or intermittently throughout recorded history, and among some simple societies without written history; and in every case the quality of ownership is the same. The life of the slave belongs to the owner, who can take it without having committed a crime or having to account for his action.[15]

Among indigenous groups in the Western hemisphere, throughout North, Central, and South America, there was a form of slavery substantially different from that in most other parts of the world: Men of enemy tribes captured in war were considered to be slaves (possessions), but they were adopted, married into the tribe, and treated as a son or brother for several years. Then, at a certain time (whose identifying parameters are not known), they would be informed that the moment for the final treatment of captured male warriors had arrived. This treatment was to be put to a painful, torturous death and, often, subjected to ritual cannibalism. Women captured in war were generally used for slave labor, but might also marry into the tribe. They were not automatically slaughtered in a ritual sacrifice; but in the case of some North American tribes which practiced ritual human sacrifice to the gods of fertility (such as the Pawnee), female slaves from another tribe were the preferred victim. Because of the small size and simple, egalitarian organization of hunter-gatherer bands and tribes, those which made slaves of captured members of enemy tribes had only a few such individuals among them; and the slaves generally lived ordinary lives indistinguishable from those of others in the group up to the time of their deaths.[16]

Slaves were also the victim of choice for human sacrifice in agrarian societies and early states in parts of the Middle East and other areas.

**Serfdom:** In many places for centuries after slavery became illegal, conditions that resemble slavery were widely practiced.[17] These are the forms of compulsory servitude identified by the following terms: coloni (in late Roman society), serf, villein, bondman, thrall, and, in more recent times, indentured servant. Most (but not all) people in these groups were farm hands; some were household servants or worked in factories or at trades. What distinguishes these conditions of servitude from slavery is that what is owned is not the body but some or all of the daily labor of the individual. The exact legal and social positions of the individuals called serf, villein, bondman, or thrall differed from one country to the next and over time. Serfs, bondmen, and thralls were never classified as "free men": villeins seem to have moved over time between the free and unfree status in England and France. For convenience, the following discussion uses the term "serf" to identify all of the "unfree" persons who were not outright slaves.

Serfs were "owned" in the sense that their own and their children's labor was owned in perpetuity; they were identified in records as being owned and sold; and they represented an enumerated part of the inheritable holdings of an estate at death. In some cases the serf could purchase his own freedom (in rare cases where he could cobble together the means to do so). In most cases, however, buying freedom was not an option not only because the serf was too poor, but also because the serf was bound to the land and would not be released by the master even for payment unless a replacement were provided—and no willing replacements were to be found.

Serfs were probably subjected to the same kinds of punishment suffered by slaves for failure to meet their masters' work requirements. A detailed multiyear daily diary of serf affairs for a mid-19th century Russian estate shows that three-quarters of the serfs were beaten, many several times, during the course of a typical year; and the average beating, conducted with a birch rod, involved 30 lashes.[18] In addition, serfs were frequently struck or beaten by their superiors; rape and forced sexual relations were common; and in Russia serfs could be transported to Siberia for disobedience.[19] In principle, the masters of serfs were not legally permitted to inflict random or arbitrary violence on them, nor to kill them, whereas masters had both rights with slaves. In practice, there was no court in which masters were held accountable for violence toward serfs, short of homicide, and they could even get away with murder. Thus, the physical abuse to which masters could subject serfs with impunity was a key difference between serfs and poor free sharecroppers.

There were feudal societies built on serf labor in the pre-Colombian American city states, in the ancient Middle East, and throughout the circum-Mediterranean area. In addition, the condition of serf or villein was common throughout the British Isles, Scandinavia, Europe, and Russia continuously or intermittently from around 1000 AD (when slavery left from late antiquity was dying out) to the mid-19th century.[20]

One remarkable feature of serfdom in Europe, which is instructive with respect to socially sanctioned violence more generally, is that it did not develop in a straightforward evolutionary sequence, arising initially as a weakened form of slavery and then gradually disappearing. In every case which I have had an opportunity to review (England, France, Spain, Hungary, and Russia), serfdom represented not a rise from slavery, but a loss of freedom by farmers who had previously been free men, but who, suffering under harsh conditions of one kind or another, found themselves increasingly deprived of various rights and freedoms. In England this occurred between 600 and 900 AD when assaults and migrations from Scandinavia were leading to the deaths of farmers and the loss of their land, and the farmers chose to place themselves under the protection of feudal lords.

In France, Catalonia, and Hungary, the transition occurred after the onset of the Plague in the 14th century, when labor was scarce and large landholders became more demanding. In Russia, serfdom was introduced between 1600, when peasants had the legal right to move from estate to estate between harvests, and 1700, when that right was abolished and the peasants were legally bound to the land. On the part of the Czar, this was part of an ongoing effort with several goals: to enforce tax law and increase tax income; to identify potential recruits for military service; and to improve agricultural productivity by establishing a system of mutual obligation between the landowners, who were bound to set aside registered lands for the private use of the serfs, and the serfs, who were bound to give a certain number of days' labor per year to farming the landowners' land. Very quickly, however, the main effect of the law was to bind the serfs to the landowners, who viewed themselves as owning the serfs and conducted business accordingly.

In nations where serfdom was practiced, serfs generally made up the great majority of the peasant population. The first Norman census of England, in 1086, for example, reckoning male heads of households, lists 283,000 individuals, of which two-thirds (195,000) were "villeins" or "bordari" (a related group). The other major groups were: slaves (25,000), major tenants who ran large estates (23,000), free men (generally small farmers who rented property) (12,000), the landowning principals and the nobility (9,000), and burghers and townspeople (8,000). The remaining 15,000 comprised craftsmen, small cottagers, religious and military professionals, and so on.[21] In Russia at the time of the last census before the abolition of serfdom, the 10th national census, held in 1859, serfs represented 37.5 percent of the population of European Russian, 22.5 million out of a total of about 60 million.[22] What these examples suggest is that even though in most nation-states the existence of a large class of slaves gradually disappeared after the fall of Rome, farm workers making up a large proportion of the population were subjected to treatment comparable to that of slaves for centuries.

## Corporal Punishment

Over the range from simple to complex societies, the punishments meted out by representatives of a society for violations of law or custom show a clear trend, first toward increasingly severe forms of corporal punishment and then away from corporal punishment and toward incarceration in prison. Simple societies of hunter-gatherers, which were organized in mobile extended family groups of 25–50 persons, had no means of imprisoning individuals who violated the accepted rules of behavior, nor could they support an individual who was maimed in a way that interfered with productive work. Many such societies had ingenious means of conflict resolution, penance or expiation, and reconciliation. Where an offense was considered so grave as to warrant punishment, the options were generally limited to two forms: death or exile (which may have led to death). Since there were no courts or police, the aggrieved party and kin, or the group as a whole, were responsible for apprehending and killing the defendant. In some cases, where the violation was particularly severe and ritual cannibalism was known, the consumption of the dead body by the group might follow the execution with an intent such as preventing any possibility of afterlife or rebirth.

In all parts of the world, more complex societies introduced a variety of forms of physical punishment. Most often, there was an effort to make the punishment fit the crime. Rape would be punished by castration; theft by cutting off a hand or a foot; slander or the betrayal of an oath by cutting out the tongue. The use of horrible forms of torture to extract confessions is well known from the Spanish Inquisition and from the practices of 20th century dictators who tortured political opponents.

In agricultural societies with rudimentary systems of law and prior to the development of prisons, blood feuds of the same kind that occurred among the simplest bands were common. Where frequent, blood feuds were generally not illegal. In theory, retribution by an aggrieved person's kin against the perpetrator of an offense was supposed to be proportionate to the crime and to put the matter to rest. In practice, however, there were self-interested agreements about both the nature of the crime and the nature of the response. This often led to perpetual and, in some cases, escalating acts of (generally lethal) violence by each group of kin against the other, each justified not by the original crime but by the lack of justice in the last preceding act of revenge or retribution.

In Anglo-Saxon England, the kings attempted to dampen the tendency to wanton violence in society and the blood feuds that followed by establishing an elaborate system of fines ("wergild" or man-money) for every conceivable form of physical aggression, and for theft, adultery, and rape. Around the year 600, King Æthelbert issued 90 "laws," the vast majority of which simply list the fine for a meticulously described violent offense.[23] Comparable laws issued by King Alfred three centuries later maintained an elaborate system of fines, but added two entirely new features: first, the laws cover many activities other than violent crime and theft, most of which involve some betrayal of trust or promise; and second, for many crimes, the fines indicated in the older law have been replaced with forms of corporal punishment.[24] In one case, where the rule seems to come directly from the Old Testament (which is the case for several other passages), it is difficult to know whether a practiced punishment is being described, or rather a general principle of equity: "If any one thrust out another's eye, let him give his own for it; tooth for tooth, hand for hand, burning for burning, stripe for stripe." In another case, the specificity of the crime suggests an actual punishment: "If a male serf commits rape on a female serf, the fine is his testicles." Several other situations of aggressive and presumably unwanted sexual advances are described, involving free men and single free women or slaves or nuns: In these cases, the penalty is a fine, or marriage or both (in the case of a free woman). Thus the main difference between the two sets of laws concerns crimes punishable by death. In the early set, there were none. In King Alfred's laws, death is listed as the only penalty (fine is not an option) in the following cases: murder (except by a priest, in which case the penalty is losing all he has and been expelled from the ministry); stealing and selling a free man; cursing one's parents; causing the death of a pregnant woman; killing a thief for breaking and entering in daylight, unless unavoidably compelled to do so; being a witch; making sacrifices to pagan gods (this may be another extract from the Old Testament); or plotting against the life of the king or the lord one is sworn to serve.

During the late Middle Ages and Renaissance, more elaborate and horrible corporal punishments were devised, such as death by burning (for women; men were hanged or had their head cut off), death by being drawn and quartered, and various forms of mutilation and branding.

The public spectacles associated with gruesome forms of capital punishment and mutilation in 16th–19th century France (and other parts of Europe) are described in detail by Foucault (1979). This is the period when deliberate cruelty and the excruciating, long-lasting pain of corporal punishment reached an apogee in the Western world. Foucault then analyses the process by which torturous forms of physical punishment and capital punishment were gradually abolished in this part of the world, and replaced with incarceration in prison.

Some forms of corporal punishment now banned as cruel and extreme in the West are still practiced elsewhere. Two examples reported in the news in recent years are the instance of flogging an American youth in Hong Kong (for vandalism, involving wantonly destroying the finish on a series of parked cars, along with some friends); and a case in Saudi Arabia of two members of the royal family (a man and a woman) being publicly beheaded for having committed adultery.

# 4.4 The Declining Tolerance for Violence

Over the last two centuries, the worldwide abolition of slavery and serfdom and the decline in physical violence as a form of legal punishment have been paralleled by two other developments. First, there has been a steady decline in social approval of various forms of violence committed by one individual against another. This is illustrated in the abolition of dueling, the outlawing of the beating of children by parents and teachers, the growing public opposition to wife-beating, and, in many countries, the banning of boxing. In Western nations, we are rapidly approaching the point at which no form of interpersonal violence is socially sanctioned.

Second, the purposes for which war is socially sanctioned have shrunk in a parallel manner, reflecting the same declining tolerance for violence. Consider, for example, the role of warfare in creating, extending, and maintaining empires. For centuries the use of armed force for this purpose was considered more or less legitimate, and service in armed forces dedicated to this end was an honorable profession. Since 1945, however, with Germany's defeat and the end of colonization, the use of force by great powers to acquire and rule far-flung empires has, little by little, been abandoned; and the morally justifying view that imperial administrations are good for the subject populations has been replaced by the view that all people have the right to self-determination.

In sum, despite the unprecedented rate of killing in war and genocide over the course of the 20th century, and the recently rising rates of violent crime in the wealthier nations (after at least a century of steady decline), there is a great deal of evidence that in Western culture and world culture over the past several hundred years, there has been a marked shrinking in the set of socially sanctioned forms of individual and group violence; and over the past century, a parallel shrinking in the set of socially accepted reasons for war.

## 4.5 The Rise of Institutionalized Forms of Violence

If mature, reasonably socialized adults in all cultures are predisposed to avoid violent behavior, then what is the source of culturally shaped beliefs about just or acceptable forms of violence in which individuals may or must participate?

A substantial body of literature in political science and sociology argues that the organization of society itself is the source of socially sanctioned violence. People band together, the argument goes, in order to form "attack" or "defense" units, that is, groupings which permit them to defend the territory and resources on which they rely for survival, or, alternatively, to attack others and seize the resources available to them.

The ethnographies of simple societies suggest, however, that this conception of the origin of society, and the origin of socially sanctioned violence, is much too narrow. Judging by the ways of life of the small bands with simple cultures which survived into the past five centuries, the primary function of the most basic social groupings was not to permit group violence nor to defend against attack, but to increase the chance of survival in other ways: that is, to provide jointly enough food, shelter, and, when needed, surrogate parents to ensure that each generation would survive long enough to raise the next generation to childbearing age. This survival function would have predisposed the earliest forms of social organization among hunter-gatherer societies, which occurred at a time when the average life spans was generally very short (about 30 years)[25] to discourage internal violence and to protect against external violence—but not to originate violence. Even later, when larger, more settled societies arose around the practices of fishing, herding, and horticulture, the chief function of the increased scale of society was not attack or defense, but the division of labor and construction of settlements which produced more stored foodstuff, giving more people access to a more reliable food supply, and thereby supporting larger populations with longer life spans.

Violent attacks by marauders and by empire builders, seeking to appropriate the wealth accumulated by others, arose alongside the more settled life style. But such predatory violence followed rather than caused the rise of settlements and accumulated wealth, and settled defenders always far outnumbered mobile predators. This means that the rise of a warrior class and organized warfare (as distinct from small-scale, haphazard theft and marauding), which was associated with the growth of agriculture and cities in all parts of the world, was less a cause of the development of early city states than a product of it.

Against this backdrop, I suggest, the earliest socially sanctioned forms of group violence are likely to have been rooted in specific experiences in which particular forms of violence undertaken in an ad hoc manner became strongly associated with survival. The predominant case would be that of a band or tribe facing starvation which found that taking food from the territory of another group, or seizing food supplies stored by another group, represented a route to survival. Over time, repeated violation of earlier inhibitions against attacking others—lapses from ordinary adult discipline made under duress—could lead to the development of a more positive ethos of conquest and destruction. An evolution of this kind might account for development of the aggression-justifying belief systems which arose repeatedly among nomadic pastoralists in the steppes of Asia—first as long ago as 2000 BC, among the Indo-European groups that spread from the Pontic-Caspian region into Europe, the Middle East, and South Asia, displacing more complex, settled, peaceful agrarian societies in those regions;[26] and then much later in the West, among the Goths (including but not limited to the Scythians, Vandals, and Huns) in the 5th century AD;[27] and in the east, among the Mongols, led by Genghis Khan, in the 12th century AD.[28] Given the millennia-long repetition of outward expansion and aggression, it seems likely, however, that the glorification of conquest and empire was not merely handed down from one generation to the next, but reappeared from time to time in response to the exigencies of a nomadic lifestyle in which a group of men on horseback could rapidly attack and plunder a farming community or, alternatively, be attacked and lose everything to another group on horseback.[29]

To take a very different example, early agricultural societies seem likely to have introduced human sacrifice in an ad hoc manner, when faced with exceptional adversity. In all parts of the world, the first sedentary societies probably used the quantities of storable produce generated by agriculture in an effort to smooth out their food supply over the course of the year. From time to time, however, this aim must have been frustrated by plagues, floods, and droughts, leading to widespread famine. Drawing a parallel with their own social and personal experience of stability and security as a function of food, the leaders of these societies conceived of a natural universe controlled by gods who needed food to stay in a good humor and keep the world stable and predictable. Scaling up from daily life, and attempting to trade one evil for another (the root concept of sacrifice), the political-religious leaders of the early societies came up with human flesh as the preferred food of the gods, or, in another manner of speaking, the sacrifice of a human being as a concession of ultimate power and authority to the gods—in either case, propitiating forces beyond their own control in the hope of being granted, in return, conditions for a good harvest during the coming year. Unlike warfare conducted for the purpose of seizing food, acts of human sacrifice generally did nothing to alleviate the crises that may have prompted the creation of this ritual. But like acts of war aimed at seizing food, acts of human sacrifice were justified on the grounds that the evil being done was the lesser of two evils in the situation.

Over the course of human history, there must have been innumerable cases in which people in a given culture experienced some link between own vulnerability to pain, loss, suffering, and death and protection from such ills with the deliberate infliction of pain or loss on others; and having made this link, inferred a more general moral rule from it, such as, "human sacrifice will lead to good crops" or, "a life of military conquest will earn glory as well as wealth and security." Moreover, through cultural dispersal, normatively loaded beliefs about just or desirable forms of group violence are likely to have spread from one culture to others which imitated or adopted them because they offered new solutions to shared problems.

## 4.6 The Demise of Institutionalized Forms of Violence

If institutionalized, socially sanctioned forms of group violence tend to appear initially as a by-product of crisis response, why and how do socially sanctioned forms of group violence end?

What we know about the cessation of once-widespread practices that have been abolished—ritual cannibalism, ritual human sacrifice, and slavery—suggests two main mechanisms:

- A practice can be abolished through some form of coercion imposed from outside the culture. This happened in many parts of the world over the past several centuries, when conquerors and missionaries from Europe encountered what they considered abhorrent and unthinkable customs.
- A practice can fall into disuse as a result of changes in society which lead to changes in the moral beliefs that once justified it. This seems to have

happened with human sacrifice in the circum-Mediterranean area in ancient times, and with ritual cannibalism throughout the world at various times.

In the latter case, within the context of a larger world view which itself is changing, the practice may be increasingly perceived as either unnecessary as a means of achieving a given end, or unnecessarily harmful in relation to the objective. In what follows, I discuss each of these processes briefly, and then look at their interactive functioning.

The US civil war is probably the most widely cited instance of the abolition of a form of socially sanctioned group violence as a result coercion imposed from outside the society: people in the North who opposed slavery imposed their view on those in the South who thought it should be legal, and the Northerners made war to impose their view. The exploration and colonization of the world by Europeans over the past five centuries offers many other examples of new standards of behavior being abruptly imposed by outsiders, with the result that many practices were changed, abolished, or died out with the populations that had practiced them. Among other practices, this applies to ritual forms of cannibalism and human sacrifice practiced in many parts of the world. In the Americas and the Pacific, explorers, conquerors, and missionaries insisted that primitive tribes instantly cease such practices. In Africa, India and other parts of Asia, British and other European colonial rulers took a hands-off approach at first, but eventually banned various customs of human sacrifice, including suttee (the burning of a widow on her dead husband's pyre) and fertility rites involving the sacrifice of human victims.

Direct and indirect evidence suggests that in the more distant past—from one millennium to several millennia ago—the practices of ritual human sacrifice and ritual cannibalism were once common, but that they ceased as a result of changes in economic and political organization. Among simple groups encountered in the modern period—bands or tribes with a basic hunter-gatherer economy, or tribes with the same supplemented by some systematic horticulture or herding—ritual cannibalism appears to have been surprisingly widespread, with an incidence of 50 percent or more. Ancient writing and some archaeological evidence suggest that in the parts of the world that developed first, when large, settled, complex agricultural societies arose in various regions, ritual cannibalism died out and ritual human sacrifice became common. For both ritual cannibalism and ritual human sacrifice, the practices, where they occurred, were associated with cultural beliefs that were common among all societies with similar economies, including societies that did not practice ritual cannibalism or ritual human sacrifice. And ritual human sacrifice was, for the most part, abandoned by cultures that had more developed economies, incorporating much more extensive reliance on money (legal tender) and on trade with other cultures. Another example of association between a given form of socially sanctioned violence and a particular stage of development is offered by slavery which was banned when modern political and industrial growth made it no longer tolerable or profitable.

The extraordinarily close correlation between successive stages of political and economic development and the rise and demise of given forms of socially sanctioned violence implies that the latter is a function of the former, unmediated by any significant contributing role of moral belief or world view. If this were the case, then we should infer that war is likely to end if and only if there is an appropriate change in worldwide political and economic development—and that moral beliefs about just war have, indeed, little bearing on the matter.

There is, however, a more plausible interpretation of the association between political and economic development and sanctioned forms of group violence. This is that increasing complexity and scale of political organization and increasing control over natural threats to physical survival are associated with world views, and changes in world view, which lend themselves to the moral justification of specific forms of sanctioned group violence. If this is the case, then we would expect to find what history shows: a given form of sanctioned violence is sometimes but not always associated with a given degree of political and economic complexity, but virtually never occurs in societies considerably more or less complex.

For both cannibalism and human sacrifice, there is evidence of the demise of the practice in given cultures not after a change in development, but while the culture was still operating at the level of development normally associated with each practice. This suggests that a change in world view and in moral beliefs about group violence may precede and help cause the change in political and economic development, rather than follow from it.

The same may be said, in a much weaker form, about the imposition of abolition from outside the practicing culture. Explorers, missionaries, and imperial conquerors typically imposed broader horizons on local cultures, requiring change not just in the practice of certain forms of socially sanctioned violence, but in a web of interlocking behaviors, beliefs, and values. In many cases, forms of ritual cannibalism by simple tribes were abolished almost instantly at the demand of imperial administrators, who (not surprisingly) treated the practices with contempt and horror, as inhuman and intolerable. The rapid collapse of practices which (anthropologists found in retrospect) were integrally incorporated in the equivalent of religious-philosophical-political organization and belief systems suggests that when confronted with an utterly alien world view, the entire set of beliefs supporting the ritual practice simply caved in. These beliefs were not replaced by alternative beliefs or practices, designed to accomplish the same ends as ritual cannibalism. Instead, people's lives were deprived of those ends and other social ends incompatible with those of the colonizing culture.

Regardless of the proximate cause of change—views imposed from outside, changing political and economic structure, or simply weakening adherence to old beliefs—the moral views that supported previously sanctioned forms of violence tended to seem solid as long as they went substantially unchallenged, yet ultimately vulnerable to rapid and comprehensive change. A metaphor for this vulnerability might be that of a thick-skinned balloon, which can withstand knocks and bounces and being seriously bent out of shape, but which will collapse instantly if pricked by a sharp object. The culturally shaped moral beliefs that support socially sanctioned forms of violence can be solid for centuries, yet collapse and vanish in a few years. I attribute this unusual combination of resilience and vulnerability to the fact that the justifications for sanctioned violence are always working against an underlying propensity to nonviolence. In terms of resilience, this means that the barrier to change must be kept high; that is, the social investment in maintaining the moral reasoning must be substantial, and the social means of fending off challenges and defections extensive. But in terms of vulnerability, it means that a moral cognitive dissonance is always waiting, like a tectonic fault, for an opportunity to settle into a more stable, consistent configuration of beliefs with regard to violence.

## 4.7 Goals, Efficacy, and Morality in Institutionalized Violence and Violation

In looking back at older forms of socially sanctioned violence, we tend to classify them according to contemporary world views and standards of socially sanctioned violence. We tend to distinguish between rituals of violence and violation which, by our lights, were based on false ideas about the world—rituals involving superstition, shamanism, magic, or implausible religious beliefs—and violent practices of a kind that continue today, which may have had the desired physical impact on the prospects for survival, or the prospects for thriving, such as socially sanctioned war to obtain food, or socially sanctioned use of foreign populations as slave labor to increase the wealth of one's own society. In other words, the modern mind gravitates toward a functional assessment of violent practices: did they serve a practical end? And if so, were they, perhaps, justified by objective interests rather than by variable, culturally determined moral beliefs?

In this discussion, the *efficacy* of a sanctioned form of violence as a means to expected or desired ends is not at issue. What is at issue is the motivation for the action among those who do it: Is the practice driven or permitted by unique, culturally shaped moral beliefs according to which the form of violence is just and acceptable? Or—and here we have the relevant alternative—is the violence motivated by human needs which are common across cultures, such as survival needs, which do not involve culturally variable moral beliefs?

The way to identify a given act of violence as rooted in culturally variable moral beliefs, on the one hand, or innate human needs, on the other hand, is by looking carefully at the claimed benefit of the action.

The issue is readily confused because most forms of socially sanctioned violence are called, or can be called, "necessary evils." Taken out of context, this term suggests that the violent action is necessary for survival. For the most part, however, the term is meant to show a link between two seemingly contrary expectations: the expectation that a given action will harm or cause pain to one person or many people (thus, it is "evil"), and the expectation that some good will come out of the (thus, it is "necessary" or, more precisely, useful). For example, a person who says "Spare the rod, spoil the child" is saying that spanking is a necessary evil. Or, to take another case, people believe that punishment which hurts criminals is a "necessary evil" because if inadequately punished, crimes will be more common.

The use of socially sanctioned lethal violence is sometimes but not often a survival-related "necessary evil" in the sense that if one person does not die, one or more others will die, with certainty and speed. Most sanctioned forms of violence, though called "necessary evils," are not actions which, if suspended, would result in the prompt and certain death of one or many individuals. (A form of lethal violence which is a "necessary evil" in this sense is a sniper's killing a crazed individual who cannot otherwise be stopped from killing people randomly with an automatic weapon.)

Most if not all socially sanctioned forms of group violence are institutionalized: that is, the context and reasons are identified in advance, the procedures are specified, and the participants (the violent actors) are known and, in many cases, go through extensive training. But violence which is carefully planned and prescribed in advance of the event is rarely undertaken as a matter of survival, strictly and narrowly speaking. Moreover, in the rare cases where preplanned violence might actually be used to ensure the survival of most members of a group, it is likely that the same energy, directed at developing a nonviolent means of survival, could prevent the rise of the situation in which lethal violence was needed.

For the most part, the claimed benefit of institutionalized, socially sanctioned group violence is a social good less urgently or comprehensively needed than survival—and, by the same token, more closely bound to a specific culture and its world view. In most cases, the physical survival of members of the society is taken for granted: what is at issue are the political, economic, or cultural conditions under which the group will live. The goals for which people in a given culture may be prepared to inflict or suffer lethal violence are many. They include political conditions like creating or preserving an empire, or achieving self-determination; acquiring, keeping, or losing wealth; the toleration or nontoleration of religious, cultural, or ethnic self-expression, and so on.

If we look back at roughly comparable societies, one of which sanctioned a given form of violence and the other did not, what we would find most often is not an association between violence and survival, but rather an association between violence and another socially defined "good" which a modern observer might or might not consider worth killing or dying for. Political scientists routinely attempt to assess war as an instrument of politics by assessing the outcome of wars in terms of costs, risks, and losses to the aggressor compared with gains to the aggressor, where the costs and gains are measured in terms of wealth, territory, population, natural resources, political influence, or other socially defined "goods." The conclusion typically drawn is that war was a rational or wise choice if the gains outweighed the costs, or an irrational or poor choice in the opposite case. The implication is that the purpose and goals of war—and in those senses, its cause—was gain of the relevant kind.

What such analyses overlook is that war can be perceived and assessed not only as a more or less successful means to given ends, but also as a means to ends which a given society may consider unacceptable. This distinction is all-important in any case where war (or another form of group violence) is not being employed as a means to survival, in the most basic, literal, physical sense of the term. Only in cases where a society is facing mass starvation (or a comparable environmentally linked catastrophe, like mass death by freezing or by drowning), or facing deliberately inflicted genocide, and when violent action might literally save more lives than it would cost in the threatened society can it be argued that a socially sanctioned form of violence may be amorally driven by objective "interests." In other words, only when many lives are immediately at stake not during the prosecution of violence but as a certain fact in the absence of violence can we infer that the violence may be entirely dissociated from a special, culturally determined system of moral beliefs. Even in such situations—for example, in a society facing mass starvation—the view that one's own survival is an adequate reason for killing another human may be morally intolerable; and in those cases, individuals may starve rather than kill, as a result of learned moral beliefs. Thus, in the final analysis, the defensive killing of attackers may be the only form of socially sanctioned violence motivated by a practical end in which the reason for killing other human beings need not be supported by culturally shaped moral beliefs, but could be the result of a culturally invariant will to kill, if necessary, in order to defend oneself (or others) from being killed.

# RITUAL CANNIBALISM

## A Case Study of Socially Sanctioned Group Violence

## 5.1 Introduction

This chapter argues that ritual or customary cannibalism shares a number of features with war, which make it a relevant precedent for the practice and potential abolition of war. Like war, ritual cannibalism:

- was relatively widespread (among hunter-gatherer societies) for centuries or millennia;
- was institutionalized as a socially sanctioned and, often, socially required practice, in which various members of society played well-defined roles;
- involved a violation of the human body which, in the abstract, was perceived as abhorrent and hateful; and
- was undertaken despite its abhorrent nature because it was believed to be justified by an important social value.

Finally, as I argue is likely to be the case for the abolition of war, when key features of the culture changed, the culturally determined reasoning that had justified customary cannibalism faded away; and once the justifying reasons disappeared, the practice not only stopped, but became an unthinkable horror.

### The Meaning of Ritual Cannibalism

In everyday usage, the word "cannibalism" conjures up the image of a tribe boiling or roasting human flesh for dinner. This is a caricature of actual cannibal practices, an ancient myth perpetuated, largely inadvertently, by modern explorers and conquerors. The evidence available today suggests that regularly practiced, socially sanctioned "food cannibalism" may have occurred in one or two cultures, but that if it ever did exist, it was extraordinarily rare.

In contrast, starvation cannibalism—individuals painfully violating an internalized taboo against consuming human flesh—has occurred in times of famine in all parts of the world. Some cases of starvation cannibalism have involved murdered victims, others have involved flesh taken from dead bodies; but there is no evidence that the practice was ever socially sanctioned as customary behavior. Cannibalism as an aberrant (not sanctioned) practice has also occurred as a product of sociopathic behavior and mental illness.

Virtually all socially sanctioned cannibalism—and nearly all of the practices which anthropologists study—are very different from food cannibalism. These practices typically involve the ritual or customary ingestion of some part of a dead member of one's own band or tribe ("endocannibalism") or of a stranger or a member of an enemy tribe ("exocannibalism") in the belief that this will have a particular impact on the life or the afterlife of the consumer or the consumed, or both. In acts of ritual or customary cannibalism, specified members of a society consume all or part of certain body parts, which are believed to contain and convey attributes of the deceased. Often, the organ to be consumed is the heart, the brain, or the liver, and the attribute to be preserved (endocannibalism) or appropriated (exocannibalism) is the soul stuff, the spirit, the courage, or the fecundity of the deceased.

In many cases of ritual or customary cannibalism, the part of the human body that is ingested does not take the form of food or resemble food; in some cases, it is obscured by food. For example, the ash of the burnt bones of a deceased relation may be dissolved in a drink; or some of his or her blood may be mixed in with some form of food or drink. Even when ritual cannibalism does involve the consumption of flesh in more substantial quantities and gruesome forms, it is still utterly unlike food cannibalism. Ritual or customary cannibalism occurs only under certain circumstances, and then at a special time set aside for the purpose. The ingestion of human substance is usually just one step in a much longer and more elaborate ritual. The activity is generally considered to be of the utmost importance as a social obligation or sacred duty.

## The Debate over the Existence of Ritual Cannibalism

To the modern mind, cannibalism in any form is so abhorrent that it is hard to credit. We find it difficult to comprehend or even imagine cannibal acts undertaken as a freely chosen activity by ordinary, sane, nonsadistic, nonsociopathic human beings. The gulf between the modern sensibility and that in societies with ritual cannibal practices is so wide that it undermines confidence in our ability to separate fact from fiction, or to avoid ethnocentric projections of feared, horrible "otherness" onto peoples whose cultures are vastly different from our own. Moreover, there were well-known tendencies among the explorers, traders, and conquistadors of earlier centuries to exaggerate the adventures and encounters they experienced during their travels, sometimes bringing to life the monsters of myth, fairy tale, and nightmare, and to plagiarize fantastic stories from one another.

Thus, it is not altogether surprising that some years ago an anthropologist challenged the accepted view that various forms of socially sanctioned cannibalism were once relatively widespread. The 1979 book by William Arens, *The Man-Eating Myth: Anthropology and Anthropophagy*, sent a shock wave through the field of anthropology with the claim that all or virtually all reports of socially sanctioned cannibal practices are myths originally invented by ethnocentric or interested parties and later credulously repeated, with little investigation and insufficient evidence, by sloppy, ethnocentric social scientists with a vested interest in sensationalizing the subjects of their study.

Though rejected by virtually all reviewers, Arens's claim left lingering doubts among anthropologists who have not studied the topic. In light of the controversy, it might have seemed wise to drop ritual cannibalism as a case study in socially sanctioned group violence. Instead, I decided to retain the study for several reasons.

First, as an instance of socially sanctioned group violence, the alleged practice of cannibalism was too central to ignore. As noted in Chapter 3, many socially sanctioned forms of violence have appeared in one culture or another over the course of human history, but only five forms of institutionalized, socially sanctioned group violence have been widely practiced in all parts of the world for millennia: war; punishment (often corporal punishment) for breaking the law, or violating law-like customs; slavery; human sacrifice; and, allegedly, cannibalism. With cannibalism included in the set, a strong case can be made that all forms of socially sanctioned group violence are culturally determined and susceptible to change, or abolition, as a function of changes in culture and in culturally determined moral ideas. If customary cannibalism did not exist, however, it might be argued that widespread socially sanctioned group violence comprises two forms (slavery and human sacrifice) which were practiced for a time and then ended, and two other forms (war and punishment) which have been practiced throughout human history. In other words, if cannibalism did not exist as a widespread, socially sanctioned group practice, the evidence for systematic, culturally determined variation in all forms of socially sanctioned violence and related moral beliefs would be considerably weaker.

Second, the controversy over the existence of cannibalism concerns the very issue which is at the heart of this study: Can behavior (like cannibalism) which is unthinkable in one period of history be institutionalized and even routine in another? And if so, can behavior (like war) which is institutionalized in a given culture become unthinkable as culture changes? While granting that ethnocentric projection could play a role in the attribution of cannibal practices to simple societies, this study underscores the potential for bias in the opposite direction. Throughout the twentieth century, anthropologists reacting against the ethnocentrism and naivete of the field's nineteenth-century founding fathers have, quite reasonably, eschewed developmental concepts and language which suggest that simple, nonliterate tribal societies were the unfortunate precursors to our own "advanced" society. The effort not to be judgmental or derogatory about simple cultures has been admirable and effective; but it can create a counterproductive form of political correctness. If cannibalism did exist, then the ostensibly politically correct critics of the literature on cannibalism, such as Arens, would be the parties guilty of ethnocentrism, for having mistakenly labeled some customs of simple societies as too terrible to be human; by the same token, the anthropologists who accepted the evidence of ritual cannibalism would be the genuinely nonjudgmental scholars.

Thus, the dispute between the two views of ritual cannibalism could not be more pertinent to the argument advanced in this essay: if ritual cannibalism did exist, that tends to confirm my hypotheses, first, that people are capable of rationalizing any action in the framework of a justifying world view and set of moral beliefs; and, second, that forms of violence believed to be vital to society at some times in history can become completely irrelevant to the preservation or loss of important social values other times.

Finally, a careful review of the Arens-related claims and counterclaims, reported in the Appendix, along with the evidence concerning the incidence of customary cannibalism given in the next section of this chapter, persuaded me that ritual forms of cannibalism not merely existed, but were widespread, being practiced by at least 50 percent of simple societies in most parts of the world, and more in some areas.

## The Organization of the Chapter

The chapter begins with a detailed discussion of the evidence concerning the global incidence and cultural correlates of ritual cannibalism. Because the prevalence and even the existence of ritual cannibalism are contentious issues even among professional anthropologists who have devoted time to this issue, I have gone to some length to identify and assess evidence concerning the global incidence of the practice.

Next, I discuss the purposes and forms of ritual cannibalism, and the morality and affect associated with it in the practicing societies. These sections highlight some remarkable similarities in the context, justification, and emotional coloring of ritual cannibalism and war.

Finally, I turn to the question of how practices of ritual cannibalism ended and the inferences we might draw from that historical precedent for the potential abolition of war.

## 5.2 The Global Incidence and Correlates of Cannibalism

Two anthropologists have attempted in very different ways to provide a global overview of the incidence, forms, and meaning of cannibalism: Evald Volhard in the 1939 study *Kannibalismus* (Cannibalism), and Peggy Reeves Sanday in the 1986 book *Divine Hunger*. Volhard, an anthropologist at the Institute for Cultural Studies at Goethe University in Frankfurt, exhaustively compiles descriptions of every reported cannibal custom, current or past, anywhere in the world, that the author could find in any source. In the first half of his study, which is organized geographically by continent, region, and tribe, Volhard gives a thumbnail sketch of the time period, the sources, the specific actions, and the purposes involved in each reported custom or practice. This text is supplemented by numbered lists of the tribes or cultures (or language groups) in each region with reported cannibal practices, and by detailed maps that use the same numbers to show the approximate location of each tribe or culture by continent and region. In the second half of the study, Volhard regroups the earlier material, giving a cross-cultural analysis of cannibal customs grouped by their main purpose or meaning. (The typologies of cannibalism given by Volhard and others are discussed in the next section.)

Drawing on primary and secondary material in English, French, and German, as well as some primary material originally published in other languages (particularly Italian, Spanish, Dutch, and Portuguese) and later translated into English, French, or German, Volhard uses roughly 800 sources to identify 914 tribes or cultures which have been reported to have practiced some form of cannibalism, in nearly all cases customary or ritual cannibalism. Of the cultures identified by Volhard as having cannibal practices, 93 percent (857 cultures, many if not most no longer extant) were located in Central or South America, Africa, or Oceania (Australia, New Zealand, the Pacific islands, and Indonesia), while a scant 7 percent (57 cultures) were located in North America and the entire Eurasian continent.

Peggy Reeves Sanday, a cultural anthropologist at the University of Pennsylvania, used the Human Relations Area Files and Murdock and White's *Standard Cross-Cultural Sample* of societies[1] to estimate the incidence of cannibalism by geographic region, and to assess the impact on its occurrence of several likely factors.[2] Out of a total cross-cultural sample of 186 cultures, Sanday found enough information to assess the presence or absence of cannibalism in only 109 cultures. Of the latter, 37 (one-third) had evidence of cannibal practices.

The geographic distribution of the cases in Sanday's sample study loosely resembles that in Volhard's global study. Most of Sanday's cases were located in Africa, Oceania, and Latin America, and only 5 percent were in located in Eurasia. (See Table 5.1 for the detailed data supporting this and the next several paragraphs.) For North America, however, Volhard's and Sanday's findings appear to diverge considerably. North American accounted for only 2.5 percent of Volhard's cases (23 out of 914) but 30 percent of Sanday's much smaller sample (11 out of 37). In Sanday's sample, the rate of cannibalism in North America was about the same as that in Latin America, Oceania, and Africa—close to 50 percent of the cultures surveyed in each area (Table 5.1, col. 5). A comparable figure cannot be given for Volhard, for whom there is no basis for judging the relative intensity of cannibal practice by region. But Volhard's low absolute figure for North America—23 cases, compared with 400 cases for Africa and 351 cases for Oceania—implies either that the universe of cultures in North America, compared with that in other regions, is, for unknown reasons, far smaller in Volhard than in Sanday; or, alternatively, that contrary to Sanday's findings, the intensity of cannibalism in North America is comparatively much lower than that in other regions; or both.

Another measure of the overall similarities and differences between Sanday's and Volhard's results is the ratio of Sanday's cultures with cannibal practices to Volhard's, by region and for the world as a whole (Table 5-1, col. 9). Globally, Sanday's cases represent 4 percent of Volhard's, and for Africa, Oceania, Central and South America, and Eurasia, the ratios lie in the plausible surrounding range of 2–6 percent. In other words, in relative counts by continent, the two sources diverge from their relative global totals by not more than 50 percent. In the case of North America, however, they differ by a factor of ten: in North America, instead of representing 4 percent of Volhard's cases, Sanday's cases represent 48 percent.

This discrepancy raises questions about possible sampling bias in Volhard (North American cultures underrepresented) or Sanday (North American cultures overrepresented). In addition, for both studies an explanation is needed to account for the very low incidence of reported cannibal practices in Eurasia compared with that in Africa, Oceania, and Central and South America. The remainder of this section addresses these two points.

**TABLE 5.1** Quantitative results of Volhard's and Sanday's global surveys of reported cannibal practices

| [1] | 1. VOLHARD'S COMPILATION OF REPORTED CANNIBAL PRACTICES | 2. SANDAY'S ANALYSIS OF MURDOCK AND WHITE'S SAMPLE OF WORLD CULTURES | | | | 3. REGIONAL DISTRIBUTION | | 4. CASES BY REGION: SANDAY AS SHARE OF VOLHARD |
|---|---|---|---|---|---|---|---|---|
| | No. of cultures [2] | No. in Sanday subset [3] | of which: Cannibalism present [4] | Intensity of cannibalism by region [5] | Region's share of world cultures [6] | Volhard [7] | Sanday [8] | Sanday [9] |
| Africa | 400 | 15 | 7 | 47% | 14% | 44% | 19% | 2% |
| Oceania | 351 | 21 | 11 | 52% | 19% | 38% | 30% | 3% |
| Central & South America | 100 | 14 | 6 | 43% | 13% | 11% | 16% | 6% |
| North America | 23 | 23 | 11 | 48% | 21% | 3% | 30% | 48% |
| Eurasia | 40 | 36 | 2 | 6% | 33% | 4% | 5% | 5% |
| World Total | 914 | 109 | 37 | 34% | 100% | 100% | 100% | 4% |

*Sources:* Volhard (1939) and Sanday (1986).

In an effort to resolve the apparent discrepancy between Volhard and Sanday for North America and to clarify the reasons for the low incidence of reported cannibal practices in Eurasia, I began by considering Sanday's statistical analysis of factors that might be expected to affect the incidence of cannibalism. Sanday assessed three such factors: (1) the degree of social or political complexity, defined as levels of superordinate authority above the local band or village; (2) the regular presence of hunger, famine, or protein deficiency; and (3) the presence of a lengthy (greater than six months) postpartum sexual taboo. The expectations in the three cases (for which Sanday gives no explanation) are that cannibalism will be more frequent in simpler societies, in societies where hunger or famine is common and where the postpartum sexual taboo is long.[3]

Sanday found strong positive correlations for all three factors (see Table 5.2). Of the three, social complexity was the dominant factor: In simple societies

**TABLE 5.2**  Results of Sanday's analysis of factors affecting the occurrence of cannibalism

| | CANNIBALISM | | | CANNIBALISM AS % OF TOTAL |
|---|---|---|---|---|
| | PRESENT | ABSENT | TOTAL CASES | |
| 1. Complexity of political organization | | | | |
| Simple societies (local only) | 25 | 32 | 57 | 44% |
| One or two jural levels above local | 8 | 18 | 26 | 31$ |
| Three or more jural levels | 4 | 22 | 26 | 15% |
| Subtotal: jural levels above local | 12 | 40 | 52 | 23% |
| Entire sample | 37 | 72 | 109 | 34% |
| 2. Added impact of food stress | | | | |
| *Simple societies* | | | | |
| Some hunger/famine/protein def. | 19 | 20 | 39 | 49% |
| Food constant | 2 | 9 | 11 | 18% |
| Unknown | 4 | 9 | 7 | 57% |
| Entire sample | 25 | 32 | 57 | 44% |
| *Societies with jural levels above local* | | | | |
| Some hunger/famine/protein def. | 10 | 23 | 33 | 30% |
| Food constant | 1 | 16 | 17 | 6% |
| Unknown | 1 | 1 | 2 | 50% |
| Entire sample | 12 | 40 | 52 | 23% |
| *Total* | | | | |
| Some hunger/famine/protein def. | 29 | 43 | 72 | 40% |
| Food constant | 3 | 25 | 28 | 11% |
| Unknown | 5 | 4 | 9 | 56% |
| Entire sample | 37 | 72 | 109 | 34% |
| 3. Added impact of lengthy post-partum sexual taboo | | | | |
| *Simple societies* | | | | |
| 6 months-2 years+ | 7 | 8 | 15 | 47% |
| Up to 6 months | 12 | 16 | 28 | 43% |
| Unknown | 6 | 8 | 14 | 43% |
| Entire sample | 25 | 32 | 57 | 44% |

| | CANNIBALISM | | | CANNIBALISM AS % OF TOTAL |
|---|---|---|---|---|
| | PRESENT | ABSENT | TOTAL CASES | |
| *Societies w/jural levels above local* | | | | |
| 6 months-2 years+ | 7 | 8 | 15 | 47% |
| Up to 6 months | 3 | 22 | 25 | 12% |
| Unknown | 2 | 10 | 12 | 17% |
| Entire sample | 12 | 40 | 52 | 23% |
| *Total* | | | | |
| 6 months-2 years+ | 14 | 16 | 30 | 47% |
| Up to 6 months | 15 | 38 | 53 | 28% |
| Unknown | 8 | 18 | 26 | 31% |
| Entire sample | 37 | 72 | 109 | 34% |

*Source:* Sanday (1986).

(no political structure or integration above the local village), the incidence of cannibal practices was about 45 percent; among modestly complex societies (one or two levels of authority above the local village), it was 30 percent; and among the most complex (three or more levels above the local) it dropped to 15 percent.

Food stress (famine) and lengthy postpartum sexual taboos were also associated with a higher incidence of cannibalism, particularly among the more complex societies. Among simple societies, some food stress increased the rate of cannibalism slightly (from 44 to 49 percent); ample food decreased it noticeably (to 18 percent). In contrast, in simple societies, the presence of a lengthy postpartum sexual taboo had no significant impact (incidence increased from 44 to 47 percent). Among societies with jural levels above the local village, 23 percent had cannibal practices; in the smaller sample of such societies with food stress the rate was 30 percent, and in the even smaller sample with lengthy postpartum sexual taboo, it was 47 percent.

**The frequency of cannibal practices in simple and complex cultures**: Sanday's statistical analysis of contributing factors did not shed any light on the differences between Volhard and Sanday regarding North America, but it did suggest a possible reason for the findings in both of an exceptionally low incidence of cannibal practices in Eurasia compared with that in other continents: the earlier development of large, complex societies on the Eurasian continent resulted in an incidence of simple societies (for the period and sources covered by Volhard and Sanday) much lower than that for other continents. Sanday does not identify the 109 cultures included in her survey, nor does she give cross tabulations of factors by region. It was possible, however, to check the complexity of cultures by region in Murdock and White's original cross-cultural sample of 186 cultures—and to review the quality of the sample itself with respect to coverage of continents.

Table 5.3 shows four Murdock and White measures of cultures by continent:

Col. 2. The number of cultures described and coded in their original *Ethnographic Atlas.*

Col. 3. The Murdock and White estimate by continent of all "adequately described" cultures in the world, some 200 of which were not yet in the *Atlas.*

Col. 4. The number of "independent clusters" of cultures in the *Atlas*, which could be considered distinct from one another for the purpose of cross-cultural comparison.

Col. 5. Murdock's estimate of the total number of independent clusters that would appear if all adequately described cultures had been included.

Out of Murdock and White's estimate of 433 independent cultures (col. 5), 129 or one-third are in Eurasia; and of the 186 cultures in the Standard Cross-cultural Sample, 62 or one-third are in Eurasia. Of these, 30 (one-half) are stateless or have only one jural level above the local. In contrast, for the world as a whole, the share of cultures with no or one jural levels above the local is 69 percent: it is 61 percent in Sub-Saharan Africa, 77 percent in Oceania, 88 percent in Central and South America, and 91 percent in North America.

Thus, the distribution of simple and complex cultures by continent appears explain part of the exceptionally low rate of cannibalism in Eurasia in both Volhard and Sanday—but it does not account for all or even most of the difference between that region and others. For example, in Sub-Saharan Africa, where simpler cultures represent just over 60 percent of Sanday's sample, nearly half of the sample have cannibal practices, but in Eurasia, where nearly 50 percent of the cultures are stateless or have minimal states, only 6 percent of the sampled cultures had such practices. (See Table 5.1.)

Although it was not possible to check directly for a relevant bias in the 109 cultures in Sanday's subset of the cross-cultural sample which had adequate evidence to judge the presence or absence of cannibal practices, the distribution of cultures by region and the overall incidence of cultures that were stateless or had minimal political organization (68 percent) were both close to those in the larger, 186-society sample (Table 5.3, compare columns 7 and 8 with columns 10 and 12).

In a final effort to clarify the source of the low incidence for Eurasia in both Sanday and Volhard, I checked the specific cultures included in the Murdock and White sample. I was stunned to find that except for some very small, outlying groups (in Europe, the Lapps, the Irish Celts, and the Basques), the Murdock and White 186-society sample includes for Europe only one society (Rome); and for the entire span from Western Russia to the East coast of China one modern

**TABLE 5.3** The global distribution of cultures, and proportions of simple cultures, in the Volhard, Murdock and White, and Sanday samples

| | VOLHARD | MURDOCK AND WHITE: WORLD ETHNOGRAPHIC ATLAS & STANDARD SAMPLE | | | | | | | SANDAY SUBSET, M&W SAMPLE | | | |
| | CULTURES W/ REPORTED CANNIBAL PRACTICES | CULTURES IN ATLAS | EST., ALL ADE. DESCR. CULT. | INDEP. CLUSTERS IN ATLAS | EST., ALL INDEP. CLUSTERS | SAMPLE OF INDEP. CULT. | OF WHICH: STATELESS & MINIMAL NO. | % | CULTURES WITH ADEQUATE: GENERAL DATA | & CANN. DATA | OF WHICH: STATEL./MIN. NO. | % |
|---|---|---|---|---|---|---|---|---|---|---|---|---|
| | [1] | [2] | [3] | [4] | [5] | [6] | [7] | [8] | [9] | [10] | [11] | [12] |
| Subsaharan Africa | 400 | 239 | 239 | 85 | 85 | 28 | 17 | 61% | 24 | 15 | | |
| Oceanea (Insular Pacific) | 352 | 128 | 178 | 70 | 80 | 31 | 24 | 77% | 27 | 21 | | |
| North America | 23 | 218 | 218 | 69 | 69 | 33 | 30 | 91% | 31 | 23 | | |
| Central & S. America | 100 | 89 | 100 | 67 | 70 | 32 | 28 | 88% | 25 | 14 | | |
| Eurasia | 40 | 188 | 343 | 121 | 129 | 62 | 30 | 48% | 49 | 36 | | |
| Circum-Mediter. | | 95 | 200 | 55 | 57 | 28 | 9 | 32% | 19 | 13 | | |
| E. Eurasia | | 93 | 143 | 66 | 72 | 34 | 21 | 62% | 30 | 23 | | |
| World Total | 914 | 862 | 1078 | 412 | 433 | 186 | 129 | 69% | 156 | 109 | 7.4 | 68% |

(Continued)

**TABLE 5.3** Continued

| | VOLHARD | MURDOCK AND WHITE: WORLD ETHNOGRAPHIC ATLAS & STANDARD SAMPLE | | | | | | | SANDAY SUBSET, M&W SAMPLE | | | |
| | CULTURES W/ REPORTED CANNIBAL PRACTICES | CULTURES IN ATLAS | EST., ALL ADE. DESCR. CULT. | INDEP. CLUSTERS IN ATLAS | EST., ALL INDEP. CLUSTERS | SAMPLE OF INDEP. CULT. | OF WHICH: STATELESS & MINIMAL | | CULTURES WITH ADEQUATE: | | OF WHICH: STATEL./MIN. | |
| | | | | | | | NO. | % | GENERAL DATA | & CANN. DATA | NO. | % |
| | [1] | [2] | [3] | [4] | [5] | [6] | [7] | [8] | [9] | [10] | [11] | [12] |
|---|---|---|---|---|---|---|---|---|---|---|---|---|
| Subsaharan Africa | 44% | 28% | 22% | 21% | 20% | 15% | 13% | | 15% | 14% | | |
| Oceanea (Insular Pacific) | 38% | 15% | 17% | 17% | 18% | 17% | 19% | | 17% | 19% | | |
| North America | 3% | 25% | 20% | 17% | 16% | 18% | 23% | | 20% | 21% | | |
| Central & S. America | 11% | 10% | 9% | 16% | 16% | 17% | 22% | | 16% | 13% | | |
| Eurasia | 4% | 22% | 32% | 29% | 30% | 33% | 23% | | 31% | 33% | | |
| Circum-Mediter. | | 11% | 19% | 13% | 13% | 15% | 7% | | 12% | 12% | | |
| E. Eurasia | | 11% | 13% | 16% | 17% | 18% | 16% | | 19% | 21% | | |
| World Total | 100% | 100% | 100% | 100% | 100% | 100% | 100% | | 100% | 100% | | |

Sources: Sanday (1986), Volhard (1939), Murdock and White (1969), and Murdock (1981).

Russian village and one modern Chinese village. Most of the 62 cultures in the "Eurasia" regional sample are found in North Africa, the Middle East, and South Asia. The stress on these areas is undoubtedly appropriate for some sampling purposes; and the paucity of historical and prehistorical cultural samplings from Europe, Russia, and China, alone, does not account for the lower than usual rate of cannibal practices among the simpler cultures of this large region. Perhaps the best explanation for the low incidence of ritual cannibalism in Eurasia is that the customs of the simpler societies in this vast region may have been influenced by the proximity and frequent intrusions of more complex societies, which must have been far more extensive and frequent than was the case for simple societies in the Americas, Oceania, and Sub-Saharan Africa.

In the case of North America, the full Murdock and White cross-cultural sample shows this region to have the highest proportion of simple cultures of any continent. This only heightens the perplexing contrast between Volhard's finding of few North American cultures with cannibal practices and Sanday's finding that 50 percent of the cultures sampled had such practices. Moreover, the low overall numbers of distinct cannibal "cultures" or "tribes" identified in the Volhard study cannot be reconciled with the numbers of cultures by continent listed in Murdock's World *Ethnographic Atlas* (see Table 5.3, cols. 1 and 3). Clearly, there were discrepancies in what Volhard, on the one hand, and Murdock and White, on the other, counted as a tribe or culture—and such definitional issues could affect even broad, general inferences about the global, historical incidence of cannibalism.

**Reconciliation of the Volhard and Sanday findings for North America**: In order to identify the sources of the sampling differences between Volhard and Sanday, I reviewed a number of checklists of tribes, cultures, and languages prepared by anthropologists who specialize in cultural geography. Initially, I had hoped to place the tribes listed in Volhard in the context of a universal list of all tribes, so as to derive estimates of cannibal practices by region to compare with those of Sanday. I found, however, that no existing checklist was sufficiently comprehensive in scope, time period, and detail to permit complete identification of the tribes listed by Volhard. Moreover, various experts disagreed on the degree of difference in language or custom that merited a distinction between one tribe and another.

Given these formidable obstacles to reconciling Volhard and Sanday globally, I decided to look more closely at the North American subset of the Volhard and Sanday studies. The purpose of this excursion was to determine the source of the statistical gap for this region; to illustrate the methodological problems that are bound to arise in any comprehensive cross-cultural study of a widespread, long-lived cultural practice; and to obtain a better sense of whether cannibalism in a region occupied mainly by simple societies may have occurred in as many as half of all cultures, as suggested by Sanday's results, or was rare and exotic, as suggested by Volhard's findings for North America.

My foray into North American Indian ethnography and linguistics, whose results are presented in Table 5.4, met these goals satisfactorily. The brief answer to the Volhard-Sanday discrepancy is that Volhard counted as single tribes all of the tribes that spoke either of two languages, Iroquois and Dakota, and either of two groups of languages, Athapaskan and Algonquian; and each of these four clusters represents hundreds of tribes, as tribes counted in the Human Relations Area Files. If we count all the tribes which use a language or language group used by any tribe with a cannibal practice—shown in Table 5-4 in parts 1, 2, and 3—then well over half of all distinctly named and located, independent tribes in North America may have had cannibal practices. More specifically, in terms of Sanday's sample, of the 31 North American tribes in Murdock and White's cross cultural sample (an unspecified 23 of which were coded for the presence or absence of cannibalism by Sanday), 8 match specific cases identified by Volhard (Table 5.4, part 1); another 4 concern tribes located in the same region and with the same language as a tribe cited by Volhard (Table 5.4, part 2); and a further 4 involve tribes with the same language as a tribe with cannibalism and located in a region for which Volhard has other reports of cannibalism (Table 5.4, part 3). These 16 cases make up over half of Murdock and White's original 31-tribe sample for North America. (For good measure, another six tribes in the sample belong to tribes with the same language family as tribes with cannibal reports in Volhard, and appear in regions for which there are cannibal reports for other language families.) In other words, the comparatively small number of North American tribes identified by Volhard as having reported cannibal practices involves several very large aggregates of tribes; and when the counting system is rebased to the tribal level which Volhard uses elsewhere (and which Murdock and White use everywhere), the result is an incidence of cannibalism among simple cultures similar to that on other continents: about 50 percent.

An independent review of the situation in North America is provided in *Kannibalismus bei den nordamerikanischen Indianern und Eskimo* (Cannibalism among the North American Indians and Eskimos), a review of evidence of cannibal practices among native North Americans conducted by German anthropologist Herman Schöppl von Sonnwalden (1992), specifically in response to the Arens' allegation that there are no firsthand witness reports of cannibal customs anywhere. Schöppl von Sonnwalden reviews the claims of cannibalism by language group, citing original sources to distinguish between some areas where there are credible eyewitness reports, and others where the evidence appears to

**TABLE 5.4** The North American tribes coded for cannibalism by Volhard and Sanday compared with all North American tribes, grouped by language and region

| SHERZER'S LANGUAGE GROUPS (SUPPLEMENTED) | | | | | MURDOCK'S WORLD CULTURES | | | VOLHARD'S CASES OF CANNIBALISM | |
| --- | --- | --- | --- | --- | --- | --- | --- | --- | --- |
| REGION | LANGUAGE FAMILY | LANGUAGE GROUP OR LANGUAGE | LANGUAGE OR DIALECT | TRIBE OR CULTURE | REGION | CODE | SAMPLE NO. | CLUSTER OR TRIBE | CASE NO. |
| 1. Tribes with reports of cannibalism In Volhard, by region and language—Language groups found mainly in the North and West | | | | | | | | | |
| Western Subartic | Nadene | **Athapascan** | | | Northern Canada | | | **Athapascan** | 798 |
| Western Subartic | Nadene | Athapascan | **Chipewayan** | **Chipewayan** | Northern Canada | ND7 | | **Tschipewayan** | 799 |
| Western Subartic | Nadene | Athapascan | **Chipewayan** | **Slave** | Northern Canada | ND14 | *128* | | |
| Western Subartic | Nadene | Athapascan | **Chipewayan** | **Yellowknife** | Northern Canada | ND14 | | | |
| Northwest Coast | Salishan | Coast Salish | **Bella Coola** | **Bella Coola** | British Columbia | NE6 | *132* | **Bilchula, Bilqula** | 795 |
| Northwest Coast | Penutian | Tsimshian | **Tsimshian** | **Tsimshian** | British Columbia | NE15 | | **Tsimschian** | 793 |
| Northwest Coast | Wakashan | Wakashan | **Helitsuk** | **Helitsuk** | British Columbia | NE5 | | **Helitsuk** | 794 |
| Northwest Coast | Wakashan | Wakashan | **Kwakiutl** | **Kwakiutl** | British Columbia | NE10 | | **Kwakiutl*** | 792, 96, 97 |
| California | Penutian | Maidun | **Maidun** | **Nisenan** | California | NS15 | | **Nishinam*** | 809, 810 |
| California | Yukian | Yuklan | **Yuklan** | **Wappo** | California | NS24 | | **Wappo** | 808 |

*(Continued)*

**TABLE 5.4** Continued

| | SHERZER'S LANGUAGE GROUPS (SUPPLEMENTED) | | | TRIBE OR CULTURE | MURDOCK'S WORLD CULTURES | | | VOLHARD'S CASES OF CANNIBALISM | |
|---|---|---|---|---|---|---|---|---|---|
| REGION | LANGUAGE FAMILY | LANGUAGE GROUP OR LANGUAGE | LANGUAGE OR DIALECT | | REGION | CODE | SAMPLE NO. | CLUSTER OR TRIBE | CASE NO. |
| —Language groups found mainly in the Plains | | | | | | | | | |
| Plains | Sioux | **Dakota** | | | West Central | | | | |
| Plains | Sioux | **Dakota** | Assiniboin | Assiniboin | Prairie | NF4 | | **Dakota** | 805 |
| Plains | Sioux | **Dakota** | Gros Ventre | Gros Ventre | West Central | NQ13 | *140* | | |
| Plains | Sioux | **Dakota** | Miniconju | Miniconju | West Central | NQ11 | | | |
| Plains | Sioux | **Dakota** | Santee | Santee | West Central | NQ11 | | | |
| Plains | Sioux | **Dakota** | Teton | Teton | West Central | NQ11 | | | |
| Plains | Sioux | **Dakota** | Yankton | Yankton | West Central | NQ11 | | | |
| Plains | Sioux | **Dakota** | Yanktonai | Yanktonai | West Central | NQ11 | | | |
| Plains | Caddoan | **Pawnee** | **Pawnee** | **Pawnee** | West Central | NQ18 | *142* | **Pani** | 807 |
| Plains | Caddoan | **Pawnee** | **Pawnee** | Arikara | West Central | NQ7 | | | |
| Plains | Caddoan | **Pawnee** | Kitsai | Kitsai | West Central | NO10 | | | |
| —Language groups found mainly in Mexico | | | | | | | | | |
| Mexico | Uto-Aztecan | Nahuatlan | **Aztec** | **Aztec** | Mexico | NU7 | 153 | **Aztec** | 811 |
| Mexico | **Otomi** | **Otomi** | **Otomi** | **Otomi** | Mexico | NU26 | | **Otomi** | 812 |
| Mexico | Uto-Aztecan | Nahuatlan | **Cora** | **Cora** | Mexico | NU15 | | **Cora** | 813 |
| Mexico | Uto-Aztecan | Nahuatlan | **Huichol** | **Huichol** | Mexico | NU19 | *152* | **Huichol** | 814 |

—Language groups found mainly in the Northeast and East

| | | | | | | | | | |
|---|---|---|---|---|---|---|---|---|---|
| Northeast | Algic | Algonquian | | | East Central | | | **Algonquian** | 800 |
| Eastern Subartic | Algic | Algonquian | **Cree** | Cree | Ontario | NG4 | | **Kri** | 801 |
| Eastern Subartic | Algic | Algonquian | **Cree** | Montagnais | Quebec | NH6 | 125 | | |
| Northeast | Algic | Algonquian | **Cree** | Naskapi | Newfoundland | N15 | | | |
| Plains | Algic | Algonquian | **Cree** | Plains Cree | Prairie | NF0 | | | |
| Northeast | Algic | Algonquian | **Miami** | Miami | East Central | NP9 | | **Miami** | 802 |
| Northeast | Algic | Algonquian | **Potawatomi** | Potawatomi | East Central | NP10 | | **Potawatomi** | 803 |
| Northeast | Iroquois | **Iroquois** | | | Northeast | | | **Iroquois** | 806 |
| Northeast | Iroquois | **Iroquois** | Cayuga | Cayuga | Northeast | NI0 | | | |
| Northeast | Iroquois | **Iroquois** | Susquehanna | Susquehanna | Northeast | NI0 | | | |
| Northeast | Iroquois | **Iroquois** | Tobacco | Tobacco | Northeast | NI0 | | | |
| Northeast | Iroquois | **Iroquois** | Cayuga | Onondaga | Mid-Atlantic | NM9 | | | |
| Northeast | Iroquois | **Iroquois** | Cayuga | Seneca | Mid-Atlantic | NM9 | | | |
| Northeast | Iroquois | **Iroquois** | Mohawk | Mohawk | Mid-Atlantic | NM9 | | | |
| Northeast | Iroquois | **Iroquois** | Oneida | Oneida | Mid-Atlantic | NM9 | | | |
| Northeast | Iroquois | **Iroquois** | Huron | Huron | Ontario | NG5 | 144 | | |

2. Other tribes with the same language group and region
*Athapaskan, Western Subartic, Northern Canada*

| | | | | | | | | | |
|---|---|---|---|---|---|---|---|---|---|
| Western subartic | Nadene | *Athapaskan* | Tanana | Han | *Northern Canada* | ND10 | | | |
| Western Subartic | Nadene | *Athapaskan* | Tanana | Tutchone | *Northern Canada* | ND10 | | | |

\* Kwakiutl includes Nimkisch and Awikenoq, which were Kwakiutl villages. Similarly, Nishiram and Loretto (Concho), two Maidun tribes, are treated as a single case.

(Continued)

**TABLE 5.4** Continued

| SHERZER'S LANGUAGE GROUPS (SUPPLEMENTED) | | | | TRIBE OR CULTURE | MURDOCK'S WORLD CULTURES | | | VOLHARD'S CASES OF CANNIBALISM | |
|---|---|---|---|---|---|---|---|---|---|
| REGION | LANGUAGE FAMILY | LANGUAGE GROUP OR LANGUAGE | LANGUAGE OR DIALECT | | REGION | CODE | SAMPLE NO. | CLUSTER OR TRIBE | CASE NO. |
| Western Subartic | Nadene | Athapaskan | Dog | Bear Lake | Northern Canada | ND14 | | | |
| Western Subartic | Nadene | Athapaskan | Dog | Dogrib | Northern Canada | ND14 | | | |
| Western Subartic | Nadene | Athapaskan | Dog | Hare | Northern Canada | ND9 | | | |
| Western Subartic | Nadene | Athapaskan | Kutchin | Kutchin | Northern Canada | ND10 | | | |
| Western Subartic | Nadene | Athapaskan | Mountain | Mountain | Northern Canada | ND9 | | | |
| Western Subartic | Nadene | Athapaskan | Tahitan | Kaska | Northern Canada | ND12 | 129 | | |
| Western Subartic | Nadene | Athapaskan | Tahitan | Tahltan | Northern Canada | ND12 | | | |
| Western Subartic | Nadene | Athapaskan | Tsetsaut | Tsetsaut | Northern Canada | ND12 | | | |
| Northwest Coast | Salishan | Coast Salish | Comox | Comox | British Columbia | NE13 | | | |
| Northwest Coast | Salishan | Coast Salish | Squamish | Squamish | British Columbia | NE13 | | | |
| California | Penutian | Miwok | Costanoan | Costanoan | California | NS8 | | | |
| California | Penutian | Miwok | Miwok | Miwok | California | NS16 | | | |
| California | Penutian | Wintun | Wintun | Wintun | California | NS26 | | | |
| California | Penutian | Yokuts | Modok | Modok | California | NS17 | | | |

| California | Penutian | Yokuts | Yokuts | Yokuts | California | NS29 | 136 |
|---|---|---|---|---|---|---|---|
| California | Yukian | Yukian | Yukian | Yuki | California | NS20 | |
| Plains | Caddoan | Caddoan | Wichita | Wichita | West Central | NO10 | |
| Plains | Caddoan | Caddoan | Caddo | Caddo | South Central | NO5 | |
| Mexico | Uzo-Aztecan | Nahuatlan | Popoluca | Popoluca | Mexico | NU30 | 154 |
| Eastern Subartic | Algic | Algonquian | Ojibwa | Ojibwa | Ontario | NG6 | 127 |
| Northeast | Algic | Algonquian | Fox | Fox | East Central | NP5 | |
| Northeast | Algic | Algonquian | Fox | Kickapoo | East Central | NP7 | |
| Northeast | Algic | Algonquian | Fox | Sauk | East Central | NP11 | |
| Northeast | Algic | Algonquian | Menomini | Menomini | East Central | NP8 | |
| Northeast | Algic | Algonquian | Menomini | Illinois | East Central | NP6 | |
| 3. Other tribes with the same language group | | | | | | | |
| Western Subartic | Nadene | Athapaskan | Tanaina | Ahtena | Alaska | NA5 | |
| Western Subartic | Nadene | Athapaskan | Tanaina | Ingalik | Alaska | NA8 | 122 |
| Western Subartic | Nadene | Athapaskan | Tanaina | Nabesna | Alaska | NA5 | |
| Western Subartic | Nadene | Athapaskan | Tanaina | Tanaina | Alaska | NA11 | |
| Western Subartic | Nadene | Athapaskan | Tanaina | Koyukon | Alaska | NA8 | |
| Western Subartic | Nadene | Athapaskan | Tanaina | Tanana | Alaska | NA8 | |
| Western Subartic | Nadene | Athapaskan | Sekani | Sekani | British Columbia | NE14 | |

(Continued)

**TABLE 5.4** Continued

| | SHERZER'S LANGUAGE GROUPS (SUPPLEMENTED) | | | | MURDOCK'S WORLD CULTURES | | | VOLHARD'S CASES OF CANNIBALISM | |
|---|---|---|---|---|---|---|---|---|---|
| REGION | LANGUAGE FAMILY | LANGUAGE GROUP OR LANGUAGE | LANGUAGE OR DIALECT | TRIBE OR CULTURE | REGION | CODE | SAMPLE NO. | CLUSTER OR TRIBE | CASE NO. |
| Western Subartic | Nadene | *Athapaskan* | Carrier | Carrier | British Columbia | NE7 | | | |
| Western Subartic | Nadene | *Athapaskan* | Carrier | Chilcotin | British Columbia | NE8 | | | |
| Western Subartic | Nadene | *Athapaskan* | Sekani | Beaver | Prairie | NF5 | | | |
| Northwest Coast | Nadene | *Athapaskan* | Casta Costa | Casta Cosa | Northwest | NR22 | | | |
| Northwest Coast | Nadene | *Athapaskan* | Casta Costa | Galice | Northwest | NR22 | | | |
| Northwest Coast | Nadene | *Athapaskan* | Kwalhioqua | Kwalhioqua | Northwest | NR10 | | | |
| Northwest Coast | Nadene | *Athapaskan* | Tolowa | Tolowa | Northwest | NR22 | | | |
| California | Nadene | *Athapaskan* | Bear River | Bear River | California | NS11 | | | |
| California | Nadene | *Athapaskan* | Hupa | Hupa | California | NS11 | | | |
| California | Nadene | *Athapaskan* | Mattole | Mattole | California | NS23 | | | |
| California | Nadene | *Athapaskan* | Oregon | Rogue River | California | NS11 | | | |
| California | Nadene | *Athapaskan* | Towola | Towola | California | NS11 | | | |
| California | Nadene | *Athapaskan* | Wailaki | Kato | California | NS23 | | | |
| California | Nadene | *Athapaskan* | Wailaki | Wailaki | California | NS23 | | | |
| Southwest | Nadene | *Athapaskan* | Chiricahua Apache | Chiricahua Apache | Southwest | NT8 | 148 | | |

| | | | | | | | |
|---|---|---|---|---|---|---|---|
| Southwest | *Nadene* | *Athapaskan* | Chiricahua Apache | Mescalero | Southwest | NT8 | *148* |
| Southwest | *Nadene* | *Athapaskan* | Jicarilla | Jicarilla | Southwest | NT8 | *148* |
| Southwest | *Nadene* | *Athapaskan* | Navajo | Navajo | Southwest | NT13 | |
| Southwest | *Nadene* | *Athapaskan* | San Carlos Apache | San Carlos Apache | Southwest | NT21 | |
| Plains | *Nadene* | *Athapaskan* | Kiowa-Apache | Kiowa-Apache | West Central | NQ16 | |
| Plains | *Nadene* | *Athapaskan* | Lipan | Lipan | West Central | NQ9 | |
| Plains | *Nadene* | *Athapaskan* | Sekani | Sarsi | Prairie | NF9 | |
| Northwest Coast | *Salishan* | *Coast Salish* | Lummi | Clallam | Northwest | NR0 | |
| Northwest Coast | *Salishan* | *Coast Salish* | Snoqualmie | Snoqualmie | Northwest | NR0 | |
| Northwest Coast | *Salishan* | *Coast Salish* | Tillamook | Tillamook | Northwest | NR21 | |
| Northwest Coast | *Salishan* | *Coast Salish* | Upper Chehalis | Quinault | Northwest | NR17 | |
| Northwest Coast | *Salishan* | *Coast Salish* | Twana | Twana | Northwest | NR15 | *133* |
| Northwest Coast | *Salishan* | *Coast Salish* | Upper Chehalis | Upper Chehalis | Northwest | NR15 | *133* |
| Plains | *Algic* | *Algonquian* | Blackfoot | Blackfoot | Prairie | NF6 | |
| Plains | *Algic* | *Algonquian* | Ojibwan | Plains Ojibwan | Prairie | NF0 | |
| Plains | *Algic* | *Algonquian* | Arapaho | Arapaho | West Central | NQ6 | |
| Plains | *Algic* | *Algonquian* | Cheyenne | Cheyenne | West Central | NQ8 | |

(Continued)

**TABLE 5.4** Continued

| SHERZER'S LANGUAGE GROUPS (SUPPLEMENTED) | | | | | MURDOCK'S WORLD CULTURES | | | VOLHARD'S CASES OF CANNIBALISM | |
| REGION | LANGUAGE FAMILY | LANGUAGE GROUP OR LANGUAGE | LANGUAGE OR DIALECT | TRIBE OR CULTURE | REGION | CODE | SAMPLE NO. | CLUSTER OR TRIBE | CASE NO. |
| --- | --- | --- | --- | --- | --- | --- | --- | --- | --- |
| Northeast | Algic | *Algonquian* | Micmac | Micmac | Maritime Provinces | NJ5 | *126* | | |
| Northeast | Algic | *Algonquian* | Malecite-Passan | Malecite-Passan | Maritime Provinces | NJ4 | | | |
| Northeast | Algic | *Algonquian* | Abnaki | Eastern Abnaki | New England | NL4 | | | |
| Northeast | Algic | *Algonquian* | Abnaki | Western Abnaki | New England | NL4 | | | |
| Northeast | Algic | *Algonquian* | Massachusett | Massachusett | New England | NL5 | | | |
| Northeast | Algic | *Algonquian* | y dialect | Mohegan | New England | NL6 | | | |
| Northeast | Algic | *Algonquian* | Conoy | Conoy | Mid-Atlantic | NM11 | | | |
| Northeast | Algic | *Algonquian* | Delaware | Delaware | Mid-Atlantic | NM7 | | | |
| Northeast | Algic | *Algonquian* | Nanticoke | Nanticoke | Mid-Atlantic | NM11 | | | |
| Northeast | Algic | *Algonquian* | r dialect | Mahican | Mid-Atlantic | NM10 | | | |
| Northeast | Algic | *Algonquian* | Ojibwa/Chippewa | Ojibwa | Northeast | NIO | | | |
| Northeast | Algic | *Algonquian* | | Pennacook | Northeast | NIO | | | |
| Northeast | Algic | *Algonquian* | | Pamlico | Northeast | NIO | | | |
| Northeast | Algic | *Algonquian* | | Powhatan | Northeast | NIO | | | |
| Northeast | Algic | *Algonquian* | Shawnee | Shawnee | Southeast | NN17 | | | |
| Southeast | Algic | *Algonquian* | | Powhatan | Southeast | NN15 | | | |
| Southeast | Iroquois | *Iroquois* | Cherokee | Cherokee | Southeast | NN8 | | | |

| Region | Language family | Tribe | Tribe | Tribe | Tribe | Region | Code | Page |
|---|---|---|---|---|---|---|---|---|
| Southeast | *Iroquois* | Iroquois | Tuscarora | Tuscarora | Tuscarora | Southeast | NN19 | |

4. Other tribes with the same language family, in regions with reports of cannibalism in Volhard

| Region | Language family | Tribe | Tribe | Tribe | Tribe | Region | Code | Page |
|---|---|---|---|---|---|---|---|---|
| Western Subartic | *Nadene* | Tlingit | Tlingit | Tagish | | Northwest | NDO | |
| Northwest Coast | *Nadene* | Eyak | Eyak | Eyak | | Alaska | NA7 | 130 |
| Northwest Coast | *Nadene* | Tlingit | Tlingit | Tlingit | | Alaska | NA12 | |
| Northwest Coast | *Chemakuan* | Chemakuan | Chemakuan | Chemakuan | | Northwest | NR16 | |
| Northwest Coast | *Chemakuan* | Quileute | Quileute | Quileute | | Northwest | NR16 | |
| Northwest Coast | *Penutian* | Chinook | Lower Chinook | Lower Chinook | | Northwest | NR6 | |
| Northwest Coast | *Penutian* | Coos | Coos | Coos | | Northwest | NR7 | |
| Northwest Coast | *Penutian* | Kalapuya | Kalapuya | Kalapuya | | Northwest | NR9 | |
| Northwest Coast | *Penutian* | Yakonan | Alsea | Alsea | | Northwest | NR5 | |
| Northwest Coast | *Penutian* | Yakonan | Siuslaw | Siuslaw | | Northwest | NR5 | |
| Northwest Coast | *Penutian* | Takelma | Takelma | Takelma | | Northwest | NR20 | |
| Northwest Coast | *Nadene* | Haida | Haida | Haida | | *British Columbia* | NE9 | 131 |
| Northwest Coast | *Wakashan* | Nootka | Nootka | Nootka | | *British Columbia* | NE11 | |
| California | *Alqic* | Yurok | Yurok | Wiyot | | *California* | NS27 | |

(Continued)

**TABLE 5.4** Continued

| SHERZER'S LANGUAGE GROUPS (SUPPLEMENTED) | | | | | MURDOCK'S WORLD CULTURES | | | VOLHARD'S CASES OF CANNIBALISM | |
|---|---|---|---|---|---|---|---|---|---|
| REGION | LANGUAGE FAMILY | LANGUAGE GROUP OR LANGUAGE | LANGUAGE OR DIALECT | TRIBE OR CULTURE | REGION | CODE | SAMPLE NO. | CLUSTER OR TRIBE | CASE NO. |
| California | Algic | Yurok | Yurok | Yurok | California | NS31 | 134 | | |
| Plains | Sioux | Chiwere | Iowa | Iowa | West Central | NQ9 | | | |
| Plains | Sioux | Chiwere | Missouri | Missouri | West Central | NQ9 | | | |
| Plains | Sioux | Chiwere | Oto | Oto | West Central | NQ9 | | | |
| Plains | Sioux | Crow | Crow | Crow | West Central | NQ10 | | | |
| Plains | Sioux | Dhegiha-Omal | Kansa | Kansa | West Central | NQ12 | 143 | | |
| Plains | Sioux | Dhegiha-Omal | Omaha | Omaha | West Central | NQ12 | 143 | | |
| Plains | Sioux | Dhegiha-Omal | Osage | Osage | West Central | NQ12 | 143 | | |
| Plains | Sioux | Dhegiha-Omal | Ponco | Ponca | West Central | NQ12 | 143 | | |
| Plains | Sioux | Dhegiha-Omal | Quapaw | Quapaw | West Central | NQ12 | 143 | | |
| Plains | Sioux | Hidatsa | Hidatsa | Hidatsa | West Central | NQ14 | 141 | | |
| Plains | Sioux | Mandan | Mandan | Mandan | West Central | NQ17 | | | |
| Mexico | Uto-Aztecan | Pima | Pima-Alto | Papago | Mexico | NU28 | 151 | | |
| Northeast | Sioux | Winnebago | Winnebago | Winnebago | East Central | NP12 | | | |

5. Tribes with language families and/or in regions with no report of cannibalism in Volhard

| | | | | | | | | | |
|---|---|---|---|---|---|---|---|---|---|
| Artic | Eskimo-Aleut | Aleut | Aleut | Aleut | Alaska | NA6 | 123 | | |
| Artic | Eskimo-Aleut | Eskimo | Eskimo | Chugash | Alaska | NA10 | | | |

| | | | | | | |
|---|---|---|---|---|---|---|
| Artic | *Eskimo-Aleut* | Eskimo | Eskimo | Nunivak | Alaska | NA13 |
| Artic | *Eskimo-Aleut* | Eskimo | Eskimo | Nunamiut, Tareumiut | Alaska | NA9 |
| Artic | *Eskimo-Aleut* | Eskimo | Eskimo | Mackenzie Eskimo | Northern Canada | ND11 |
| Artic | *Eskimo-Aleut* | Eskimo | Eskimo | Caribou Eskimo | Northern Canada | ND6 |
| Artic | *Eskimo-Aleut* | Eskimo | Eskimo | Copper Eskimo | Northern Canada | ND8 |
| Plateau | *Salishan* | Interior Salish | Lilloeet | Lillooet | British Columbia | NE12 |
| Plateau | *Salishan* | Interior Salish | Shuswap | Shuswap | British Columbia | NE12 |
| Plateau | *Salishan* | Interior Salish | Thompson | Thompson | British Columbia | NE12 |
| Plateau | *Salishan* | Interior Salish | Colville | Colville | Northwest | NIO |
| Plateau | *Salishan* | Interior Salish | Coeur d'Alene | Coeur d'Alene | Northwest | NR19 |
| Plateau | *Salishan* | Interior Salish | Flathead | Flathead | Northwest | NR8 |
| Plateau | *Salishan* | Interior Salish | Flathead | Kalispel | Northwest | NR19 |
| Plateau | *Salishan* | Interior Salish | Flathead | Spokan | Northwest | NR19 |
| Plateau | *Salishan* | Interior Salish | Middle Columbian | Columbian | Northwest | NR19 |
| Plateau | *Penutian* | Cayuse | Cayuse | Cayuse | Northwest | NR18 |
| Plateau | *Penutian* | Chinook | Upper Chinook | Upper Chinook | Northwest | NR23 |

124

(Continued)

**TABLE 5.4** Continued

| | SHERZER'S LANGUAGE GROUPS (SUPPLEMENTED) | | | | MURDOCK'S WORLD CULTURES | | | VOLHARD'S CASES OF CANNIBALISM | |
| --- | --- | --- | --- | --- | --- | --- | --- | --- | --- |
| REGION | LANGUAGE FAMILY | LANGUAGE GROUP OR LANGUAGE | LANGUAGE OR DIALECT | TRIBE OR CULTURE | REGION | CODE | SAMPLE NO. | CLUSTER OR TRIBE | CASE NO. |
| Plateau | *Penutian* | Klamath | Klamath | Klamath | Northwest | NR9 | 138 | | |
| Plateau | *Penutian* | Molala | Molala | Molala | Northwest | NR23 | | | |
| Plateau | *Penutian* | Sahaptin | Nez Perce | Nez Perce | Northwest | NR12 | | | |
| Plateau | *Penutian* | Sahaptin | Sahaptin | Sahaptin | Northwest | NR18 | | | |
| Plateau | Kutenai | Kutenai | Kutenai | Kutenai | Prairie | NF8 | 139 | | |
| *California* | Aztec-Tanoan | Uto-Aztec, 1 | Luiseño-Cahuilla | Cahuilla | California | NS20 | | | |
| *California* | Aztec-Tanoan | Uto-Aztec, 1 | Luiseño-Cahuilla | Cupeño | California | NS20 | | | |
| *California* | Aztec-Tanoan | Uto-Aztec, 1 | Luiseño-Cahuilla | Luiseño | California | NS14 | | | |
| *California* | Aztec-Tanoan | Uto-Aztec, 2 | Shoshone-Comanche | Tübatulabal | California | NS22 | | | |
| *California* | Aztec-Tanoan | Uto-Aztec, 3 | Ute-Chemehuevi | Kawaiisu | California | NS13 | | | |
| *California* | Aztec-Tanoan | Uto-Aztec, 4 | Mono-Bannock | Western Mono | California | NS25 | | | |
| *California* | Aztec-Tanoan | Uto-Aztec, 5 | Gabrielino | Gabrielino | California | NS10 | | | |
| *California* | Aztec-Tanoan | Uto-Aztec, 6 | Serrano | Serrano | California | NS20 | | | |
| *California* | Hokan | Chimariko | Chimariko | Chimariko | California | NS6 | | | |
| *California* | Hokan | Chumash | Chumash | Chumash | California | NS7 | | | |
| *California* | Hokan | Esselen | Esselen | Esselen | California | NS19 | | | |

| | | | | | | | |
|---|---|---|---|---|---|---|---|
| *California* | Hokan | Karok | Karok | Karok | California | NS12 | |
| *California* | Hokan | Palainihan | Palainihan | Achomawi | California | NS5 | |
| *California* | Hokan | Palainihan | Palainihan | Atsugewi | California | NS5 | |
| *California* | Hokan | Pomo | Coast, etc. | Pomo | California | NS18 | 135 |
| *California* | Hokan | Salinan | Salinan | Salinan | California | NS19 | |
| *California* | Hokan | Shasta | Shasta | Shasta | California | NS21 | |
| *California* | Hokan | Yana | Yana | Yana | California | NS28 | |
| *California* | Hokan | Yuman | S & Baja Cal | Diegueño | California | NS9 | |
| Great Basin | Aztec-Tanoan | Uto-Aztec | Mono-Bannock | Northern Paiute | Northwest | NR13 | 137 |
| *Plains* | Tonkawa | Tonkawan | Tonkawan | Tonkawan | West Central | NO7 | |
| Great Basin | Aztec-Tanoan | Uto-Aztec | Shoshone-Comanche | Panamint Shoshone | West Central | NQ19 | |
| *Plains* | Aztec-Tanoan | Kiowa-Tanoan | Kiowa | Kiowa | West Central | NQ15 | |
| Great Basin | Aztec-Tanoan | Uto-Aztec | Shoshone-Comanche | Wind River Shoshone | West Central | NQ19 | 142 |
| *Plains* | Aztec-Tanoan | Uto-Aztec | Shoshone-Comanche | Comanche | South Central | NO6 | 147 |
| Great Basin | Aztec-Tanoan | Uto-Aztec | Shoshone-Comanche | Shoshone | Southwest | NT22 | |
| Great Basin | Aztec-Tanoan | Uto-Aztec | Ute-Chemehuevi | Southern Paiute | Southwest | NT16 | |
| Great Basin | Aztec-Tanoan | Uto-Aztec | Ute-Chemehuevi | Ute | Southwest | NT19 | |
| Great Basin | Hokan | Washo | Washo | Washo | Southwest | NT20 | |
| Southwest | Aztec-Tanoan | Uto-Aztec | Hopi | Hopi | Southwest | NT9 | |

(Continued)

**TABLE 5.4** Continued

| | SHERZER'S LANGUAGE GROUPS (SUPPLEMENTED) | | | | MURDOCK'S WORLD CULTURES | | | VOLHARD'S CASES OF CANNIBALISM | |
| --- | --- | --- | --- | --- | --- | --- | --- | --- | --- |
| REGION | LANGUAGE FAMILY | LANGUAGE GROUP OR LANGUAGE | LANGUAGE OR DIALECT | TRIBE OR CULTURE | REGION | CODE | SAMPLE NO. | CLUSTER OR TRIBE | CASE NO. |
| Southwest | Aztec-Tanoan | Uto-Aztec | Pima | Papago | Southwest | NT0 | | | |
| Southwest | Aztec-Tanoan | Uto-Aztec | Pima | Pima Alto | Southwest | NT0 | | | |
| Southwest | Aztec-Tanoan | Uto-Aztec | Pima | Pima Bajo | Southwest | NT0 | | | |
| Southwest | Aztec-Tanoan | Kiowa-Tanoan | Tiwa | Isleta | Southwest | NT10 | | | |
| Southwest | Aztec-Tanoan | Kiowa-Tanoan | Tiwa | Sandia | Southwest | NT10 | | | |
| Southwest | Aztec-Tanoan | Kiowa-Tanoan | Tiwa | Taos-Picuris | Southwest | NT17 | | | |
| Southwest | Aztec-Tanoan | Kiowa-Tanoan | Tiwa | Tiwa | Southwest | NT10 | | | |
| Southwest | Aztec-Tanoan | Kiowa-Tanoan | Tewa | Tewa | Southwest | NT18 | | | |
| Southwest | Aztec-Tanoan | Kiowa-Tanoan | Towa | Jemez | Southwest | NT11 | | | |
| Southwest | Hokan | Yuman | Delta River | River Yumans | Southwest | NT15 | | | |
| Southwest | Hokan | Yuman | Up River | Mohave | Southwest | NT14 | | | |
| Southwest | Hokan | Yuman | Upland | Havasupai | Southwest | NT14 | 150 | | |
| Southwest | Hokan | Yuman | Upland | Yavapai | Southwest | NT0 | | | |
| Southwest | Coahuiltecan | Coahuiltecan | Coahuiltecan | Coahuilteca | Southwest | NT0 | | | |
| Southwest | Keresan | Keresan | Keres | Keres | Southwest | NT12 | | | |
| Southwest | Zuni | Zuni | Zuni | Zuni | Southwest | NT23 | 149 | | |
| Southeast | Gulf | Atakapa | Atakapa | Atakapa | South Central | NO4 | | | |
| Southeast | Gulf | Chitimacha | Chitimacha | Chitimacha | South Central | NO4 | | | |
| Southeast | Gulf | Tunica | Tunica | Tunica | South Central | NO4 | | | |
| Southeast | Gulf | Natchez | Natchez | Natchez | South Central | NO8 | 146 | | |

| Southeast | Gulf | Muskogean | Alabama-Koasa | Alabama | South Central | NO8 | 146 |
|---|---|---|---|---|---|---|---|
| Southeast | Gulf | Muskogean | Chatot | Chatot | South Central | NO8 | 146 |
| Southeast | Gulf | Muskogean | Mikasuki-Hitchiti | Hitchiti | South Central | NO8 | 146 |
| Southeast | Gulf | Muskogean | Chocktaw-Chickasaw | Chickasaw | Southeast | NN9 | |
| Southeast | Gulf | Muskogean | Chocktaw-Chickasaw | Choctaw | Southeast | NN10 | |
| Southeast | Gulf | Muskogean | Creek-Seminole | Creek | Southeast | NN11 | 145 |
| Southeast | Gulf | Muskogean | Creek-Seminole | Seminole | Southeast | NN16 | |
| Southeast | Gulf | Muskogean | Cusabo | Cusabo | Southeast | NN12 | |
| Southeast | Gulf | Muskogean | | Calusa | Southeast | NN7 | |
| Southeast | Timucua | Timucua | Timucua | Timucua | Southeast | NN18 | |
| Southeast | Yuchi | Yuchi | Yuchi | Yuchi | Southeast | NN20 | |
| Southeast | Sioux | Tutelo | Ofo/Mosopelea | Ofo | Southeast | NN13 | |
| Southeast | Sioux | Catawba | Catawba | Catawba | Southeast | NN13 | |
| Southeast | Sioux | Tutelo | Tutelo | Tutelo | Southeast | NN13 | |
| Southeast | Sioux | Biloxi | Biloxi | Biloxi | Southeast | NN14 | |

*Sources:* Volhard (1939), Sanday (1986), Murdock and White (1969), Murdock (1981), and, for the identification of Indian tribes and languages groups Sherzer (1976), supplemented by Campbell and Mithun (1979), Driver (1969), Heizer and Whipple (1971), Jenness (1933), Kehoe (1981), Landar (1973), Sapir et al (1990), Sebeok (1976), and Swanton (1952).

*Notes:* In part 1, the language families, language groups, languages, and tribes which Volhard identifies as having cannibal customs are shown in bold, and the smallest aggregate with the name Volhard uses is underlined. In subsequent parts, the groupings that are underlined in Part 1 are italicized, and in cases where they are found in the same region that Volhard identifies as having cannibal customs (for that grouping), the region is also italicized. The successive parts are arranged in declining order of cultural and regional closeness to the groups shown in Part 1. This arrangement identifies the cultures in Murdock's sample of world cultures which, given Volhard's terminology, could be counted as having cannibal customs: they are the Murdock sample cases identified in italic in parts 2 and 3.

be nothing more than sensationalistic hearsay. He sums up his conclusions in a passage worth citing in full (p 91, Forsberg translation):

> Cannibalism among North American Indians and Eskimos did not assume the extensive form which it took in, for example, Melanesia, Central and West Africa, or Central and South America; generally speaking, it was not practiced. It did, however, occur in a region that stretched from Labrador across the eastern woodlands, through Florida and to the Gulf of Mexico. [This huge region is represented in Volhard by just two tribes, which are actually language groups encompassing a large fraction of North America: Algonquian and Iroquois. RF] Then, with an interruption for the non-cannibal areas, across Northeast New Mexico into Central America and the Caribbean. A second small area included parts of the Northwest Pacific Coast. Among the Eskimos, there was a tradition of eating dead relatives and tribe members in cases of extreme hunger. The eating of dead tribe members was nowhere practiced with the exception of the Pacific Northwest Coast. (In any case, as practiced by the Kwakiutl, it did not involve "patrophagie"—killing one's seniors to eat them—but rather the use of mummified corpses for ritual purposes.)

Schöppl von Sonnwalden supplements Volhard's sources with another 125 sources available (in the original or in translation) in English or German. After reviewing these, Schöppl von Sonnwalden comes to conclusions that match extremely closely both Volhard's original account of incidence by language group and Sanday's account of incidence by subgroup or tribe (as identified by me from within the larger White and Murdock sample).

While this does not fully account for the Volhard-Sanday differences in counts for North America compared with those for other regions, it increases confidence in the main conclusions suggested by both scholars:

First, ritual or customary cannibalism has been far more frequent in simple societies than in societies with complex, multilevel political organization.

Second, taking into account a sampling bias (simple cultures in the regions of Europe, Russia, and China lie so far back in prehistory that they are missing from the sample), we can assume that the high incidence of cannibal practices in the Third World and the low incidence in Eurasia are products of the length of time that certain societies in each region have had complex political systems with widespread cultural influence.

Third, given the extraordinarily good convergence between Volhard and Sanday (after North America is reconciled)—two fully independent studies—it is reasonable to conclude that the incidence of ritual or customary cannibalism among simple societies is likely to have been as high as 50 percent or more.

# 5.3 The Purposes and Forms of Cannibalism

Several authors who survey cannibalism in various cultures offer schematic representations of its purposes and forms. It is useful to start with that provided by Volhard, who divided cannibal practices into four main forms:

- Profane cannibalism (treating human flesh as food, whether by preference to other food or as a means of preventing starvation)
- Legal or punishment cannibalism
- Magical cannibalism
- Ritual cannibalism, including:

> Worship of gods
> Mortuary (death and burial) rituals Ancestor preservation
> Celebration of victory in war
> Puberty rites
> Fertility rites[4]

In *Cannibals!* (1994), a book for the general public, Hans Askenasy makes a useful distinction among various forms of what Volhard calls "profane" cannibalism and what others call "food" or "gastronomic" cannibalism. Askenasy divides the eating of flesh as food into five subcategories, each with a slightly different connotation from the others. First, he treats starvation cannibalism (cannibalism by necessity) as a special case of food cannibalism. Then he distinguishes among cases of starvation cannibalism according to the cause of the starvation:

1. Natural famines
2. Man-made famines, such as the siege of a city in wartime
3. Travel accidents that leave people stranded in remote locations, such as at sea, while traversing mountains, or in plane accidents

He then adds to these forms of starvation cannibalism two forms of "food cannibalism":

4. Cannibalism among sadists and the mad
5. Cannibalism by tribes which chose human flesh by preference over other available food.

My review of cases of cannibalism among sadists and the mad suggests that the causation here is probably much closer to that in cases of ritual or customary cannibalism than to that in food cannibalism: generally, the cannibal actions sadists and the mentally ill are driven by a construction of feelings and motives in which the ingestion of part of another human does not serve as food, but has an important symbolic role. There also appears to be a special related subcategory for a few butchers who seem otherwise completely sane but who secretly killed people on a regular basis during times of famine or near famine in order to process their flesh into meat for sale, from which they made a profit. This kind of behavior is sociopathic: deadly violence which seems to involve little if any insanity except in the utter lack of conscience and guilt. (In some cases of human butchery, however, the butchers killed themselves before they could be brought to trial, indicating their expectation and fear of unbearable shame.)

Eli Sagan, who does not cite Volhard or the large body of German and French literature on cannibalism, offers an independent yet largely overlapping scheme of categorization.[5] The examples of cannibalism on which Sagan draws, all taken from English-language publications, include anthropological ethnographies, popular books, and the accounts of travelers. Since many of Sagan's sources are the same as those of Volhard, it is not surprising that Sagan's list of ritual forms of cannibalism overlaps to some extent with that of Volhard. Both discuss funeral customs, rites to aid fertility, and rites to mark great occasions. Sagan adds to Volhard's list several other special purposes which are probably more typical of rituals of human sacrifice with a cannibal component than of cannibal rituals more narrowly defined: the passing on the powers of the king, and rites to expiate sin, to enhance the general welfare, or to insure success in warfare.

A war-related category not listed prominently by either Volhard or Sagan but extremely common in ethnographic descriptions of exocannibalism is the consumption of the blood, or heart, and/or in some cases others parts of enemies slain in battle and of war captives tortured and killed after the return to the victor's village.[6] The foremost objective seems to have been to deprive the opponent's tribe of the soul stuff or courage or fighting strength of this warrior, and to transfer one or more of those qualities to one's own tribe. The consumption of enemies was also intended to convey disrespect of the enemy tribe and demoralize them.

Not surprisingly, the main objective of endocannibalism, particularly in tribes which practiced both, was often a mirror image of the purpose of exocannibalism: the goal was to retain the soul stuff, courage, strength, and fertility in the tribe, for the good of the group. In other cases, such as the South American Waari (which practiced both endo- and exocannibalism), described by Conklin (1995), the purpose of endocannibal customs was to insure the successful passage of the dead into the afterworld, to make sure that the soul did not linger in some kind of limbo, and in some cases, to make sure that the soul would proceed to a place or state from which a cycle of reincarnation would later be completed, with the individual's returning either in another human body or else in a prescribed animal intermediary form. In the case of the Waari, being buried, rather than consumed by relatives, was expected to result in the soul getting stuck in the mucky ground forever and not being able to participate in an unending cycle of reincarnation. For this reason, in the 1950s, after Europeans insisted that the Waari abandon cannibalism and bury their dead, the last person to be consumed after death (secretly) was an old woman who on her deathbed begged her relatives to do her a favor and violate the ban so that she would not be lost forever.

The two main purposes and forms of customary cannibalism in China—which was a complex rather than simple society by the time of the first reports—are substantially different from those most common elsewhere, though not entirely unrelated. First, there are many reported cases in which emperors and warlords used cannibalism as form of punishment for treason, disloyalty, or opposition. In some cases the victims were tortured, killed, and then eaten as a form of disrespect worse than death. In other cases, punishment involved the victims being forced to consume parts of their own bodies or of the bodies of relatives (children or parents).

Second, the offering of flesh to an ill parent or a superior was recognized as an expression of filial piety or loyalty. In the most frequent example of this form of cannibalism, children cut a piece of flesh out of their thigh or arm, and turned it into broth in an effort to save the life of a parent suffering from a life-threatening illness. There is also substantial evidence of medicinal forms of cannibalism—that is, the use of powdered, dried, or otherwise reduced forms of human body parts in medical prescriptions—in 18th and 19th century Europe and North America.[7] In the conclusion of the only major study on cannibalism in China, Chong (1990) provides a useful statistical summary of the specific, historically documented cases of cannibalism which the book describes. It is quite remarkable (the more so because apparently not noticed by Chong) that out of 653 documented cases of cannibalism for reasons of filial piety, only six involve the cutting out of flesh by males; all of the others involve younger, subordinate females making the precious donation (see Table 5.5).

**TABLE 5.5**  Chong's analysis of reported incidents of cannibalism in China by purpose and form

A. The causes of cannibalism in China

| SOURCE | W/F | W/H | N/D | P/H | LOYALTY | F/P | TASTE | OTHERS |
|---|---|---|---|---|---|---|---|---|
| Tso Chuan | 2 | 4 | | | | | | |
| Chan Kuo Ts'e | 1 | 2 | | | | | | |
| Lieh Tzu | | | | | | | | |
| Chuang Tzu | | | | | | | 2 | |
| Han Fei Tzu | | | | | | | 3 | |
| Kuo Yü | | | | 1 | | | | |
| Meng Tzu | 1 | 1 | | | | | | |

(Continued)

**TABLE 5.5**  Continued

| SOURCE | W/F | W/H | N/D | P/H | LOYALTY | F/P | TASTE | OTHERS |
|---|---|---|---|---|---|---|---|---|
| Hsün Tzu | | 1 | | | | | | |
| Li Chi | | 1 | | | | | | |
| Shih Chi | 6 | 11 | | 2 | | | | |
| Han Shu | 11 | 1 | 13 | | | | | |
| Hou Han Shu | 15 | | 11 | | | | | |
| San Juo Chih | 4 | | 3 | | | | | |
| Chin Shu | 16 | 1 | 13 | 2 | | | | |
| Wei Shu | 6 | 1 | 1 | | | | | |
| Nan Shih | 12 | 3 | 3 | | | | | |
| Pei Shih | 3 | 3 | | | | | | |
| Pei Ch'i Shu | 2 | | | | | | | |
| Sung Shu | 1 | 1 | | | | | | |
| Liang Shu | 5 | 2 | 2 | | | | | |
| Ch'en Shu | 1 | | | | | | | |
| Sui Shu | 2 | 3 | 3 | | | | | |
| H/W/T/S | 10 | 4 | | | | | | |
| C/W/T/S | 3 | 1 | 1 | | | | | |
| Chin Shi | | | 3 | | | | | |
| Liao Shi | | | 1 | | | | | |
| Yüan Shih | 5 | 1 | 27 | | | | | |
| Sung Shih | 4 | 4 | 14 | | | 20 | 1 | |
| Ming Shih | 5 | | 22 | | | 17 | 1 | |
| C/S/K | 3 | | 15 | | | 58 | | |
| T/P/Y/L | 14 | 12 | 19 | 2 | 1 | 2 | | 7 |
| T/S/C/C | | | | | | 653 | | |
| T/F/Y/K | 21 | 17 | 25 | 1 | 10 | 16 | 3 | |
| Total | 153 | 74 | 176 | 8 | 11 | 780 | 10 | 7 |

Table key:

w/f: war-related famine    H/W/T/S: Hsin Wu Tai Shih

w/h: war-related hatred    C/W/T/S: Chiu Wu Tai Shih

n/d: natural disaster    C/S/K: Ch'ing Shih Kao

p/h/: peace time hatred    T/P/Y/L: T'ai P'ing Yü Lan

f/p: filial piety    T/S/C/C: Tu Shu Chi Ch'eng

T/F/Y/K: s'e Fu Yüan Kuei

**TABLE 5.5**  Chong's analysis of reported incidents of cannibalism in China by purpose and form

B. The conditions related to learned cannibalism

| R/O | DL/FL | DL/ML | D/M | D/F | S/M | S/F | W/H | GD/GM | YS/OB | YB/OB |
|---|---|---|---|---|---|---|---|---|---|---|
| ku (thigh) | 68 | 305 | 75 | 73 | 3 | 1 | 14 | 2 | | 541 |
| pi (arm) | 5 | 25 | 9 | 3 | | 1 | 5 | | 1 | 49 |
| kan (liver) | 1 | 23 | 6 | 4 | | | | | | 34 |
| ju (breast) | | 1 | 1 | | | | | | | 2 |
| jou (flesh) | | 8 | 3 | 1 | | | | 1 | | 13 |
| hsüeh (blood) | | 3 | 1 | | | | | | | 4 |
| hsiung (chest) | | 1 | 2 | | | | | | | 3 |

| R/O | DL/FL | DL/ML | D/M | D/F | S/M | S/F | W/H | GD/GM | YS/OB | YB/OB |
|---|---|---|---|---|---|---|---|---|---|---|
| chih (finger) | | 1 | 1 | | | | | | | 3 |
| lei (rib) | | 1 | | | | | | | | 1 |
| nao (brain) | | | | 1 | | | | | | 1 |
| hsi (knee) | | | | 1 | | | | | | 1 |
| fei (lung) | | | | 1 | | | | | | 1 |
| Total | 74 | 368 | 98 | 84 | 3 | 2 | 19 | 3 | 1 | 653 |

Table key:

r/o: relations above and organs below    s/m: sons/mothers

dl/fl: daughters-in-law/fathers-in-law    s/f: sons/fathers

dl/m/: daughters-in-law/mothers-in-law    w/h: wives/husbands

d/m: daughters/mothers    gd/gm: granddaughters/grandmothers

d/f: daughters/fathers    ys/ob: younger sisters/older brothers

yb/ob: younger brothers/older brothers

# 5.4 Morality and Affect in Customary Cannibalism

The reason that cannibalism, human sacrifice, and slavery represent such appropriate and important parallels to war is that in these cases, just as in the case of war, a destructive practice is sanctioned and enabled by a powerful sense of moral righteousness, which outweighs less powerful senses of moral wrongdoing, repugnance, horror, shame, and sadness.

Given the complex mixes of moral belief and affect associated with each practice, and the differences in those mixes among different individuals, we should expect the process of identifying and characterizing the feelings involved to be difficult. This is all the more true because inherent in the social sanction is having been taught that one will be respected and applauded for doing a given action, and condemned and despised for failing to do it. The feelings of the practitioner about the expected social punishments or rewards thus become intertwined with feelings about the action itself in a manner that is hard to extricate. The sense of doing something wrong and of being hurt by doing it, or feelings of sadness for the victim or remorse for the act—feelings which I hypothesize exist in most people—are likely to be concealed and repressed beneath an emotional barrier created by the social acceptability of and requirement for the action, and the moral reasoning by which it is justified. This means that we are likely to find evidence of a sense of wrongdoing and hurt in indirect forms of expression more than in explicit, verbal statements.

In the case of ritual and customary cannibalism, there are a variety of ways in which repugnance and revulsion are associated with the actions in different cultures. Among the Kwakiutl of British Columbia, a designated cannibal goes through a series of ritual processes which result in small bits of flesh being consumed whole and then vomited up and rigorously accounted for. In this case and many others, the designated consumer becomes contaminated and must undergo cleansing rituals which last for weeks, months, or even a year. During the period of purification various forms of separation are required: for example, the cannibal may be forbidden to speak to or live with his family, and sexual activities are forbidden. In some societies, where many people are expected to partake of small symbolic bits of flesh, it is recognized that some of the less hardy individuals will secretly spit theirs out. In other cases, rites of passage in puberty are required to harden the individual sufficiently to be able to consume flesh.

In cases of endocannibalism where large parts of the body are consumed by relatives, it is common that the deceased will not have the funeral ritual until all of the appropriate relatives have gathered, which can take one or two days. The degree of decomposition of the body then makes the consumption of flesh particularly difficult, even after it is cooked. The test of love for the deceased is how much of the flesh the relations manage to consume rather than cremate. In some cultures only blood relatives consume the dead, while in others only in-laws do so: in either case, the task is a duty (not a pleasure) in which the consumers are supported (though not aided) by the nonconsumers.

The Chinese forms of cannibalism reflect parallel feelings about exo- and endocannibalism: Used as a punishment, the important qualities of cannibalism were that because it violated the dignity and integrity of a person, it was revolting and it showed disrespect. Used as an expression of filial piety, the important quality was that of self-sacrifice—such a great sacrifice that only the lowest person on the family totem pole was expected to make it.

## 5.5 The Demise of Customary Cannibalism

My hypotheses about the about the causes and variability of socially sanctioned group violence do not pertain narrowly to any single case: that is, the implications for the abolition of war of the rise and demise of ritual or customary cannibalism, discussed in this chapter, do not differ substantially from the implications for war of the rise and demise of the practices discussed in Chapter 4. It may be useful, nonetheless, to pause here and consider the more general points briefly in light of the material on cannibalism.

Customary cannibalism adds an important case to the universe of socially sanctioned forms of group violence. It is an important case in part because any form of cannibalism is so alien to the modern mind and in part because the practice seems to have been relatively common among simple societies—quite possibly more common than war has been in recent centuries among complex societies.

As a form of socially sanctioned group violence, what features does cannibalism have in common with war which might help us understand the tenacious roots of war and the possibility of its abolition? The key features are that, like war, customary or ritual cannibalism was relatively widespread; was institutionalized as a socially sanctioned routine in which various members of society played well defined roles; involved forms of behavior which, in the abstract, were perceived as abhorrent and hateful; and was undertaken in spite of its abhorrent aspects because it was believed to be extremely important to the survival or thriving of society.

Finally, the practice and subsequent demise of cannibalism is relevant to the potential abolition of war because, as is likely to be the case for war, cannibalism involved justifying reasons which were embedded in a larger cultural framework and which became irrelevant or invalid when key features of the culture changed. As the main form of socially sanctioned violence in simple societies, cannibalism addressed the most serious issues in the world view of hunter-gatherers: death and rebirth, immortality, and soul stuff as a finite resource whose retention, revitalization, possession, or loss was all-important to the survival of the group.

When economic structure, scale, and political organization changed from hunter-gatherer, roving and small, and simple to agricultural, settled and large, and complex, the central preoccupations of the group changed from soul stuff, reincarnation, and the roles of the hunter and the hunted, to crops and herds; and the means to survival changed from holding together body and soul, maximizing soul stuff, and keeping up courage, fighting strength and fertility to having good weather and fertile soil. This externalization of the means of survival, combined with the growth of the social unit, led to the decline of cannibalism as a means of surviving and thriving, and the rise of pantheons of gods, who controlled weather and disease, and who, like humans, had to be fed to be happy. Thus cannibalism, like human sacrifice, was a justifiable evil which was centrally associated with survival in the societies in which it was practiced.

# SANCTIONED VIOLENCE, MORALITY, AND CULTURAL EVOLUTION

## 6.1 Introduction

The thesis that moral beliefs change with changes in the practice of socially sanctioned violence has ramifications not only for the feasibility of the abolition of war, but also for theories of morality, human nature, and society more generally. This chapter explores some of those ramifications. The purpose is not so much to try to make a case for a particular view of the larger issues as to illuminate the thesis itself. For if the larger views which are implied by the thesis and tend to support it do not seem plausible, that would cast doubt on the thesis.

The material is organized in three main sections. Section 6.2 explores the relationship between the perceived utility of certain forms of violence and the degree of complexity of the cultures in which they are practiced. I argue that sanctioned forms of violence are associated with particular problems in a given form of social organization; and that the moral beliefs which justify given forms of socially sanctioned violence concern not merely the actual or perceived utility of the practice as a means to certain ends, but the perceived significance of the ends themselves. The social goals that are perceived as vital in a given culture are always embedded in a world view which gives those goals value and meaning. World views, in turn, are both product and a determinant of the forms of political, social, and economic organization.[1]

Section 6.3 presents an hypothesis about cultural evolution which explains the rise and potential demise of war and other forms of socially sanctioned large-group violence as a function of priorities among human needs. The hypothesis

128

is that, given limited life expectancy in simple hunter-gatherer societies, people accepted a coercive, hierarchical form of social organization which, by increasing the food supply, fostered population growth and longevity at the price of a reduction in individual dignity and autonomy and an increase in human-on-human violence; but once a certain degree of physical security had been achieved, priorities switched back to favoring egalitarian forms of social organization which foster dignity, autonomy, and peace, as well as physical security. This model helps reconcile the intuitively plausible but conflicting propositions that beliefs about acceptable forms of violence vary with culture and that there exists a universal moral objection to deliberate violence by some people against others. In addition, by underscoring that recognition of the dignity and autonomy of the individual is the main issue addressed by democratic forms of social organization, it supports the thesis that the spread of democratic institutions is likely to lead to the abolition of war.

Finally, in Section 6.4, I conclude with a brief discussion of the prospects for the abolition of all forms of socially sanctioned violence.

# 6.2 The Pattern of Successive Forms of Socially Sanctioned Violence

Two quite different issues are posed by the historical sequence of successive forms of socially sanctioned violence, each highly correlated with a particular stage (or stages) in the emergence of increasingly large societies with increasingly complex forms of political and economic organization. The first issue concerns particulars: Why did specific forms of socially sanctioned violence arise in many different places and times independently, in the context of specific forms of social organization (which themselves arose in different places and times independently)? The second issue is more general: The historical pattern of successive forms of institutionalized violence suggests even if war ends, socially sanctioned, institutionalized violence will never end; only the form will change. This inference is discussed in Section 6.4.

## The Forms of Social Organization and the Forms of Sanctioned Violence

One interpretation of the most widely practiced forms of socially sanctioned violence and violation, which developed independently in various parts of the world, is that they arose at points of vulnerability typical of the forms of social organization in which they arose—that is, around threats which a given form of organization did not protect against, or around the potential for self-interested human exploitation associated with mechanisms that provided a social benefit.

**Ritual cannibalism:** The frequency of ritual cannibalism among simple societies, and its rarity among more complex societies, is, I believe, related to the greater intensity of fears about "death and the regeneration of life" among simple societies, combined with the focus among such societies on food-gathering and eating as the predominate necessity and the most structured activity of life.[2] In the great majority of cases, the purpose of rituals involving the ingestion of symbolic body parts of a deceased person, whether a relative who is mourned or a stranger who is feared, is to control the impact of the death on both the dead and the living.

Ritual cannibalism differs from most forms of socially sanctioned violence in that the action need not involve violence toward a living being (although lethal violence is part of the ritual in most cases of exocannibalism): the traumatic event is, instead, *the violation of the body* (and, implicitly, the individual) inherent in treating the flesh of the deceased like food. The violation of human dignity entailed in such a process is underscored if we contrast ritual cannibal practices with modern medical practices in which the body parts of some individuals (the blood and some organs) are "consumed" by others in the form of blood transfusions and organ transplants. These procedures, which involve the same body parts that are involved in cannibal rituals, do not appear to the modern mind as "cannibal" practices for one reason: the "consumption" of organs is not through the mouth and alimentary tract, like food, but through surgical means long associated with healing and wholeness.

In the simple societies with cannibal rituals, as much as the practitioners may have been loathe to ingest some part of a dead human body, the act had a symbolic meaning which transcended its physical nature. In embracing the fearful, conquering it by making it intimately familiar, the practitioners inflicted as much violation and degradation on themselves as on their victims. By making themselves one with the victim, they eliminated or blurred the most terrifying aspect of death: the disappearance of the living into the unknown.

Later, as the scale and complexity of social organization grew, death must have become a less traumatic feature of life. Unlike the death of an individual in a group of 25 persons, the death of an individual in a society of many thousands or millions would affect those who knew the deceased but not the society as a whole. With growth in the scale, complexity, and anonymity of society, the shadow of death must have shrunk and, by comparison, much more energy must have been given to the trials and tribulations of life in a complex society. Once this happened, ritual cannibalism would no longer be needed as part of the routine of daily life as a means of vitiating the terror of death: the split between the personal and the public imposed by the large scale of social organization would have already eliminated death's worst threat, which in simple societies would be the shrinking of the group below the scale of viability.

**Religious human sacrifice:** Human sacrifice as a form of socially sanctioned violence is extremely rare among simple societies, which do not have anthropomorphic "gods" that would require or receive sacrifices. (In place of gods, the spiritual concepts and origin myths of simple societies are generally organized around spirits that are immanent in the natural world, that is, in certain animals or plants, in the sky, the wind, the sun and moon, the earth, and so on. These spirits have great power, but they tend not to be omnipotent anthropomorphic beings like the later gods.)

Among the early agrarian states which created the first cities, built monumental architecture, and had pantheons of gods who controlled the vicissitudes of life, human sacrifice was universal. In most cases, the purpose of religious human sacrifice was to ensure the fertility of the land and the bounty of the crops, or to seek relief from a plague, drought, or other calamitous natural condition. We can infer from this correlation that the critical vulnerability of agrarian society was the susceptibility of farming to fail badly and cause devastating famines in times of bad weather; and the susceptibility of concentrations of population to decimating diseases. Since the weather and plagues were believed to be inflicted or controlled by the gods, trying to keep the gods happy with gifts and sacrifices of society's most valued possessions was the best that could be done to ward off these dangers. Like ritual cannibalism, human sacrifice was perceived as a necessary evil; but in a mirror-image reversal of the cannibal practitioners' violation of themselves by embracing their worst nightmares, the victim of religious human sacrifice was endowed with godlike qualities, as was required for communication between man and god. In virtually every culture, the very act of being sacrificed made the victim a god. In addition, in many cultures, the individual being prepared for sacrifice was treated as having already become godlike, or as the most revered person in the community.

**Slavery, war, and burial sacrifice:** The spiritual or religious transforming quality of human sacrifice and ritual cannibal practices, and the limited degree of violence in each distinguish those practices from the coinciding and later continuing practices of slavery and war, which involved massive violence and violation, and which did not involve any transforming symbolic meaning which bound victim and perpetrator together in a shared experience. The same can be said of the burial sacrifices of the wives, concubines, servants, soldiers, and other retainers of very highly placed individuals, though on a smaller scale.[3] Slavery and war were first institutionalized as large-scale, routinized instrumental means to social ends at about the same time that human sacrifice was introduced; and like human sacrifice, slavery and war both arose in places where the mobile subsistence economy had given way to fixed habitats, agriculture, the accumulation of wealth, a high degree of differentiation in the specialization of labor, and an extremely hierarchical form of social organization, with a king-god at the top, in some cases, and a mass of slaves at the bottom.

On the one hand, war and preparations for war must have been established as a means of defending territory and wealth from marauding bandits. Indeed, the hierarchical power structure of the early state, and, in particular, the extreme concentration of power in the hands of a divinely invested king, must have arisen at least in part specifically as a means of giving farmers an effective defense against thieves. On the other hand, the war-based conquests involved in the creation of virtually all of the early states suggests that the benefits of protection and economies of scale were only part of the motivation for the early state formation: it is likely that the rest of the motivation lay in the desire for wealth and power among the chief warriors and rulers. Similarly, the establishment of large-scale institutionalized slavery cannot be explained away as an essentially defensive reaction to a pressing social vulnerability: on the contrary, the creation of institutionalized slavery must have been a direct and immediate perversion of the concept of the accumulation of wealth, in which human beings became an owned form of wealth and human slave labor a means to wealth.

Of the three practices introduced at the time of the earliest states, human sacrifice ended the soonest, at least as a socially sanctioned practice. Slavery (or serfdom) and war, however, continued into modern times as means of securing and protecting wealth. Only when an individual-centered view of the world, according equal dignity and worth to every human being, made slavery and serfdom appalling did the legal institutions perpetuating them end.

In the case of war, many observers have argued that the nature of wealth and power have changed so much during the 20th century that territorially based warfare is increasingly irrelevant to obtaining or protecting either one.[4] Modern societies and their great wealth are vulnerable to many forms of destruction and disruption; but their complexity, vulnerability, vast lines of communication, and global economic interdependence make them difficult if not impossible to seize and exploit militarily. Slowly but steadily, the means of coercion and exploitation by some people over others have shifted from military to economic, contributing to the growing sense that apart from defense and humanitarian intervention, war is neither an effective means nor an appropriate means to any ends.

# 6.3 Directed Cultural Evolution and Priorities Among Human Needs

The ultimate question about war is, Why war? Why would human beings invent such an awful practice, and, having experienced its horrors, repeat it over and over again for thousands of years? This question is reciprocal to the main subject of this essay: Having invented and practiced war, how might we end it? Addressing these questions, this section suggests that the rise and potential demise of war can be understood as part of a larger pattern of cultural evolution directed toward meeting a range of basic human needs.[5]

## Costs and Benefits of the Shift from Small Hunter-gatherer Groups to Large Warring States[6]

Some of the hunter-gatherer cultures that have survived into modern times have practices which resemble war in some respects: two groups prepare for an armed confrontation; they identify each other in denigrating terms, often referring to each other as subhuman or nonhuman; they engage in an armed confrontation; and they retreat. Most such practices, however, have other features that make them unlike war: the participants do not kill or injure one another; the confrontation consists mainly of displays of ferocity and shouting; and the confrontation ends as soon as any injury has occurred on either side (if it has not already ended).

The simplest hunter-gatherer bands are mobile groups typically comprising 15–25 individuals, making up several families or an extended family. They have no domesticated animals or horticulture; they carry everything they own when they abandon their base camp after the food in an area is depleted; and they have few personal possessions. This means that they do not own the wealth or other natural resources, such as land, that are typically the object of war. Warlike rituals and, in some cases, raids by one group against another have three main purposes, none of which requires the mass killing or control of territory that are the defining features of war: first, distancing and frightening the unknown "other" (that is, the group living nearest at hand); second, acquiring soul stuff; and third, winning renown and prestige for the display of courage in a dangerous situation. Warfare by a group with a growing population, aimed at seizing a certain area by systematically killing or driving off those who are currently using it, is not unknown; but this true warfare generally does not occur until a culture has domesticated plants or animals and grown to comprise more than one local band (in which case, it may be called a tribe, or, if it is still larger and more complex, a chiefdom).

War was not institutionalized in the form we know until the development of early agricultural societies, in which people began to store food surpluses against future times of need, and thereby created wealth which others could steal. Later, as agrarian societies became larger and more complex, with large cities, specialization of labor, and the accumulation of wealth in the form of manufactured goods, the object of war turned from merely seizing food to seizing nonperishable forms of wealth, and, finally, seizing and incorporating into an existing polity the land and the people that generate the surplus wealth.

The correlation between the development of warfare as a social institution and the rise of large, complex societies capable of accumulating great wealth suggests the following hypothesis about the direction of cultural evolution: Economies which generated food surpluses and, through the specialized labor permitted by these surpluses, nonperishable forms of wealth must have offered some benefit to the mass of individuals at the bottom of their hierarchical structures—a benefit that was worth the loss of autonomy and the increase in sanctioned and nonsanctioned violence which they experienced. Because the price was steep, and because throughout the world population size and longevity have increased as a function of the growing complexity of society, it is reasonable to assume that the benefit was increased life expectancy for oneself, one's spouse, and one's children. This interpretation leans toward the "population push" view of the rise of complex societies because it suggests that the desire for better survival conditions for more people lay behind the development of new forms of technology and social organization, which increased per capita productivity.[7]

One argument against this thesis is that the hunter-gatherer societies that survived into modern times generally gather enough food to meet the group's needs in a few hours of work per person per week, leaving the remaining time for leisure activities. Life in these groups seems to have been healthy, happy, diverse, and fulfilling (at least until the introduction of previously unknown diseases by foreigners), suggesting that people may have been both materially and emotionally better off in hunter-gatherer groups than in later complex societies.

I speculate, however, that the hunter-gatherer groups which survived into modern times did so because they represented particularly successful adaptations to their ecological environments. In other cases, the gradual early expansion of the populations in one region or another must have pushed offshoot groups into borderline ecological environments—for example, where it was cold, or where water was in short supply, or seasonal changes made the food supply unreliable, or disease was rampant. Such conditions would have made the hunting and gathering lifestyle much more stressful, with frequent hunger, malnutrition, or starvation, and low life expectancy. In those cases, the opportunity to secure a more predictable, less stressful, and longer life, with higher rates of survival into child-bearing years, would have been greatly desired. There is substantial archaeological evidence to support the hypothesis that the desire to improve life expectancy was the motive for the development of agriculture and of large, complex societies. This evidence is reflected in the estimates of world population size and regional longevity shown in Table 6-1. Although all figures for population size before the last century, shown in part A, are tentative (and more speculative the further back they go), anthropologists, archaeologists, and demographers generally agree about the patterns of regional increase or decrease and the orders of magnitude involved. The estimates of longevity in the Eastern Mediterranean region from 30,000 BC to the present, shown in Table 6-1, part B, are based on the scientific analysis of skeletons excavated from areas where people of all ages were buried. For most of the sample years shown, 100 or more skeletons of each sex were available. Table 6.1, part C, gives life expectancies for European countries with comprehensive and carefully assessed written documents. The Mediterranean and European estimates are not directly comparable, because the Mediterranean data represent average age at death for those who had reached 15 (the beginning of child-bearing years), whereas the European estimates represent life expectancy at birth. If the Mediterranean data were rebased to life expectancy at birth, the longevity ages would fall by 5–10 years.

**TABLE 6.1**   Comparative historical estimates of world population size (in millions) and life expectancy, 40,000 BC to 1850 AD

| | BC | | | | | | AD | | | | | | | |
|---|---|---|---|---|---|---|---|---|---|---|---|---|---|---|
| | 40,000 | 35,000 | 7000 | 5000 | 1500 | 650 | 1 | 120 | 600 | 1000 | 1400 | 1500 | 1650 | 1750 | 1850 |
| A. World population | 0.5 | >5 | >10 | 50 | | | 296 | | 312 | | 487 | | | 791 | 1262 |
| of which | | | | | | | | | | | | | | | |
| China | | | | | | | 80 | | 65 | | 125 | | | 200 | 430 |
| India-Pakistan | | | | | | | 75 | | 75 | | 110 | | | 190 | 233 |
| Mid-East & N. Africa | | | | | | | 50 | | 35 | | 35 | | | 45 | 60 |
| Other Africa | | | | | | | 22 | | 30 | | 45 | | | 96 | 96 |
| Other Asia | | | | | | | 15 | | 20 | | 25 | | | 46 | 64 |
| Europe | | | | | | | 35 | | 35 | | 65 | | | 125 | 208 |
| Central & S. America | | | | | | | 10 | | 35 | | 45 | | | 15 | 38 |
| USSR | | | | | | | 7 | | 10 | | 15 | | | 42 | 76 |
| Japan | | | | | | | 1 | | 6 | | 20 | | | 30 | 31 |
| N. America | | | | | | | 1 | | 2 | | 2 | | | 2 | 26 |

*(Continued)*

**TABLE 6.1**   Continued

| | | BC | | | | | | AD | | | | | | | | |
|---|---|---|---|---|---|---|---|---|---|---|---|---|---|---|---|---|
| | | 40,000 | 35,000 | 7000 | 5000 | 1500 | 650 | 1 | 120 | 600 | 1000 | 1400 | 1500 | 1650 | 1750 | 1850 |
| B. Eastern Mediterranean adult longevity (life expectancy among those 15+ only) | | | | | | | | | | | | | | | | |
| Male | | 33 | 34 | 34 | 39 | 45 | | 40 | 36 | | 38 | | | | | 40 |
| Female | | 23 | 30 | 29 | 32 | 36 | | 35 | 31 | | 31 | | | | | 37 |
| C. European Life Expectancy at Birth | | | | | | | | | | | | | | | | |
| Elites | | | | | | | | | | | | | | | | |
| British Peers | Male | | | | | | | | | | | | | 30 | 45 | 55 |
| | Female | | | | | | | | | | | | | 33 | 46 | 63 |
| Geneva bourgeoisie | Male | | | | | | | | | | | | | 31 | 43 | 55 |
| | Female | | | | | | | | | | | | | 37 | 48 | 60 |
| National Populations | | | | | | | | | | | | | | | | |
| Sweden | Male | | | | | | | | | | | | | | 34 | 45 |
| | Female | | | | | | | | | | | | | | 37 | 48 |
| France | Male | | | | | | | | | | | | | | | 39 |
| | Female | | | | | | | | | | | | | | | 42 |
| Britain | Male | | | | | | | | | | | | | | | 42 |
| | Female | | | | | | | | | | | | | | | 44 |
| Netherlands | Male | | | | | | | | | | | | | | | 39 |
| | Female | | | | | | | | | | | | | | | 42 |

*Sources:*

**Part A**: For 1750 and 1850, J Durand, "The Modern Expansion of World Population" (repr from Proc of the American Philosophical Society, June 1967), in Charles B Nam, ed., *Population and Society: A Textbook of Readings*, Boston: Houghton Mifflin, 1968. For AD 1, 1000, and 1500, J Durand, "Historical Estimates of World Population: An Evaluation," *Population and Development Review* Vol 3, No 3, 1977, cited in Boserup (1981). For 40,000, 35,000, 7,000 and 5,000 BC, Jean Noel Biraben, "Essai sur l'evolution du nombre des hommes," in Herve Le Bras, ed., *Population*, Paris: Hachette, 1985, pp 56–68 (drawing on Durand 1967).

**Part B**: J Lawrence Angel, "Paleoecology, Paleodemography and Health," in Steven Polgar, ed., *Population, Ecology, and Social Evolution*, The Hague: Mouton (US distributor Aldine).

**Part C**: O V Glass, "Introduction," in *Population in History: Essays in Historical Demography*, O V Glass and O E C Eversley, eds., Chicago: Aldine Publishing Co., 1965.

Taken together, the estimates in Table 6.1 show the following overall relationship between stages of economic and social organization, on the one hand, and changes in population size and longevity, on the other. The first modern humans are estimated to have reached a population size of up to 5 million relatively early in the history of hunter-gatherers (35,000 years ago) and to have taken the next 30,000 years to double, reaching at most 10 million by the time of the introduction of agriculture. Life for the early *homo sapiens sapiens* must have been hard, since only half of all children survived to 15, and half of the remaining population was dead by about the age of 30. Disease and death in childbirth were important causes of early death. Until the medical advances of the last century, these factors kept life expectancy from rising higher than 50. Other factors which must have contributed to the low life expectancy among prehistoric hunter-gatherers were malnutrition, which lowered resistance to disease, starvation, wild animals (including poisonous snakes), severe weather, and accidents.

Though conditions may have been harsh, it is generally agreed that the low rate of overall population growth was due to relatively low birth rates as well as high death rates. Long breast-feeding led to "child spacing" (intervals between pregnancies of 2–3 years), which was supplemented by abortion (induced in part by carrying infants while gathering food) and infanticide. In areas where survival was somewhat easier and the population did grow, population growth led to migration and dispersal, as new groups of 15–25 individuals broke off and moved further afield.

Increased local population density leading to innovations that would increase the productivity of a given area did occur in some places, but only gradually. This led to the earliest forms of horticulture, animal husbandry, and coastal harvesting of fish and shellfish; and it was associated with the development of semisedentary groups of bands (tribes or chiefdoms).[8]

After the earliest settlements based on agriculture appeared in 7000–8000 BC, the world's population grew by a factor of 5 in 2000 years, from 10 million to 50 million (in absolute terms, 10 times the growth that occurred over the previous 30,000 years). During the early flowering of agriculture between 5000 BC and 1AD, in the Middle East (including Egypt), the Indian subcontinent, and China, there was another fivefold increase in the world's population, from 50 million to over 250 million.

During the same period (between 5000 BC and 600 BC), the quality of life for the average person in the Eastern Mediterranean improved so radically that life expectancy rose from 34 and 29 for men and women, respectively, to 45 and 36. Subsequently, however, this area suffered from overpopulation, urban crowding, lack of new conquered farm labor, a decline in nutrition, and rampant malaria and other diseases. In the first centuries AD, both the size of the population and life expectancy declined throughout the Eastern Mediterranean, from Rome to Carthage. Similarly, the Chinese population, which was the largest and the most dense in the world in 1AD, suffered from disease, drought, and war, and declined over the period to 1000 AD. Over the same period, the emergence of the early agricultural city states of Central and South America brought substantial growth to the population there, which continued to grow until the 16th—17th centuries, when it was decimated by diseases introduced by Europeans.

In Europe, growth of industry and intensification of agriculture after the Renaissance led to a new spurt of population growth and, more important, a steady rise in life expectancy for the growing population. This is particularly clear in estimates for British peers and for the bourgeoisie of Geneva (for both of which unusually detailed and reliable figures are available), which show a remarkably close match in average life expectancies over the period from 1650 to 1850: both sets start in the low 30s, move by 1750 to the mid 40s, and by 1850 reach the high 50s. (Again, these figures are shifted down by 5–10 years compared with those for the Eastern Mediterranean because they include child mortality.) Sweden shows the same trend for its entire national population, but lagged by 100 years; for France, Britain, and the Netherlands, gains in life expectancy for the population as a whole lag about 150 years behind those of the upper class. The differences for all of these populations horizontally across time and vertically across classes are largely attributable to reliable (lifelong) access to food in sufficient quantity and with sufficient diversity to meet essential nutritional needs. The important issue in modern Europe was not so much early death by starvation (although that did occur periodically throughout Europe), but weakened resistance to life-threatening diseases and injuries.

In sum, the introduction of large, hierarchically organized complex societies, in which a small minority of city-based rulers, priests, warriors, craftsmen, and servants were supported by a large majority of agricultural workers in the surrounding countryside, did create enough food to support both an increase in world population of between one and two orders of magnitude (from 10–50 million at the start to 300–800 million between 1 AD and 1750 AD), and an increase in average life expectancy at birth of 10–15 years, from the low to mid 20s to the high 30s. Within the boundaries of this general increase in quantity and quality of human life, there was, however, no steady growth trend in any part of the world. Instead, there were wide swings, in some cases enormous swings, in population size, and wide swings in life expectancy at different times in different regions, as a function of the decline and collapse of the system of agricultural intensification, due to pandemics, war, soil exhaustion, or political collapse. Not until the industrial revolution in the 18th century did steady, substantially unbroken growth in both population size and life expectancy take hold in virtually all parts of the world. (Even now, setbacks can occur, as in the recent substantial decline in life expectancy in Russia, due to a combination of inadequate nutrition and the virtual collapse of the medical system.)

I have reviewed the evidence on population size and longevity at some length in order to underscore what I hypothesize was a powerful motivation for the mass of ordinary people at the bottom of the heap to put up with the violence, indignity, and inequity of hierarchically structured agricultural and feudal societies and empires, instead of returning to (or remaining with) the simpler but more peaceful, dignified, and egalitarian lifestyle of the hunter-gatherers. This motivation was to have a better chance at surviving and, on average, a better quality of life physically. It is likely that during periods of social collapse, as well as during plagues and famines, the quality of life and life expectancy in hierarchical societies were at least as bad as and sometimes worse than those of hunter-gatherers. But on the whole, this was not the case. In addition, the more cosmopolitan and diverse context of life in a large society would have been appealing even for those with very few resources. Markets, holidays, church services, and ceremonies would have all provided occasions for interaction with the larger society which replaced the small, insular groups of hunter-gatherers.

## A Symmetrical Transition from Warring States to a Nonwarring International System

My thesis about what may have originally made war acceptable as an institution has a corollary about what may make it unacceptable in the foreseeable future. The modern period has seen a transition very nearly opposite to the transition from small hunter-gatherer group to large agricultural societies, in two important respects. First, over the last two centuries, in parallel with an unprecedented growth in world population size and extension of life expectancy, there has been the first fundamental change in social and political organization since the shift from "acephalous" hunter-gatherer bands to hierarchical city states. The modern change, embodied in democratic institutions, has been toward asserting egalitarian values and establishing ways to increase the opportunity for the average person to influence decisions made on behalf of the entire society. The common thread in the political, social, and economic changes of the modern period is the rise in the perceived dignity and worth of the individual, at the expense of the hierarchically structured world order of earlier times and, in particular, at the expense of the top ranks in that order. This has led to a devolution and dispersal of political power from the center to the periphery, reflected both in the establishment of popularly elected representative government within nation-states, and in the dismantling of colonial empires (and attitudes) among nation-states.

Second, the rise in the dignity and worth of the individual and the leveling of power, in turn, have been associated with a change in the role of violence in society. Hierarchically structured polities have always been maintained through threats of the use of force by the ruling elites. The authority of the top ruler, which was generally very broad, was largely arbitrary: it was based not on merit or popular selection, but on the arbitrary factors of inheritance backed up by wealth, with which the ruler purchased superior armed force to enforce his rule. An usurper with more powerful armed forces was generally recognized as the legitimate ruler as soon as he had demolished the fighting forces of his predecessor. This was not because people approved of armed takeover, but because the position of ruler was itself treated as a somewhat unpleasant necessity: someone has to do it, otherwise there will be anarchy and everyone will lose. The use of violence as a means to power was, thus, routinely practiced, recognized, and accepted.

The rise of an individual-centered view of the world has been associated with (and, I believe, caused) a declining tolerance for violence in general, and, specifically, the replacement of violence with verbal persuasion as the means of maintaining or changing a government and its policies.

Implicit in this interpretation of political and cultural developments over the past several centuries is a view of predominant individual priorities that determine the direction of cultural evolution. In contrast to the early change in social organization that introduced war—a change in which individuals sacrificed the autonomy, dignity, and nonviolence of hunter-gatherer groups for the physical security and longevity offered by large agrarian states—the focus of contemporary social organization has been to move beyond mere physical security in ways that reestablish the long-lost conditions of autonomy, dignity, and nonviolence.

Of course, these values are altered by the differences between the modern world and the small hunter-gatherer band or tribe. In small, self-sufficient bands, each individual's autonomy and dignity and the group's tendency to nonviolence were practiced in a community in which each individual was well known (and probably related) to every other, and the welfare of each was of immediate concern to the others. In modern society, the situation is very nearly the reverse: the autonomy, dignity, and nonviolence of each individual and of society as a whole exist within a framework in which people live at close quarters (in cities and towns) with innumerable strangers, and where the supporting roles of the community and the extended family are often modest. This difference in context gives the qualities of autonomy and dignity a different meaning. Earlier, the granting of autonomy and respect for the dignity of others were based on familiarity and love. Today, in towns where most people walk past or interact with scores or hundreds of strangers on a daily basis, recognizing the dignity and autonomy of others requires that each individual learn to apply the qualities of justice, fairness, tolerance, and reciprocity. Crime-ridden inner-city locales, the drug subculture, and the tendency of teenagers to rely on peers instead of parents for socialization all undermine this crucial learning process, producing uneven results.

In sum, in trying to account for the existence of destructive institutions, such as war and slavery, and to reconcile these institutions with our everyday sense of human nature, it is reasonable to infer that at a certain stage, people gave a higher priority to physical security and longevity than to autonomy, dignity, and nonviolence; but that once a certain degree of security and life length had been achieved, the quality of life was accorded an equal or greater priority, with stress on the qualities of dignity, autonomy, and freedom from war.

This view of the direction of cultural evolution in general, and of the causes of the rise and potential demise of war in particular, suggests that we should expect *all* forms of socially sanctioned, institutionalized violence, not just war, to end in the foreseeable future. Similarly, so long as present trends continue, new forms of socially sanctioned violence should not arise.[9]

The idea that the rekindling of egalitarian values and the creation of democratic institutions are likely to lead to the end of war has been challenged by scholars who point to the frequency with which democratic countries have been involved in war. It is, however, generally accepted that democracies tend not to go to war with each other; and this fact is central to the prospects for the spread of egalitarian values—specifically, the growth of respect for the dignity and worth of the individual—to lead to the end of war.

Since the American revolution, democratic nations have maintained a double standard regarding the use of force: they have supported the commitment to nonviolence which is central to an egalitarian political system at home, while continuing to play the old game of power politics abroad. This suggests that the spread of democracy has *not* fostered commitment to defensive nonviolence as a moral position on war, or else that this standard is not easily interpreted and applied in the international arena. The truth is, I believe, different and less discouraging to the prospects for the abolition of war.

In conflicts with nondemocratic societies, the democracies have betrayed the standard of defensive nonviolence in a way they are unlikely to do in conflicts with other democracies. In conflicts with nondemocratic societies, the leaders of democratic societies have assumed that they are always on the defensive, and that their opponents are always the aggressors. Of course, political leaders always advance self-serving interpretations of questionable behavior in international politics; but in this case, objective aspects of the domestic politics and military alliances of the "communist" countries have fostered this view. First, leaders and citizens in the democracies have assumed that *governments that are oppressive at home will be prone to aggression abroad*. Second, they have assumed that *since nondemocratic governments do not represent the will of their own people, trouncing them in an international conflict will help liberate an oppressed people*—an action that can be interpreted as inherently defensive in nature. Third, during the bipolar era of the Cold War, political leaders in the democracies assumed that an overall policy of limiting the influence of the leading nondemocratic nation, the former Soviet Union, justified giving armed support to nondemocratic but capitalist governments or factions in smaller countries. The rationale was that *nondefensive action on the local level—taking the side of repressive, autocratic governments—was an acceptable tactical move in the global strategic conflict with the Soviet Union, in which the democracies were (in their own view) on the defensive.* Finally, democratic leaders assumed that *governments which were undemocratic but capitalist were more likely to become democratic than those which were undemocratic and socialist.*

From this set of *a priori* assumptions, democratic governments drew the conclusion that in any international or civil war, socialist governments and allies and clients of the former Soviet Union could reasonably be assumed to be the attackers and their opponents the defenders. For the large Western nations, particularly the United States, the effect of this blanket inference was to create a morally ambiguous public policy, in which the burden of decision on whether to use armed force in a given conflict rested on the old just war standard, while the public rhetoric justifying actual uses of armed force stressed the contemporary standard of defensive nonviolence. The US debate on the Gulf War, held in Congress and in the press during the period between Iraq's invasion of Kuwait (August 1990) and the US armed intervention to expel Iraqi troops (beginning in January 1991), provides an extraordinarily transparent view of the duality in Western grand strategy. In October 1990, President Bush floated the idea that the United States should use force to repel Iraq from Kuwait because an Iraqi stranglehold on Middle East oil would lead to economic setbacks in the United States and other Western nations, including a loss of jobs in the United States. This "just war" reasoning was not popular with the public, however: in opinion polls, the majority of people expressed the view that economic costs would not justify armed intervention. As a result, by December 1990, the Bush administration had switched to a entirely different reason for intervention, one that was consistent with commitment to defensive nonviolence and supported by a majority of the public: this was that to deter future cases of armed international aggression in the new and unstable post-Cold War world, the United States would have to take a principled stand against this early and blatant example. From the sequence of events, we can reasonably infer protecting national economic interests was the primary motive for the use of force on the part of the decisionmakers; but taking a principled stand against international aggression, not advancing economic interests, was the primary motive for public acceptance of the use of force. The moral ambiguity that was common during the Cold War is now gradually giving way to the greater moral consistency to be expected in conflicts among democratic societies.

When both sides in a conflict have democratic governments, neither has a ready excuse to assume that all aggressiveness lies on one side and all defensiveness on the other. Given the democratic character of the opposing government, neither side's leaders can justify war as fundamentally protective of the longer-term interests of the opponent's people, or as essential to larger, longer-term goals for global peace and democracy. In place of the traditional "us and them" mentality, the spread of democratic institutions creates an assumption of shared values, including the ultimate goal of developing an international society in which commitment to defensive nonviolence is the rule. This assumption puts pressure on leaders on both sides in any conflict between democracies to identify nonviolent means of conflict resolution.

Over the course of the 20th century, uses of armed force beyond national borders have been increasingly (albeit slowly) confined to situations that can be considered defensive or humanitarian. But as the standard of democratic commitment to nonviolence has become stronger, the governments of the democracies have increasingly characterized ambiguous or self-interested uses of force as "defensive." The effect has been to corrupt the concept and language of "defense." The word "defense" has become a *portmanteau* for any military action; used as an adjective, it routinely replaces the more neutral word "military," as in the phrase "defense budget." Ironically, even the name Department of Defense, which was introduced in the United States at the close of World War II, replacing "Department of War" which had served since the country's founding, was introduced at the very moment that the United States was becoming a great power, whose armed forces were intended for use mainly overseas, not for the defense of US territory.

Despite the corruption of the language of defense, the stringency with which the criterion of defensiveness constrains the use of force is likely to increase in direct proportion to the worldwide spread of democratic values and institutions. The governments of democratic societies, where most people believe that the use of force should be limited to defense, will tend not to initiate aggression. The constraint will be particularly powerful in conflicts with other democracies, where the populations on both sides will be extremely reluctant to support any government inclination to go to war. As democracy spreads and there are fewer conflicts whose treatment is amenable to the old just war standard, society's sense of the relevance and appropriateness of this standard in any conflict will disappear.

# 6.4 The End of Socially Sanctioned Forms of Violence

In illustrating the tremendous variability in socially sanctioned forms of violence across time and culture, this essay documents successive forms of socially sanctioned violence that stretch back for thousands of years, deep into prehistory. While appropriately conveying a sense that no particular form (such as war) is likely to be immutable, this list may also give the impression that for whatever reason, human societies have always been prone to invent and conduct sanctioned forms of group violence, and they are therefore likely to do so in future.

This argument is important not only in its general form, but also specifically in the context of the abolition of war, because for most people the idea that war cannot be abolished is probably only loosely and casually tied to particular obstacles to abolition. To the extent that this is so, references to "innate aggressiveness" or other obstacles are equivalent to a throwaway phrase, such as "the human propensity for war, whatever that might be." In other words, for many people, the view that war cannot be abolished probably boils down to the following argument: "Since war or, if not war, some other form of group violence has been present throughout human history, sanctioned violence must not be susceptible to being abolished."

This argument is based on an assumption contrary to modern thought: Since something has not happened in the past, it cannot happen in the future. Why would this contrary perspective be applied to war, when, in this century, people have done so many things which were previously not only undoable but virtually unthinkable, such as walk on the moon, or fly, or get a new heart?

There are, I believe, three aspects of war (and, in lurking behind war, other not yet identified future forms of socially sanctioned violence) which lend it a special aura of immutability: First, it is morally profoundly controversial, at once terrible and just. To say that war could end would mean to acknowledge or embrace the notion that war is (at least potentially) no longer controversial, no longer just, only terrible. People do not believe that war can end because they believe that some wars are just: this means that they do not wholeheartedly want for it to end.

Second, war is haphazard. From time to time, regularities appear in the incidence of war, the conditions under which war breaks out, or the parties to war. But to the specialist as well as the lay person, war remains unpredictable. How can we expect an activity that is sporadic and unpredictable to end?

Third, war has long served as the apotheosis of human ills, as illustrated in the phrase "the scourge of war." For many people, the image suggested by the idea of ending war is probably something like creating a heaven on earth, a paradise in which there is no violence or iniquity and all people can live productive, happy, healthy lives. This is, of course, not the case. Ending war would not end any of life's other mass woes: disease, poverty, starvation, malnutrition, illiteracy, greed, crime, unequal distribution of wealth, population explosion, environmental destruction, corruption, betrayal, and so on.

To make the idea of ending war conceivable, "war" must be extricated from its larger-than-life symbolic meaning and scaled back to its ordinary, nasty self. The fact that societies stop a particular practice of death and destruction that has been historically sanctioned would not mean that the individual human beings who make up societies will have become more altruistic, generous, truthful, rational, or farseeing; it would mean only that societies had abandoned one more barbarous custom, along with the others abolished earlier.

This discussion constitutes part of my response to the view that because some form of socially sanctioned violence has always been with us, some form always will be: specifically, I suggest that the claim itself, which entails no particular evidence or argument, represents nothing more than an amalgam of the various sources of resistance to thinking through the meaning and conditions of abolition.

In addition, however, there is a direct response to the concern about unending socially sanctioned violence. The reason that we can expect to find that all forms of socially sanctioned group violence are ending is suggested by my characterization of modern social organization as an effort to retrieve the autonomy, dignity, and freedom from violence that were put on the back burner, so to speak, during humanity's long quest for physical security and longevity. If this characterization is correct, this effort is likely to produce a general rejection of all forms of socially sanctioned violence as no longer justifiable or tolerable.

# Appendix: The Debate on the Existence of Cannibalism

In 1979 a heated debate in the field of anthropology on the existence of cannibalism was sparked by the publication of *The Man-Eating Myth: Anthropology and Anthropophagy* by William Arens, an anthropologist at the State University of New York at Stoneybrook. Before turning to Arens' claims and the responses of his critics, I give some general background on the nature and sources of scholarly studies of cannibalism, and other bodies of literature on the topic. There is far more nonfiction material on the topic than is generally known, and the idea of cannibalism is far more pervasive than we realize as a metaphor, a fear, and a reality among nonhuman fauna. When considering whether many cultures once had rituals involving the ingestion of human body parts, it is useful to have a sense of the larger universe of sources and references which surrounds the alleged practice.[1]

## Scholarly Studies of Cannibalism

Anthropology, archaeology, history, and historical documents contain the main body of literature on cannibalism, and virtually all of the literature on socially sanctioned ritual or customary cannibalism. Histories record both starvation cannibalism and customary or ritual cannibalism. Archaeological studies may occasionally refer to recovered hieroglyphics or other ancient written or pictorial representations of customary or ritual cannibal acts; but they are more likely to involve the study of fossilized bones left from starvation or food cannibalism than the interpretation of material pertaining to customary or ritual cannibalism.

This social scientific literature involves five large and distinct subsets:

1. Reports of starvation cannibalism and customary cannibalism in the official and unofficial histories of various Chinese dynasties going back to the second millennium BC [discussed in Chong, *Cannibalism in China* (1990)].[2]
2. Western historical reports of cannibal practices, from Herodotus to Marco Polo. [Surveys of the oldest written Western sources on cannibalism are given in Peter-Rocher (1994) and Tannahill (1975).]

3. Post-Columbian reports by travelers, explorers, missionaries, settlers, colonial governors, and the first amateur and professional anthropologists on cannibal practices among previously unknown simple cultures in Africa, North and South America, Southeast Asia, and Oceania. These start with the first reports from Columbus' trips and continue through the first half of the twentieth century. One typical and widely cited example (which I scanned in a nineteenth-century French translation of the original Spanish), written in 1568, is an 850-page diary, *The True Story of the Conquest of New Spain*, reconstructed from notes by Hernando Díaz del Castillo, who accompanied Hernando Cortes on several long trips to Cuba, Central America, and South America between 1514 and 1547 (1877).

4. More carefully compiled ethnographies dating from the late nineteenth century to the present, generally prepared by professional anthropologists, describing and explaining the meaning of cannibal practices among little-known cultures, along with cross-cultural anthropological studies based on such ethnographies. An excellent recent example of an ethnographic study of cannibalism is that by Beth Conklin: "'Thus Are Our Bodies, Thus Was Our Custom': Mortuary Cannibalism in an Amazonian Society" (1995). An excellent cross-cultural analysis of exocannibal practices associated with war is given in *The Comparative Ethnology of South American Indians*, Volume V of the classic five-volume *Handbook of South American Indians* (Steward 1946–1959), in a chapter entitled "Warfare, cannibalism, and human trophies" by Alfred Metraux, the world's foremost expert on warfare among South American indian tribes. Two other fine cross-cultural studies, which look at both endo- and exocannibalism in many parts of the world, are Peggy Reeves Sanday, *Divine Hunger* (1986) and Maurice Bloch and Jonathan Parry, *Death and the Regeneration of Life* (1982).

5. Archaeological studies of human bones revealing signs of the consumption of flesh as food by other humans. Such studies have become scientifically complex over the past 20 years, with growing reliance on the study of bone breakage and cutmarks with electron microscopes and on radioisotopic dating. One outstanding example is Timothy D. White's *Prehistoric Cannibalism at Mancos SM TUMR-2346* (1992), a natural-scientific study of the skeletal remains of 29 individuals at a single pueblo site in Colorado, dating from around 1100 AD—a study conducted, photographed, and written up as a model for rigorous assessment of archaeological evidence of cannibalism, and endorsed by reviewers as excellent for this purpose.

In addition to these kinds and contexts of thought and observation relating to cannibalism, there are related journalistic variants, prepared mainly for public entertainment and amusement. Works by Bernheim and Marriner are moderately sensationalistic books of this kind. These books and others like them typically recount a selection of stories drawn from the other kinds of sources described above. In some cases, such books may involve extensive research among primary sources (such as missionaries' letters and reports) and secondary sources; and they may document instances of cannibalism not previously mentioned in the professional anthropological literature. Bernheim, for example, provides a detailed and well-documented review of cannibalism associated with famine in all parts of the world (Bernheim 1992, "Part II. Chronique de l'extrême faim," pp 123–239). Popular nonfiction books on cannibalism and human sacrifice by Hogg (1966), Tannahill (1975), and Tierney (1989) are all carefully researched and documented, and all three are cited as sources in subsequent works by professional anthropologists.

Among cultural anthropologists, there are noticeable differences in the national bodies of literature on cannibalism published over the past 50 years. German scholars, more than others, have conducted semiquantitative cross-cultural studies oriented to producing social-scientific generalizations. See, for example, Frank (1987), Wendt (1989), Volhard (1939), Peter-Rocher (1994), and Menninger (1995). French studies, more than others, tend to stress the psychological and social-psychological sources, meanings, and implications of customary cannibalism. See, for example, Erikson (1986), Pilette (a French Canadian, 1990, 1993), Siran (1989), Thomas (1980), Detienne (1979), Halm-Tisserant (1993), and Hubert and Mauss (1964). English-, Spanish-, and Portuguese-language anthropologists tend to eschew cross-cultural generalizations as well as psychological interpretations, and to focus instead on the particular ethnographic context of cannibal customs: that is, the ritual perceived within the larger framework meaning, importance, action, and need in a given culture. They also tend to look for signs of reaction in the practices of primitive tribes to encounters with the explorers, missionaries, colonialists, and slave traders with whom they were interacting when their practices were being observed and recorded. Good examples of this form of cultural anthropology are the collected articles in *The Anthropology of Cannibalism*, edited by Paula Brown and Donald Tuzin (1983), and in *Warfare, Culture, and Environment*, edited by R. Brian Ferguson (1984a). Finally, there are ethnologies and anthropological studies of specific cultures which devote considerable attention to cannibalism. Good examples are those by Abler and Logan (1988), Albert (1988), Balée (1984), Basso (1990), Castro (1992), Clastres (1974), Combès (1992), Dole (1974), Eves (1995), Goldman (1981), Halm-Tisserant (1993), Hassig (1988), MacCormack (1983), McGee (1983), Molet (1956), Saignes (1985), Walens (1981), Whiffen (1915), White (1993).

Given the contentious nature of the subject of cannibalism, it is unfortunate that there seems to have been relatively little cross-referencing and mutual fertilization among what we might call the French, German, and Anglo-American-Spanish traditions of study on the subject. Specifically, there has been no attempt to synthesize the results of quantitatively oriented, global studies of the phenomenon of cannibalism with the rich, psychologically and ethnographically oriented material derived from the careful study of specific cultures. This appears to be a result of linguistic limitations as well as intellectual orientation: Many scholars reference only works in English or French, or in English or German; some reference only works that appear (in the original or in translation) in their own language.[3]

## Other Bodies of Literature about Cannibalism

Allusions to cannibalism appear frequently in disparate contexts. Along with reproduction, eating is the foremost activity required for the survival of the species; and the earliest form of eating, breast-feeding, combines the positive experiences of comfort, security, love, and probably sexual arousal with that of satiating hunger through food produced by the body of another person. Moreover, the aphorism "eat or be eaten" expresses the primary relationships between humans and other species and between flora and fauna generally (McNeill 1980). Thus, it is not surprising that eating and the fear of being eaten are pervasive metaphors for many aspects of human existence.

**Psychology:** In the realm of psychology, cannibalism arises as a metaphor derived from—or an actual extension into adult life of—the ambivalent infantile impulse toward "oral incorporation." This is the postulated desire of the infant not merely to nurse at the mother's breast, but to consume, that is, to physically incorporate and possess, the source of food, physical comfort, security, and love, that is, the breast of the mother. Freud's important work, *Three Essays on Sexuality*, originally published in 1905 and revised in several subsequent editions through 1925 (*Complete Works*, Vol. VII, pp 130–243), includes an essay on "Infantile Sexuality," in which Freud identifies the oral and anal loci of the earliest sexual sensations. About the oral he says (p 198):

> We shall give the name of "pregenital" to organizations of sexual life in which the genital zones have not yet taken over the predominant part. We have hitherto identified two such organizations. . . .
>
> The first of these is the oral or, as it might be called, cannibalistic pregenital sexual organization. Here sexual activity has not yet been

separated from the ingestion of food; nor are opposite currents within the activity differentiated. The object of both activities is the same; the sexual aim consists in the incorporation of the object—the prototype of a process which, in the form of identification, is later to play such as important psychological part. A relic of this constructed phase of organization . . . may be seen in thumb-sucking, in which the sexual activity, detached from the nutritive activity, has substituted for the extraneous object one situated in the subject's own body.

Like the ritual practices of cannibalism discussed later, the impulse toward oral incorporation combines two opposing impulses: loving a person or object—to the point of wanting to integrate that object into oneself; and being prepared to destroy the person or object for the sake of one's own needs or desires. For infants, the hostile aspect of the desire to incorporate may be associated with frustration that food does not appear promptly on demand, or with the fear that when it does appear, it will never suffice.

A substantial body of literature at the boundary between psychology and anthropology explores several sets of relationships relevant to the role of innate oral-cannibalistic impulses: first, relationships among oedipal, incestuous, and oral-cannibalistic impulses;[4] second, the relationship between impulses to oral incorporation and destruction on the one hand, and the development of the ego and the sense of identity on the other;[5] and third, relationships between these impulses and their expression in various aspects of culture, including myths, literature, and alleged ritual and customary practices involving cannibalism.[6]

**Fairy tales, myths, and literature**: Around the world, myths and children's stories are replete with tales of the cannibal consumption of children by parents or of human beings by gods or monsters.[7] Hansel and Gretel, Jack and the Beanstalk, and Little Red Riding Hood are the most well known fairy tales in which the main element of suspense and drama is the child's fear of being eaten. In all three cases, the child lacks ordinary adult protection: Hansel and Gretel are lost; Jack has no father and is off seeking to help support his mother; and Little Red Riding Hood has been sent on an errand through what might be expected to be dangerous woods. In all three cases, the child is at risk of being eaten by a less-than-human adult (an old crone, a giant, a wolf).

It is remarkable that in these and other fairy tales, the danger posed to children by villains—goblins, trolls, giants, witches, crones, and wolves—is not a plausible horror, such as being kidnapped, enslaved, sexually abused, beaten, or killed, but the implausible horror of being eaten. The underlying fear for which this is a metaphor is probably the fear of the loss of identity and control entailed in all of the more plausible horrors. However, the combination of the implausible fear of being eaten by a less-than-human adult and the absence of protective parents suggests the worst of all possible dangers: in time of need, parents, far from being protective, will abandon the child and save themselves by performing the monstrous act of killing and eating their own children.

There is a chilling truth which lies behind this nightmarish terror. Histories of famines suggest that eating children is generally the first form of starvation cannibalism, and, thus, the most frequent form. At the same time recognizing that (according to psychoanalytic theory) fears are generally paired with wishes, we can also interpret the child's fear of being eaten as an inverted expression of the infantile desire not merely to nurse, but to gobble up the breast of the mother.

Several Greek myths involve cannibal acts in which children are eaten by parents or other older relatives (see, for example, Arfouilloux 1993; Halm-Tisserant 1993). The original creator-father, Chronos, eats his children, swallowing them whole before they can murder him to get at his throne. Because in Greek mythology "father-son antagonism is essentially that of eater and eaten," the genealogical origin of the Greek gods is "a succession of devouring fathers and castrating sons that ends only with Zeus, who takes rather drastic precautions against filial rebellion," (swallowing his own wife, Metis, so that he can possess her cunning and not be dethroned in turn by the sons he and she might produce) (Kilgour 1990, p 14). Other mythic cannibal events which recur as prominent themes in Greek culture are the consumption of Dionysus by the Titans, an act incorporated in religious rituals by worshipers of Dionysus; and Tereus' unwitting consumption of his own child, served to him by his wife which is echoed in the Oedipus tragedy (Detienne 1979).

In Homer's *Odyssey*, Odysseus, a Zeus-like King, is in danger of being eaten by Polyphemos, the cyclops, who symbolizes chaos; but Odysseus avoids that risk through quick, clever action. Ovid's later *Metamorphoses* revolves around the same mythic acts of murder and cannibalism in Latin garb (for an extended analysis of both cases, see Kilgour 1990, pp 20–45).

**Ancient written records:** In addition to ancient Greek literature and art, ancient records from other parts of the world refer to cannibal threats or acts. The Old Testament alludes to starvation cannibalism as a form of punishment inflicted on parents by God. In Leviticus and in Deuteronomy, God tells Moses and Moses tells the Israelites that if they fail to keep God's commandments, they will be besieged and reduced to eating their own children: "The Lord shall bring a nation against you from afar, from the ends of the earth, swooping down like a vulture. . . . They shall besiege you . . . so that you shall have to eat your own offspring, the flesh of the sons and daughters whom the Lord your God has given you in the stress of the siege."[8] Later, during a famine, a woman admits having killed and eaten her son (Kings II, 6:24–29), an act that is subsequently mourned in Lamentations (2:20) "See, o Lord, and behold; to whom else hast thou done thus: Whether it be women devouring their own offspring, their petted children; Or priest and prophet slain in the sanctuary of the Lord?" and (4:10) "Tenderhearted women with their own hands have cooked their children; They became their food, at the downfall of the daughter of my people."

This sequence of Old Testament references is discussed by Lasine (1991), who points out (p 30) that "Parental cannibalism is also mentioned in several Assyrian treaties, as well as in Mesopotamian texts as old as the *Curse of the Agade* (lines 237–238 and *Atrahasis* (Neo-Assyrian version 2.6.35–37, 48–50). Although not all scholars agree that the curses in Deuteronomy 28 are modeled on Assyrian treaties, it is probable that readers of Deuteronomy would have taken the references to parental cannibalism as a conventional way of epitomizing the devastating results of treaty violation, whether or not the book's author had intended to emulate Assyrian practice."

In China the earliest reported reference to cannibalism, cited by Chong (1990, p 47), involves Chou Wang, a Yin ruler whose reign ended in 1122 BC. According to the ancient historian Han Fei Tzu, Chou Wang punished three officials who rebuked him for cannibalism and cruelty by cooking, preserving, and eating their flesh. The first reported case of starvation cannibalism in China occurred during a wartime siege of the capital of Sung in May 594 BC. As Chong describes the incident (p 45), "When the city ran out of provisions, the people sent one of their agents, Hua Yuan, under cover of night into the enemy camp. The agent told the general of the Ch'u army, 'My master has sent me to inform you of our distress. In the city, we are exchanging our children and eating them and splitting up their bones for fuel.' Soon afterwards, peace was declared." Chong comments that the event "is described in many Chinese classics with the words *i tzu erh shih* (people exchanging one another's children for food)" (p 45) and he cites five primary historical sources.

In ancient India and Egypt—the other parts of the world for which there are documents dating to 1000 BC—cannibalism appears as a metaphor in creation myths and related religious practices. For example, in the *Rig Veda*, which dates from the second millennium BC, the earliest the gods, who were children of the primeval man Prajapati, sacrificed Prajapati to himself to create the universe (*Flesh and Blood: A History of the Cannibal Complex*, Tannahill, pp 22–23):

> From his body he made the animals
>     of air and wood and village. . . .
> Thence were born horses,
>     and all beings with two rows of teeth.
> Thence were born cattle,

and thence goats and sheep. . . ,
From his navel came the air,
  from his head there came the sky
from his feet the earth, the four quarters from his ear,
  thus they fashioned the worlds. . . [9]

While this creation story was not explicitly a cannibal event, the language suggests images of body parts being consumed and transformed. Similarly, as the ancient Egyptian myth of the murder, dismemberment, and dispersed burial of Osiris by his brother Set, followed by the reassembling and resurrection of Osiris through the efforts of his wife Isis, is echoed in an indirect form of cannibal sacrifice in which the flesh, bones, and blood of sacrificed individuals are scattered over the fields so that the gods who control the earth and heavens can "swallow up" the sacrificial victim and, in exchange, make the fields fertile (Tannahill, pp 20–21).

**Religious practices**: Religious practices that involve the sacrifice of an animal often include consumption of parts of the animal by priests; and many comparative studies of the origin and meaning of religious sacrifice include discussion of certain associated cannibal practices.[10] In Aztec human sacrifices, priests extracted (but did not eat) the heart and the blood pumping through the heart as the principal offering to the gods, and then pushed the body down the pyramid steps to those who had captured the victim, who cooked and ate the arms and legs (Davies 1981). As discussed later, cannibal rituals in simpler societies, rather than being an adjunct to human sacrifice to gods, tended to be the central religious or spiritual ritual, for which the killing of captives was, in some cases, an integral part.

The Christian ritual of the "Eucharist" offers a contemporary parallel to early religious forms of sacrifice and cannibalism. In this case, the consumption of bread and wine, representing the body and blood of Jesus, is conducted in remembrance of, and to benefit from, the sacrifice of his life, which was made to expiate the sins of humanity. This symbolism resembles that of non-Christian religious practices, in which the consumption (or dispersal throughout fields) of some part of a sacrificed human or animal by priests on behalf of the community, or by members of the community, creates a line of communication that permits or persuades the gods to endow human beings with benefits, such as a good crop or fertility, or, in a later era, grace, forgiveness, and redemption.

The parallel between the Christian ritual of communion and early forms of human sacrifice and cannibalism are discussed less in the theological and religious literature of Christianity than in anthropological and humanistic literary studies. The exception that proves this rule is provided by John Fenton, honorary canon of Christ Church, Oxford, in a 1991 article entitled "Eating People," published in the venerable quarterly *Theology*. Fenton argues that the seeming parallels between the Christian Eucharist and primitive practices of human sacrifice-cum-cannibalism must involve a misinterpretation, perhaps fostered by the disciple Paul (believed to be a Greek gentile who had converted to Judaism), because to Jews of Jesus' era, sacrifice and cannibalism represented an abomination, not an accepted form of religious ritual. Noting that throughout the Bible, cannibalistic metaphors indicate hostility, aggression, and destruction,[11] Fenton suggests (p 421) that in the Gospel account of the Last Supper, Jesus "commanded the disciples to take the bread and he passed them the cup to drink, in order to symbolize their responsibility for his death."

**Primate and other nonhuman biology:** In the biological sciences, the "conspecific" consumption of newborn offspring by parents, by each other, or by other adults has been studied in recent years as a counterintuitive example of how genetic endowment and environment may combine in survival-oriented behavior. A review published in *Science* (Mock 1992) of the first book-length collection of survey articles on this topic, *Cannibalism: Ecology and Evolution among Diverse Taxa*, is worth citing at some length:

> In the 1960s and '70s, refinements of natural selection theory led most biologists to realize that phenotypic traits, including behavior patterns, evolve because of net benefit to the individual's inclusive fitness. One consequence of this paradigm shift . . . was that sporadically reported cases of vile or unsavory behaviors performed by animals (such as rape, slavery, infanticide, mate-desertion, and cannibalism) could not simply be assumed to be pathological or aberrant any more. . . . One could no longer seek comfort in the meager records (many such behaviors are inherently rare and hard to witness) or dismiss them airily as mere by products of captivity. . . .
>
> . . . . This led to exponential growth on several fronts. Ecological predictions began to emerge, specifying the context in which these behaviors should be found. Eventually, reviews began to appear. The current volume can be viewed, therefore, as the formal rite of passage for the fascinating topic of cannibalism as a very respectable area in evolutionary biology.
>
> Fifteen review chapters by 17 scientists make it abundantly clear that there is nothing particularly astonishing or freakish about the ingestion of conspecific tissue. Such habits have evolved repeatedly as a solution to various problems, often (but not always) involving food shortages.[12]

While most cases of cannibalism in animals involve insects, fish or amphibians, cannibalism of the young by mammals has been observed. For example, lions which take over a pride may eat the young of their predecessors (Leakey and Lewin

1977, p 220). In recent decades, close observation of chimpanzees (the anthropoid apes which most closely resemble *homo sapiens*) has revealed cannibal behavior by at least one mother (observed by Jane Goodall) and by a few chief males in family clusters who have eaten a newborn male in cases where there was reason to doubt the paternity (see Hamai et al 1992; Nishida and Kawanaka 1985; Tartabini 1991).

**Criminology:** The literature of crime and criminology contains occasional references to the law pertaining to cannibalism or to cases of individuals convicted of murder and cannibalism. The latter generally fall into two groups: psychotic or sociopathic serial murderers, and individuals at risk of starving to death after being stranded in a shipwreck or comparable accident. Bernheim and Stavridès (1992) and Marriner (1992) provide brief accounts of the cannibal acts of the following convicted cannibal-murderers (in most cases, multiple murderers) of the nineteenth and twentieth century:

1817 the farmer's wife at Selestat (Bernheim)
1824 Leger (Bernheim)
1824 necrophage de Saint-Amand (Bernheim)
1826 Maria de las Dolores (Bernheim)
1858 Comstock (Bernheim)
1864 Tirsch (Bernheim)
1872 Verzeni (Bernheim)
1879 Garayo (Bernheim)
1881 Mc T (Bernheim)
1891 Eugene L. (Bernheim)
1894 Vacher (Bernheim)
1897 Luetgert (Marriner)
1913–1921 Carl Wilhelm Grossman (Bernheim/Marriner)
1918–1924 George Haarmann (Bernheim/Marriner)
1921–1924 Karl Denke (Marriner)
1928 Albert Fish (Bernheim/Marriner /Heimer)
1929 Peter Kurten (Bernheim)
1949 John George Haigh (Bernheim/ Marriner)
1950 Edward Howard Gein (Bernheim)
1955–1976 Kroll (Marriner)
1969 Modzieliewski (Bernheim)
1970 Frazier (Marriner)
1970 Kemper (Marriner)
1970 Mullin (Marriner)
1970 Stanley Dean Baker (Marriner)
1976 Chase (Bernheim)
1979 Clement X (Bernheim)

1980 Djoumagaliev (Bernheim)

1981 Anna (Marriner)

1981 Issed Sagawa (Bernheim)

1986 Heidnik (Marriner)

1986 Weber (Marriner)

1989 Rakowitz (Marriner)

1991 Dahmer (Bernheim)

1992 Chikatilo (Bernheim)

Marriner also recounts in some detail a case mentioned in many sources: In 1611 Countess Elisabeth of Báthory, who ruled a large castle and estate after her husband's death in 1604, was convicted of having tortured and killed some 600 girls and young women between 1604 and 1610 in order to daily bathe in and drink their blood, which she thought would keep her young. At the time of her arrest on 30 December 1610, her chief means of "harvesting" blood was to put a girl in a narrow iron cage, with nails pointed inward to puncture the skin, and suspend the cage from the ceiling while she sat under it, bathing in a shower of blood (Marriner, pp 129–130).

**Stranded, starving travelers**: The best known cases of starvation cannibalism by travelers are those of the Donner party members, who were stranded in snowstorms in Nevada while trying to cross the Rocky Mountains in November 1846; by crew members of the *Mignonette*, which sank in the ocean on 3 July 1884, leaving several officers in a dinghy hundreds of miles from land; and by survivors of the plane crash in the Andes in October 1972, who lived on the flesh of the dead (whose bodies had been frozen) for 70 days. In these cases, the cultures concerned (US, British, and Argentine) tended to judge the cannibal actions as morally warranted and legitimate if the victims were already dead, and as morally wrong and criminal, but only slightly more so, if the victims were on the verge of death or if they were selected to be killed in order to help save a larger group. The British trial of the *Mignonette* survivors, who had killed to eat, involved the first legal use of the "necessity" defense for cannibal murder. In that case, the defendants, who openly admitted what they had done and argued that it was justified, were convicted of murder and sentenced to death; but Queen Victoria commuted the death sentence to six months in jail (Marriner).

# William Arens and His Critics: A Comprehensive Review

As noted in Chapter 5, only one attempt has ever been made to systematically identify, assess, and analyze all reported practices of customary cannibalism in all parts of the world: a 550-page work entitled *Kannibalismus* by anthropologist

Evald Volhard, published in Germany in 1939 and unfortunately never translated into English or French. Volhard uses some 800 sources to identify 914 cultural or linguistic areas (bands, tribes, or larger groupings) for which there are reported practices of cannibalism. Though catalogued in the Harvard library since 1948 and universally cited by German anthropologists writing on the topic, the book was not used as a reference by any of the three English-speaking scholars who have attempted, on a much more modest scale, to provide some useful generalizations about the practice of cannibalism around the world: William Arens, who claims that customary cannibalism did not exist, and Peggy Reeves Sanday (author of *Divine Hunger*, 1986) and Eli Sagan (author of *Cannibalism: Human Aggression and Cultural Form*, 1974), who attempt to give global overviews of ritual or customary cannibalism as a cultural practice with examples drawn from diverse cultures.

In this instance, the barriers of language and conflicting scholarly traditions have led to neglect of important sources of a kind that would not be tolerated in the natural sciences because it precludes cumulative learning. Due to the scale of his undertaking, Volhard relied in part on nineteenth-century secondary compilations of primary source material; and nearly all of the many primary sources he cites were published before 1930. No survey article or book on cannibalism reviews the main findings of respected scholars over the past 60–70 years, regardless of language or scholarly tradition. As a result, Arens' sweeping claims put anthropologists who attempt to critique his work, along with those reviewing the critiques, in the position of providing a less than thorough assessment of his claims, or producing the equivalent of a survey article as the basis of a thorough assessment. Between the material in Chapter 5 and that presented here, I have attempted, in a very brief fashion, to provide a survey article.

When claiming that there is no hard evidence for the existence of food cannibalism or for widespread practice of the consumption of human body parts in customary or ritual cannibalism, Arens argues that early anthropologists' reports regarding such practices represented projections in which they extrapolated from circumstantial evidence, expressing ethnocentric expectations of "the other" which have been common in all cultures. Moreover, Arens claims, recent anthropological studies of cannibalism have accepted and repeated the earlier reports uncritically, with equally ethnocentric credulity.

To support these claims, Arens reviews some of the original source material for a few of the most widely cited cases of cannibalism. His assessment, presented in three main chapters, covers three groups of cases:

- "Classic" man-eaters discovered by Columbus and others in Central and South America in the sixteenth century: the "Caribs" (from whom the term cannibal derives), the Aztecs of Mexico, and the Tupinamba of Brazil.

- "Contemporary" man-eaters studied by twentieth-century social scientists: the Amahuaca of Brazil, the Fore of New Guinea, and the Azande and several other tribes in Africa
- "Prehistoric" man-eaters of North America studied by contemporary anthropologists and archaeologists: the Iroquois and the Anasazi.

Arens argues that classic cases of cannibalism represented: (1) the wishful thinking or deliberate lies of Spanish slave traders in the Caribbean and Mexico, who were legally forbidden to enslave indigenous people except from among tribes that practiced cannibalism; (2) sensationalism by early travelers and missionaries to Brazil, who wanted to impress their European audience and sell books or impress their denominational financial supporters; or (3) plagiarism of earlier writers by later ones. Regarding contemporary cases, Arens argues that purported eyewitness reports by modern scientists (Dole in the case of the Amahuaca, and Alpers and Gadjusek in the case of the Fore) are faulty because there is reason to believe that they were extrapolations or presumptions based on observed activities that actually stopped short of eating. Finally, Arens argues that the archaeological evidence adduced to support pre-Columbian cannibalism among the Iroquois and the Anasazi is inconclusive and could represent evidence of other processes, such as "secondary burial," disturbances of graves by wild animals, or accidents.

Because Arens accuses living and dead professional anthropologists of being ethnocentric and sloppy, his book caused a great stir; and it is cited in virtually every subsequent study, occasionally in contexts that support his claims, mainly by scholars who disagree with him.

Several of the original reviewers cast doubt on Arens's thesis, but do so in such a cautious manner as to leave the reader uncertain about the actual practice of cannibalism. For example, Ivan Brady of SUNY Oswego, writing in the *American Anthropologist*, asks, rhetorically, whether cannibalism exists "on the scale and in the manner in which anthropologists (some or all) have assumed in the past?" In reply Brady answers: "Arens does not think so. I agree, but suggest that the discrepancy is neither so wide as he thinks—not everyone is equally reckless with wisdom and facts—nor exists for exactly the same reasons." Similarly, Vincent Crapanzano of Queens College and the City University of New York Graduate Center, writing in the *New York Times Book Review*, comments that "Mr. Arens' book is poorly written, repetitive, snide. His sloppiness is especially regrettable because it lessens the impact of his basic, significant suggestion: that the degree which cannibalism has been practiced has been exaggerated."

Other reviewers are much more critical, explicitly condemning Arens for his own sloppy scholarship and for egregiously misrepresenting the extent of overstatement and underdocumentation in primary sources, based on their knowledge of the literature on which he draws.

Ulla Wagner of the University of Stockholm states: "[H]is presentation of the data shows the bias and selectivity that furthers his case. Nowhere does he take up cases where the informants themselves have stated that they practiced cannibalism. For example, when he quotes Hallpike (on p 99), we are led to believe that it is only others that impute cannibalism to certain Papuan groups, when in fact Hallpike gives several quotations which refer to the informant's own group (Hallpike 1977)." Citing Arens's sweeping condemnation of the tendency of anthropologists to give credence to reports of cannibalism, "Merely entertaining the possibility of a universal taboo on cannibalism would affect the public's image and support of the discipline," Wagner comments that Arens is implying, first, that anthropologists are not to be trusted; second, that they deal only with the exotic; and third, that they have vested interests in maintaining cultural boundaries. To these points she responds that the integrity of anthropologists is probably neither better nor worse than that of scholars in other fields, and that "the other two points are obviously nonsense. Cultural differences are definitely not figments of the anthropological imagination. They are very real, and I cannot see how the endeavor to make understandable that which is strange and alien could ever be construed as being its very opposite."

In the *Anthropological Quarterly*, James W Springer of Northern Illinois University says: "His methods of evaluation are faulty and his critical attitudes amount to little more than a refusal to believe any statement of the existence of cannibalism, combined with a variety of impeachment of the motives of those who report it." Springer then cites one of Arens's many sweeping but incorrect claims about specific sources and cultures: "The collected documents of the Jesuit missionaries (Thwaites 1959), often referred to as the source for Iroquois cruelty and cannibalism, do not contain an eyewitness description of the latter deed." Springer observes that the source in question, a 72-volume work called the *Jesuit Relations*, contains abundant eyewitness accounts of cannibalism by Indians. For this he cites the index page on which references to these accounts may be found (vol. 72: 124). As specific examples, Springer points out that the "narratives of Father Jogues (vol. 39: 19–221) and donne Regnaut (vol. 34: 25–37) show firsthand knowledge" of the practice.

Thomas Abler of the University of Waterloo, another specialist on the Iroquois, reviewing Arens's book in *Ethnohistory*, argues that Arens cannot possibly have looked even at the volume indexes to the *Jesuit Relations*, which contain references to "Cannibalism—Iroquoi" in 31 volumes of the 72-volume series. Having reviewed all of the indexed references, Abler argues that even if one discounts most of the Indian statements on the grounds that the informants may have tended to boast about their own valor with references to cannibal acts and to vilify enemies with exaggerated claims about their barbarism, there are firsthand accounts by Jesuits, captives, and others which there is no reason to doubt; and he cites, in addition to the two accounts cited by Springer, the following passages: vols. 39: 81, 52:169–171, 53: 139, 62: 75, and 62: 91. Abler also cites four seventeenth-century eyewitness reports from sources other than the *Jesuit Relations*. In addition, both Springer and Abler review a variety of archaeological sources for claims of cannibalism among the Iroquois in the prehistoric period (roughly 1300–1500), and portions of the evidence supporting the view that cannibalism did occur in that period as well.

The two most damning critiques of Arens work are those of P.G. Rivière of Oxford, a student of the Tupian peoples of Brazil, and Marshall Sahlins, the pre-eminent expert on sixteenth to nineteenth century sources concerning cannibalism on the Fiji and Marquesas Islands and among the Maori of New Zealand. Writing in the journal *Man*, Rivière details examples of Arens' inaccuracy, incompleteness, and unwarranted inferences in dealing with the primary sources on Tupi cannibalism. He concludes his review as follows (pp 204–205):

> [Arens's book] has forced me to look again at the sources on Tupi cannibalism and, without doing a complete assessment of the material, I am more than ever confirmed in the opinion that the Tupi-speaking Indians of the Brazilian coast in the sixteenth and seventeenth centuries practiced cannibalism.
>
> Bad books do not usually deserve long reviews, and I have given this one more attention because it is also a dangerous book. With little work and less scholarship, it may well be the origin of a myth.

As indicated the discussion of later anthropological sources below, this fear has been fulfilled to some extent.

In late 1978 in the *New York Review of Books*, Marshall Sahlins reviewed *Cannibals and Kings* by Marvin Harris, a book which argues, among other things, that the main reason for cannibalism among simple societies was protein deficiency. Sahlins's review, which stressed the ritual and symbolic nature of most cannibalism, prompted Arens to write an article-length letter to the editor laying out the main arguments and some of the evidence from his forthcoming book and concluding:

> From what I can gather from an extensive review of the literature, every human culture, sub-culture, religion, cult and sect, including our own, has been labeled cannibalistic at one time or another by someone. Yet no one has ever observed this purported cultural universal. This should give pause to consider whether we are dealing with historical reality or an extremely satisfactory myth.

Arens's letter was published in the March 22, 1979 *New York Review of Books*, along with a response by Sahlins, under the heading "Cannibalism: An Exchange." In his response, Sahlins gives long excerpts from the primary sources of eyewitness reports of cannibalism in the seventeenth to nineteenth centuries among the Aztecs, the Maoris, and the Fijians. Noting that he has seen an advance copy of *The Man-Eating Myth* and is outraged that peer review notwithstanding, Arens is "about to publish a book under the imprint of a famous university press [Oxford] which expounds on the thesis of his letter," Sahlins concludes with the following scathing attack:

> It all follows a familiar American pattern of enterprising social science journalism:
>
>> Professor X puts out some outrageous theory, such as the Nazis really didn't kill the Jews, human civilization comes from another planet, or there is no such thing as cannibalism. Since facts are plainly against him, X's main argument consists of the expression, in the highest moral tones, of his own disregard for all available evidence to the contrary. He rises instead to the more elevated analytical plane of ad hominem attack on the authors of the primary sources and those credulous enough to believe them. All this provokes Y and Z to issue a rejoinder, such as this one. X now becomes "the controversial Professor X" and his book is respectfully reviewed by nonprofessionals in *Time*, *Newsweek*, and *The New Yorker*. There follow appearances on radio, TV, and in the columns of the daily newspapers.
>>
>> The effect is to do away with the usual standards of scholarly value, such as use of evidence or quality of research, as criteria of academic success. Like the marketing of automobiles or toothpaste, academic research is submitted to the one characteristic sense of criticism left to American society: *Caveat Emptor* [no guarantees unless expressly stated]. So the publishing decisions of academic presses, and ultimately the nature of scholarly research are drawn irresistibly into the orbit of the average common opinion of the consuming public. It's a scandal.

In my view, the evidence adduced by these reviewers and their more general professional judgment about the integrity and interpretation of the primary sources they cite and others like them provide a sufficient reason to conclude that Arens is wrong: the cultures widely believed to have practiced ritual and customary cannibalism did so. Because of the importance to my own study of not falling prey to ethnocentric exaggeration, I was, however, left with nagging doubts about the real extent of ritual cannibalism, as distinct from wanton treatment of body parts which might have been cooked and preserved as trophies but not actually eaten, and which natives might claim to have eaten in order to elicit approval or shocked disapproval from European observers.

To lay these doubts to rest, I surveyed the professional anthropological literature on cannibalism published after Arens's book had appeared, in order to see whether professional anthropologists had subsequently assembled more comprehensive and carefully reassessed evidence of the practice of cannibalism.

I found that most professional books and articles on cannibalism published since 1980 list Arens as a source and explain their reasons for disagreeing with him. In some cases, Arens's claims are dismissed briefly in introductory remarks. The following passage from Sanday illustrates this approach: "Although [Arens] is correct in asserting that the attribution of cannibalism is sometimes a projection of moral superiority, he is incorrect in arguing that cannibalism has never existed. Contrary to his assertion that no one has ever observed cannibalism, reliable eyewitness reports do exist." Sanday cites five eyewitness reports from diverse periods, including two from the twentieth century.

In other recent studies, new assessments of historical and contemporary material are presented with the purpose, in part, of showing that cannibalism was commonly practiced as a ritual or custom in the cultures in question. Generally speaking, the larger purpose of these studies has been to provide an anthropological description and interpretation of the practice, not just mere confirmation of its existence. The following 20 articles and books published since 1983 all cite Arens's book, dispute his claims, and offer new evidence concerning actual practices of cannibalism:

Abler (1992) "Scalping, Torture, Cannibalism and Rape: An Ethnohistorical Analysis of Conflicting Cultural Values in War"

Abler and Logan (1988) "Florescence and Demise of Iroquoian Cannibalism: Human Sacrifice and Malinowski's hypothesis"

Barber (1992) "Archaeology, ethnography and the record of Maori cannibalism before 1815: A critical review"

Bowden (1984) "Maori Cannibalism: An Interpretation"

Brown and Tuzin, eds. (1983) *The Ethnography of Cannibalism*

Castro, Viveiros de (1992) *From the Enemy's Point of View*

Chong (1990) *Cannibalism in China*

Clunie (1987) "Rokotui Dreketi's human skull: yaqona cup?"

Combès (1992) *La Tragedie Cannibale Chez les Anciens Tupi-Guarani* [The cannibal tragedy among the ancient Tupi-Guarani]

Conklin (1995) "'Thus Are Our Bodies, Thus Was Our Custom': Mortuary Cannibalism in an Amazonian Society"

Ernandes (1992) "Serotonin Deficiency Hypothesis Explaining the Aztec Human Sacrifice/Cannibalism Complex"

Forsyth (1985) "Three Cheers for Hans Staden: The Case for Brazilian Cannibalism"

Jamieson (1983) "An Examination of Prisoner-Sacrifice and Cannibalism at the St. Lawrence Iroquoian Roebuck Site"

Liep (1987) "Kannibaler og Kulier: Antropofagiske Scener fra en Sydhavso" [Cannibals and coolies: anthropophagic scenes from the South Pacific]

Obeyesekere (1992) "British Cannibals: Contemplation of an Event in the Death and Resurrection of James Cook, Explorer"

Saignes (1985) "La Guerre Contre l'Histoire" [War against history]

Sanday (1986) *Divine Hunger: Cannibalism as a Cultural System*

Schöppl von Sonnwalden (1992), *Kannibalismus bei den noramerikanischen Indianern und Eskimo* [Cannibalism among the North American Indians and Eskimos]

Spennemann (1987) "Cannibalism in Fiji: The Analysis of Butchering Marks on Human Bones and the Historical Record with an Appendix on Experimental Butchering with Bamboo Blades"

Whitehead (1984) "Carib Cannibalism: The Historical Evidence"

Reading these studies convinced me, first, that cannibalism not only existed as a practice (not just as a metaphor or symbolic ritual), but that it once occurred in many cultures around the world—mainly though not exclusively in simple cultures, with no more than two levels of political hierarchy (the chief of a given tribe and the chief of a group of tribes). In addition, these studies show that both mortuary cannibalism, showing respect and care for deceased members of one's own band, and cannibalism consumption of parts of fallen enemies, intended to show disrespect toward or to kill the spirit as well as the body, occurred in diverse, widely separated cultures, with little or no opportunity for "diffusion" of a practice from one culture to the next.

The length of this rejection of Arens's claim that cannibalism was not widely practiced is largely a function of the disturbance which his unwarranted accusations have created in the anthropological literature. In addition to some of the early book reviews, many of the later sources which confirm the existence of cannibalism equivocate about its extent. Here, too, Sanday's work is illustrative. While writing a lengthy and important monograph on the diverse meanings of cannibal practices in a dozen different cultures, and while claiming that some cases unquestionably involved the physical ingestion of human flesh, Sanday distances herself from any assertion that cannibal acts were common by treating mythical, symbolic cannibal behavior and literal cannibal behavior as identical for the purposes of her study. Thus, in reviewing the literature on a representative sampling of cultures to assess the incidence of cannibalism, she treated cannibalism as present not only in cultures where ritual or starvation cannibalism was practiced, but also in cultures for which there were "reports of past practice, legend, or hearsay," and cultures for which "fantasized incidents of cannibalism are feared and take the form of belief in cannibal sorcerers or witches." This is not to say than Sanday herself was unable to distinguish in the sources between purported real and fantasized cases of cannibalism; but only that for analyzing the meaning of cannibalism, she did not treat the distinction as important.

This is the case in several of the post-Arens studies listed above, in which the authors observe that literal cannibalism undoubtedly occurred in a given culture at some point in the past, but that rituals, myths, and stories involving cannibal behavior are equally good, if not better, for the purpose of exploring and understanding the meaning of the cannibal practice in a given culture.

In addition, there are a few anthropologists who have continued to cite Arens as a credible source; and there have been have been several review studies prompted by his work, which reconsider the primary sources and find many lacking in the degree of detail and credibility one would want. One of the most controversial cases concerns the Fore of New Guinea, among whom women (and some children) transmitted an invariably fatal infectious disease with a 5–25 year incubation period (kuru) either by eating or by handling the decomposing brain of deceased relatives. In an article published in the *American Anthropologist* in 1982, Steadman and Merbs, anthropologists at Arizona State University who cite Arens and build on his methods, argue that the case for eating was circumstantial at best, and the evidence contained many contradictory and unsubstantiated points. In 1992, however, a research doctor who contributed an article to a book on *Human Biology in Papua New Guinea*, without citing or showing any evidence of having read the Steadman and Merbs piece, used some of the same evidence to describe the outstanding scientific detective work through which it was found that the disease was transmitted through cannibal consumption of the brains of dead victims. In the meantime, Steadman and Merbs are continuing to be cited by anthropologists as documenting the ease with which fact and the rumor about cannibalism can be confused. The main studies of the usefulness of primary sources prompted by Arens's work are four German books: Frank (1987), *"Y se lo comen": kritische Studie der Schriftquellen zum Kannibalismus der panosprachigen Indianer Ost-Perus und Brasiliens* [A critical study of the written sources on cannibalism among the Pano-speaking Indians of East Peru and Brazil]; Menninger (1995) *Die Macht der Augenzeugen: Neue Welt und Kannibalen-Mythos, 1492–1600* [The Power of the Eyewitness: The New World and Cannibal Myths 1492–1600]; Peter-Rocher (1994), *Kannibalismus in der prähistorischen*

*Forschung: studien zu einer paradigmatischen Deutung und ihren Grundlagen* [Cannibalism in prehistoric research: Studies of a paradigmatic interpretation and its foundations]; and Wendt, *Kannibalismus in Brasilien: eine Analyse europaischer Reiseberichte und Amerika-Darstellungen für die Zeit zwischen 1500 und 1654* [Cannibalism in Brazil: An analysis of European Travel Reports and Images of America for the Period between 1500 and 1654].

Arens-based doubts also continued to be raised, with damaging effects for cultural anthropology, in the largely unrelated area of the archaeological study of human bones which may show signs of food cannibalism. For example, Trinkhaus (1985), Bullock (1991, 1992), Bahn (1990, 1991, 1992), Pickering (1988), and Russell (1987a, 1987b) argue that archaeological evidence at particular sites is insufficient to warrant a claim of cannibalism, particularly since no reliable evidence of cannibalism in any age exists—a claim for which they cite Arens as the main authority.

Since there is a great deal of undisputed evidence of cannibalism in periods of famine, and this could account for at least some of the archaeological findings pointing to cannibalism, the claim by these authors that there is no proof that *any* form cannibalism ever occurred is unlikely to have much impact in the field. A much more seriously damaging dissemination of misinformation based on Arens's book is the analysis of ritual and customary cannibalism presented by White (1992). Since White's book is intended as a textbook on the archaeological study of cannibalism and since all of the reviewers (except Bahn, who refuses to recognize any form of cannibalism anywhere) agree that the book is excellent for this purpose, White's treatment is likely to shape the thinking of a generation of archaeologists. After citing Arens and his reviewers briefly and dismissing Sanday because she includes some societies with cannibal myths in her study, White concludes that cultural anthropology cannot be of much use on this subject:

> As Arens has suggested, many if not most historical sources on cannibalism are inadequate or inaccurate. "Because ethnographic research no longer seems possible, the study of cannibalism must, of necessity, be accomplished by a historical science. A man in a position to know, Matos Moctezuma, the excavator of a site at which Spanish accounts suggest that human sacrifice took place (the Aztec Templo Mayor in Mexico City) puts it this way (1987: 185): 'Documentary sources provide us with historical information that is either exaggerated or faithful to observations, depending on the bias of the chronicler and how he has chosen to present his material. Such ethnohistorical information serves as a basis for the hypotheses that are corroborated or invalidated by excavation and archaeological evidence. Archaeology then either validates

the written information or demonstrates its unreliability.' Archaeology seems, therefore, to be the only remaining tool for investigating the existence and extent of cannibalism."

There are two main problems with this statement: First, even though cannibal practices and, in most cases, the cultures that still had retained them in historical periods have now died out, considerably more research in the cultural anthropology of ritual cannibalism has been conducted since Arens's book was published—including superb monographs by Combès (who relied entirely on historical sources) and by Castro (who lived with a small band intermittently over a period of years)—and a great deal more remains that can be done with ethnographies and other written sources. Second, unlike cultural anthropology, archaeology offers little if any hope of clarifying the nature, context, and meaning of the great majority of reported cannibal practices, because these practices, unlike food cannibalism or starvation cannibalism, tend not to leave marks on bones; and in most cases (involving the consumption of blood, or of a small bit of soft tissue, or of ash following cremation), they will not have left any detectable archaeological relic.

In conclusion, while ritual and customary endo- and exocannibal practices undoubtedly occurred in many simple societies, this fact has not yet been fully rehabilitated in anthropology and archaeology in the wake of Arens's critique.

# Notes

**EDITORS' INTRODUCTION**

1. The editors, to whom Randy Forsberg was a friend and mentor since the early 1980s, have found it difficult not to call her by her first name, as nearly everyone did. We hope readers will indulge our flouting of academic convention.

2. See Matthew Evangelista, *Unarmed Forces: The Transnational Movement to End the Cold War* (Ithaca: Cornell University Press, 1999), Mary Kaldor, *Global Civil Society: An Answer to War* (Cambridge: Polity Press, 2003), and Lawrence S. Wittner, *Toward Nuclear Abolition: A History of the World Nuclear Disarmament Movement, 1971 to the Present* (Stanford: Stanford University Press, 2003).

3. Jürgen Habermas, "Discourse Ethics: Notes on a Program of Philosophical Justification," in *Moral Consciousness and Communicative Action* (Cambridge: MIT Press, 1990), pp. 43–115; Jürgen Habermas, *Justification and Application: Remarks on Discourse Ethics* (Cambridge: MIT Press, 1993).

4. Randall Caroline Watson Forsberg, "Toward a Theory of Peace: The Role of Moral Beliefs," PhD diss., Massachusetts Institute of Technology, June 1997; the summary version is available as "Socially-sanctioned and non-sanctioned violence: On the role of moral beliefs in causing and preventing war and other forms of large-group violence," in Matthew Evangelista, ed., *Peace Studies: Critical Concepts in Political Science*, 4 vols. (London: Routledge, 2005), vol. I, ch. 5. Elise Boulding and Randall Forsberg, *Abolishing War: Dialogue with Peace Scholars Elise Boulding and Randall Forsberg* (Boston, MA: Boston Research Center for the 21st Century [now the Ikeda Center],1998). In a respectful and friendly exchange, Boulding emphasized the role of peace education, whereas Randy stressed changes in institutions and moral beliefs, as in this book.

5. Forsberg, *Toward a Theory of Peace: The Role of Moral Beliefs*, Preface.

6. Quoted in https://www.sipri.org/about/history.

7. Randall Forsberg, *Resources Devoted to Military Research and Development* (Stockholm: Almqvist & Wiksell, 1972). Randy's work on Soviet military R&D set the standard for research on that secretive and difficult topic and engendered much discussion and follow-on research in the US Central Intelligence Agency and Defense Department. See, for example, *Comparison of Military Research and Development Expenditures of the United States and the Soviet Union* (https://www.gao.gov/assets/80/78897.pdf), a General Accounting Office staff study for the Subcommittee on Research and Development, US Senate Committee on Armed Services, 31 January 1972, which compares the Defense Department's estimates to those in the 1969 *SIPRI Yearbook*.

8. Application from archives of Stockholm International Peace Research Institute, quoted in Neta Crawford's remarks at "The End of War: A Conference in Honor of Randall Forsberg," City College of New York, 5 May 2008.

9. Ibid.

10. https://web.archive.org/web/20080214014251/http://web.mit.edu/ssp/people/alumni.html.

11. Christopher Paine, "On the Beach: The Rapid Deployment Force and the Nuclear Arms Race," *MERIP Reports* #111 (January 1983).

12. Other contributors were Phyllis Morrison, George Sommaripa, and Martin Moore-Ede.

13. The Boston Study Group, *The Price of Defense* (New York: Times Books, 1979), republished as *Winding Down: The Price of Defense* (San Francisco: W. H. Freeman, 1982).

14. The Boston Study Group, *The Price of Defense*, p. 11.

15. We are grateful to Judith Reppy for this point.

16. IDDS Brochure, 1984. 2001 Beacon St., Brookline, MA.

17. Lawrence S. Wittner, "The Nuclear Freeze and its Impact" (https://www.armscontrol.org/act/2010_12/LookingBack), *Arms Control Today*, 5 December 2010; Andrew Lanham, "Lessons from the Nuclear Freeze" (https://bostonreview.net/politics/andrew-lanham-lessons-nuclear-freeze), *Boston Review*, 14 March 2017.

18. See David S. Meyer, *A Winter of Discontent: The Nuclear Freeze and American Politics* (New York: Praeger, 1990); Wittner, *Toward Nuclear Abolition*.

19. John Steinbruner, "Fears of War, Programs for Peace," *The Brookings Review*, vol. 1, no. 1 (Fall 1982): 6–10.

20. Randall Forsberg, "A Bilateral Nuclear Weapons Freeze," *Scientific American* (November 1982).

21. American Academy of Arts and Sciences, *The Nuclear Weapons Freeze and Arms Control: Proceedings of a Symposium held at the American Academy of Arts and Sciences, January 13–15, 1983* (Cambridge: Harvard University, 1983).

22. Randall Forsberg, "The Freeze and Beyond: Confining the Military to Defense as a Route to Disarmament." *World Policy Journal*, vol. 1, no. 2 (1984). For a video clip of Randy describing the relationship between nuclear and conventional forces, see http://openvault.wgbh.org/catalog/V_F6CC542AF94B434FBC7E1DBE45F07024.

23. Forsberg, "Confining the Military to Defense: A Sensible and Popular Route to Disarmament," first draft, September 1979, Institute for Defense and Disarmament Studies, Brookline, MA, p. 7. Institute For Defense And Disarmament Studies Records, 1974-2007 (http://rmc.library.cornell.edu/EAD/htmldocs/RMM08588.html), Collection Number 8588, Division of Rare and Manuscript Collections, Cornell University Library, Box 8, Folder 20.

24. Kaldor, then at the University of Sussex, invited Forsberg to engage in a published discussion about contradictions and compatibilities between END and the Freeze in a periodical published there. See Randall Forsberg, Matthew Evangelista, and Mark Niedergang, "END and a Nuclear Weapon Freeze," *ADIU Report* [Armament and Disarmament Information Unit, Sussex, England], July/August 1981.

25. Evangelista, *Unarmed Forces*, pp. 310–315.

26. Forsberg, "The Freeze and Beyond," p. 313.

27. Institute for Defense and Disarmament Studies, *American Peace Directory 1984* (Cambridge, MA: Ballinger Books, 1984), ed. by Melinda Fine and Peter M. Stevens; Institute for Defense and Disarmament Studies, *Peace Resource Book: A Comprehensive Guide to the Issues, Organizations, and Literature* (Cambridge, MA: Ballinger Books, 1986); an updated version was edited by Carl Conetta and published by Ballinger in 1988. The Institute also produced a periodical newsletter, *Defense and Disarmament News*, from 1985 to 1988.

28. Jeffrey W. Knopf, *Domestic Society and International Cooperation: The Impact of Protest on U.S. Arms Control Policy* (Cambridge: Cambridge University Press, 1998); Knopf, "Did Reagan Win the Cold War?" *Strategic Insights*, vol. 3, issue 8 (August 2004); Wittner, *Toward Nuclear Abolition*; Meyer, *A Winter of Discontent*.

29. Randall Forsberg, "Parallel Cuts in Nuclear and Conventional Forces," *Bulletin of the Atomic Scientists* (August 1985).

30. Randall Forsberg, ed., *The Arms Production Dilemma: Contraction and Restraint in the World Combat Aircraft Industry* (Cambridge, MA: MIT Press, 1994).

31. Barton Wright, *Soviet Missiles* (Lexington, MA: Lexington Books, 1986); Neta Crawford, *Soviet Military Aircraft* (Lexington, MA: Lexington Books, 1987).

32. Forsberg, *Arms Production Dilemma*, pp. 2–3.

33. Forsberg, *Arms Production Dilemma*, pp. 289–290.

34. "Global Action to Prevent War," reprinted in Matthew Evangelista, ed., *Peace Studies: Critical Concepts in Political Science*, 4 vols. (London: Routledge, 2005), vol. IV, ch. 59, and in various versions on the web.

35. Dennis Hevesi, "Randall Forsberg, 64, Nuclear Freeze Advocate, Dies," *New York Times*, 26 October 2007.

36. Forsberg, *Toward a Theory of Peace*, p. 23.

37. Forsberg, *Toward a Theory of Peace*, section 2.1. The term "defensive nonviolence" is not ideal, as Randy acknowledged. Christopher Paine has pointed out to us that it risks conveying something quite different, that massive nonviolent resistance be used as a substitute for armed force in national defense. He suggests that the phrase "solely defensive use-of-force" would be truer to Randy's intent to describe the only form of socially sanctioned group violence that would be morally acceptable.

38. Forsberg, *Toward a Theory of Peace*, sections 2.1 and 2.2.

39. Forsberg, *Toward a Theory of Peace*, p. 24.

40. Forsberg, *Toward a Theory of Peace*, p. 24.

41. Forsberg, *Toward a Theory of Peace*, p. 17.

42. Forsberg, *Toward a Theory of Peace*, p. 27.

43. See Bruce Russett, *Grasping the Democratic Peace: Principles for a Post-Cold War World* (Princeton: Princeton University Press, 1993); Joshua S. Goldstein, *Winning the War on War: The Decline of Armed Conflict Worldwide* (http://winningthewaronwar.com/) (New York: Dutton, 2011); Steven Pinker, *The Better Angels of Our Nature: Why Violence Has Declined* (New York: Viking, 2011). For a critical response to some of this work, see Michael Mann, "Have wars and violence declined?" *Theory and Society* 47, issue 1 (February 2018): 37–60.

44. Azar Gat, *War and Human Civilization* (Oxford: Oxford University Press, 2006); Andrew Linklater, *The Problem of Harm in World Politics: Theoretical Investigations* (Cambridge: Cambridge University Press, 2011); Andrew Linklater, *Violence and Civilization in the Western States-System* (Cambridge: Cambridge University Press, 2016); Norbert Elias, *The Civilizing Process* (Oxford: Blackwell, 1994).

45. Oona A. Hathaway and Scott J. Shapiro, *The Internationalists: How a Radical Plan to Outlaw War Remade the World* (New York: Simon & Schuster, 2017).

46. Kwame Anthony Appiah, *The Honor Code: How Moral Revolutions Happen* (New York: W. W. Norton, 2010).

47. Neta C. Crawford, *Argument and Change in World Politics: Ethics, Decolonization and Humanitarian Intervention* (Cambridge: Cambridge University Press, 2002).

48. Jürgen Habermas, "What is Universal Pragmatics?" in Jürgen Habermas (translated by Thomas McCarthy), *Communication and the Evolution of Society* (Boston: Beacon Press, 1979), pp. 1–68. Also see Jürgen Habermas, (translated by Thomas McCarthy), *The Theory of Communicative Action*, vols. 1 and 2 (Boston: Beacon Press, 1984 and 1987), and Jürgen Habermas, *Between Facts and Norms: Contributions to a Discourse Theory of Law and Democracy* (Cambridge: MIT Press, 1996).

49. See Habermas, "What is Universal Pragmatics?" pp. 26–29.

## CHAPTER 1

1. See MacAloon (1981) and Mandell (1976).

2. The proceedings and results of the first Hague conference and of a second conference held in 1907 are found in Scott (1908), Anon. (1916), and Anon. (1918).

Government instructions to delegates and official national viewpoints are reported in Great Britain Foreign Office (1899), Groupe parlementaire (1907), United States Commission (1899), United States Department of State (1899), and the collected papers of Baron Mikhail Aleksandrovich Taube, Russian envoy in the Hague in 1907 (Taube n.d.).

The hopes of peace organizations that the Hague conferences would end war are illustrated in the following sampling of publications from the participating countries: American Peace Society (1899), Darby (1899), Estournelles de Constant (1907), Ferguson (1899), Halpert-Berlin (1899), Hull (1908), London Committee of the International Peace Crusade (1899), Tryon (1910), and Tolstoy (1899).

Early scholarly analyses of the two conferences, also from various participating countries, are given in Boidin (1908), Bourgeois (1910), Choate (1913), Docteur en droit [anon] (1908), Foster (1904), Holls (1900), Scott (1909), Stead (1899), Wehberg (1918), and Schücking (1912–17).

Results of the several dozen cases of arbitration brought before the International Court under the terms of the Hague conventions are summarized in Wilson (1915).

More recent assessments of the context of the Hague conferences and the later impact of the agreements they produced are provided by Davis (1975), Dülffer (1981), and Pomerance (1973).

3. Jane Addams, already well known for her work against poverty and for immigrants' rights, child labor laws, trade unions, and women's suffrage, expanded her reform agenda to include peace at the outbreak of World War I, commenting "[A] finely tempered sense of justice . . . cannot possibly be secured in the storm and stress of war. . . . [T]he spirit of fighting bums away all those impulses, certainly towards the enemy, which foster the will to justice" (Addams 1960/1922, p 4).

Along with European feminist leaders like Dr. Aletta Jacobs, head of the Dutch suffrage movement, Addams convened an antiwar International Congress of Women in the Hague on 28 April—1 May 1915, which brought together over 1,100 participants from 12 countries. Congress representatives seeking a negotiated end to the war subsequently met with the heads of government of England, Germany, Hungary, Italy, and France (belligerents), and the Netherlands, Denmark, Norway, Switzerland, and the United States (neutrals) (Addams 1960/1922, pp 17–18). Addams established a Women's Peace Party in January 1915 and helped found the Women's International League for Peace and Freedom, which in 1917 became the first secular peace organization to establish lobbying headquarters in Washington, DC (Foster 1989, p 18).

4. See Philip Noel-Baker (1979).

5. A lifelong pacifist, Russell opposed Britain's entry into World War I and US and British entry into World War II. From 1945 until his death, Russell participated in many antinuclear weapon protests and supported efforts for disarmament; he also opposed the Vietnam war and helped organize the Russell International War Crimes Tribunal against it [see Duffett (1968)]. Russell's views are explored in his autobiography (1967–69) and by Aiken (1963), Blackwell (1985), Brink (1989), Ryan (1988), Vellacott (1981), Wickham (1970), and Wood (1958).

6. Albert Schweitzer, awarded the Nobel Peace Prize in 1954, lectured on "reverence for life" in 1922 at Oxford (the Dale lectures) and at the University of Uppsala (the Olaf Petri lectures). The lectures were published in English and German as *The Decay and Restoration of Civilization* [*Verfall und Wiederaufbau der Kultur*] and *Civilization and Ethics* [*Kultur und Ethik*], respectively (Schweitzer 1923). Schweitzer argued that civilization and the reverence for life on which it is based are incompatible with war. The two original books were later published as parts I and II of *The Philosophy of Civilization* (1949), which was Schweitzer's original plan (along with two additional parts, which never materialized). Schweitzer's first published work (1899), prefiguring his future interests, concerned Kant's

philosophy of religion, *Die Religionsphilosophie Kants von der Kritik der reinen Vernunft bis zur Religion innerhalb der Grenzen der blossen Vernunft.*

7. See Allsebrook (1986), Eichelberger (1965), Luard (1982), Reid (1983), and Russell (1958).

8. A comparative overview of proposed paths to peace is given in the last part of Chapter 2.

9. In 1993, the Peace Studies Association, founded in the mid-1980s, had members representing 126 recognized interdisciplinary peace study programs at colleges and universities. Other associations of scholars concerned with peace include the Consortium for Peace Research, Education, and Development (COPRED), the International Peace Research Association (IPRA), and the Peace Studies Section of the International Studies Association, all founded in the 1970s.

10. There is not a significant body of literature in the sense that there has not been a tradition of cumulative, interreferencing work over a period of years or decades. There are, however, many publications which address the abolition of war more or less comprehensively. The most widely cited of these is *Perpetual Peace* by Immanuel Kant (1963/1784). Recent studies which offer more or less comprehensive approaches to peace include Boulding (1978), Etzioni (1962), Evans (1993), Ferencz (1985), Galtung (1980), Galtung (1984), Glossop (1987), Hollins et al. (1989), Noel-Baker (1958), Pauling (1958), Russett (1990a), Russett (1995/1993), Schell (1984), Sharp and Jenkins (1990), Smoke and Harman (1987), and Starke (1968). Intelligent, informed observers have been pondering the conditions for the abolition of war for centuries, as illustrated by Starke (1968) in a "Table of notable historical peace plans," which gives brief summaries of 25 essays on the conditions for peace published between 1300 and 1900.

11. *Webster's Unabridged Dictionary of the English Language* (1989) gives the following definition of abolish: "1. to do away with; put an end to; annul; make void; *to abolish slavery.* 2. to destroy (a person, thing, etc.) totally."

12. Starke (1968) makes the same distinction, but what I call the achievement of peace he calls the "restoration" of peace. This reflects his view that since peace is the normal condition of relations between nations, the first task to be addressed by a theory of peace is how to maintain peace; the second is how to restore it. This is also a more time-neutral approach; by comparison, my approach, as indicated earlier, involves a sequence of events with specific starting and ending conditions.

## CHAPTER 2

1. The phrase "defensive nonviolence" is not a logically correct expression of the moral position, since in this approach it is not the nonviolence that is defensive, but the violence that is permitted. I have, however, felt that it would be equally incorrect to use the phrase "commitment to defensive violence," which suggests a positive commitment to using violence, rather than a reluctant employment of a means of last resort. In an earlier draft of this essay, I used the phrase "commitment to nonviolence," which is, in my view, an accurate brief reference to the position in which one is committed never to initiate violence, and never to use violence except as a last resort, used to defend against acts of physical aggression, and even then used to the minimum extent needed to stop the aggression and (in the case of nations) restore preaggression borders. Public policies which have this character are supported by individuals who are fully committed to nonviolence in their own lives and in the lives of their families, community, and nation. Several readers objected to this use of the phrase "commitment to nonviolence," however, on the grounds that the phrase is commonly used to identify the position of those committed to nonviolence without exception for defense. For this reason, as a temporary expedient, I have inserted "defensive" before nonviolence. Underlying the problem of wording, there is, of

course, a more fundamental issue concerning the meaning and application of the concept of "nonviolence": As I note in the last section of the chapter, those who use the concept of nonviolence in a strictly pacifist meaning object to the erosion of the concept represented by making an exception for defense; meanwhile those who support defensive nonviolence feel that their commitment to nonviolence is equally powerful and does not deserve to be treated as a form of commitment to violence.

2. As indicated later, my fully stated position is qualified: the initial abolition of war is likely to be achieved most quickly if commitment to defensive nonviolence is supported by an effective international peace enforcement regime, but the least-change conditions for the initial abolition to be achieved over a longer period of time do not include the establishment of such a regime. Throughout most of the essay, however, I focus on the least-change near-future conditions, rather than the least-change, longer-term conditions.

3. In neither the Israeli-Palestine conflict nor the British-Irish conflict can the current level of violence be considered a "war" as war is defined in this essay. But if the levels of violence in the two conflicts during March 1996 (on the order of 100 casualties per month) were sustained for an extended period, they might qualify as wars.

4. An important feature of states in which democratic commitment to nonviolence is fully developed and deeply rooted is the existence of a constitutional means of secession without war. In a formal, "least-change" sense, legal means of secession represent the principle nonviolent alternative to civil war as a means of establishing a new state. (By comparison, civilian resistance represents the principle nonviolent alternative to civil war as a means of overturning authoritarian rule or fostering democratic processes in an existing state.) With the spread of democratic institutions and the rise of internal wars, the thorny political and legal issues of secession have become increasingly important. Buchanan (1991) gives an excellent overview of these issues.

5. See Doyle (1983a, Table 1), Huntington (1989, pp 6–7), and Russett (1990b, pp 132–137) for different sources and methods but convergent conclusions about the rate and extent of the spread of democratic institutions over the course of the past century.

6. A number of cases are reviewed by Sharp (1980), Sharp and Jenkins (1990) and Ackerman and Kruegler (1994).

7. Consistent with the tendency of political science to stress material factors over ideas and moral beliefs in accounting for institutional change, the literature on the relationship between democracy and peace which has appeared over the past two decades has stressed practical factors as the source of the tendency of democracies not to go to war with each other. The key initial works in this literature are those by Small and Singer (1976), Rummel (1983), and Rummel's students, Chan (1984) and Weede (1984), all of whom conducted empirical assessments of the hypothesis that liberal democracies do not fight each other; and by Doyle (1983a, 1983b, 1986), who explored the contemporary relevance of Kant's view that liberal constitutional republics were likely to end war among themselves. Kant's thesis was that a government requiring the consent of the governed would be, first, generally cautious about going to war because war inflicts great material and financial costs on the majority of people, and, second, loathe to make war on another constitutional republic in which the self-governing populace were "moral equals." Other reasons to expect peace between liberal states, in part inferred from Kant, involve the desire to promote free trade, shared cultural values, and the ability of a self-governing population to learn from the (hard) experience of war. Neither Kant nor the contemporary analysts [except Russett (1990a, 1995/1993)] stress the commitment to nonviolent conflict resolution inherent in democratic, constitutional states as the main reason to expect peace between democracies.

In 1989, articles by Russett (1990a), Levy (1988, 1989), and Maoz and Abdolali (1989) extended the earlier empirical studies of Small and Singer, Rummel, Chan and Weede; a new book by Mueller (1989) expanded on Doyle's thesis; and an article by Fukuyama

(1989a, 1989b) offered another take on the Kantian idea. In one of several respondents to Fukuyama's provocative essay, Samuel Huntington (1989) related Fukuyama's claims to the earlier empirical and theoretical work on democracy and peace. A spurt of new publications on the topic in 1992–1993 included five articles in a special issue of the *Journal of Peace Research* (Starr (1992), Sørenson (1992), Gleditsch (1992), Russett and Antholis (1992), and Weede (1992), and a book by Russett, *Grasping the Democratic Peace* (1995/1993).

Since 1994, the question of whether and under what conditions democracies tend not to go to war with one another, and if so why, has been vigorously debated in five books (Diamond and Plattner (1994), Klingemann (1994), Czempiel (1995), MacMillan (1998), Ray (1995) and in the leading journals in the field, including the *America Political Science Review, Ethics and International Affairs, Foreign Affairs, International Affairs, International Security, International Studies Quarterly,* the *Journal of Conflict Resolution,* and the *Journal of Peace Research*. See, for example, Benoit (1996), Bregman (1995), Dixon (1994), diZerega (1995), Farber and Gowa (1995), Gochman et al. (1996), Hagan (1994), Hermann and Kegley (1995), Hermann and Kegley (1996), Kegley and Hermann (1996), Lynch (1994), Mansfield and Snyder (1995a), Mansfield and Snyder (1995b), Russett et al. (1995), Smith (1994), Spiro (1994), Thompson (1996), Wolf et al. (1996).

Bruce Russett (1990a, 1990b, and 1995/1993) has argued along lines similar to those put forward here, first, that "the basic norm of liberal democratic theory" is that "disputes can be resolved without force through democratic political processes"; second, that "[w]ithin a transnational democratic culture," acknowledgment of the right of self-determination in other democracies "both prevents us from wishing to dominate them and allows us to mitigate our fears that they will try to dominate us;" and, finally, that in international affairs, "the principle of self-determination may actually work better [as the source or guarantor of peace] in the absence of a common government" (1990b, pp 124–129).

8. One example of this view is given in Waltz's "realist" classic, *Man, the State and War* (1959, p 228): "[W]ere world government attempted, we might find ourselves dying in the attempt to unite or uniting and living a life worse than death." See also Aron's classic *Peace and War* (1973), part 3, "The Antinomies of Diplomatic-Strategic Conduct."

9. The idea of a voluntary federation for the purpose of mutual defense is central to Kant's proposal in *Perpetual Peace* (1963). The main difference between Kant's concept and that put forward here lies in the moral and intellectual foundation of the federation: In Kant's version, the constituent republics are prevented from using war as an instrument of national policy (a tool for the achievement of any end except defense) by the rational self-interest of their citizens in avoiding the calamities and costs of war. In the present version, the states that make up the federation would reject war as an instrument of policy out of recognition of and respect for the dignity and worth of the individual human beings that would otherwise be subject to attack.

10. As noted earlier, Bruce Russett (1990a, 1990b) has proposed the similar notion that the democracies may maintain peace with one another indefinitely without the creation of a strong world government as a result of their shared commitment to and practice of self-determination, that is, government by the consent of the governed, without resort to coercive violence. Kant's concept of a peace enforcement federation among constitutional states also stresses the importance maintaining full national sovereignty within the federation as a safeguard against tyranny (Kant 1963).

11. The only exception to the rule of nonrecurrence might occur in the event of an historically unprecedented but imaginable complete loss of cultural memory, leading to a reversion to an much earlier stage of political and economic development—that is, the kind of apocalyptic regression that could occur after a massive global ecological catastrophe, and economic and political collapse.

12. Although I argue that a shift to defensive nonviolence could catalyze the transition to abolition, I do not see such a shift as a "first cause." On the contrary, as I suggest elsewhere in the chapter, I believe that the potential for such a shift is rooted in a much larger amalgam of political, economic, cultural, and moral changes which have been under way for several centuries.

13. See *The First World Disarmament Conference 1932–1934, and Why It Failed*, by Philip Noel-Baker (1979), a member of the British negotiating team.

14. Chapter 4, "A World Peacekeeping Federation," in Hollins et al. (1989, pp 38–53) contains a useful discussion of the political context, ambitions, and failures of both the Clark and Sohn plan and the McCloy-Zorin agreement.

15. Details of all arms control negotiations and treaties since 1982 are given in the monthly reference journal *Arms Control Reporter*, published by the Institute for Defense and Disarmament Studies in Cambridge, Massachusetts. Earlier surveys of arms control negotiations are given in the annual *SIPRI Yearbook of World Armaments and Disarmament*, published by the Stockholm International Peace Research Institute in Stockholm, Sweden, starting in 1968.

16. The approach advocated by this school of thought is fully compatible with and tends to reinforce and facilitate that put forward in this essay. The two differ in that my approach stresses mainly the defensive role of the use of force—its strategic purpose of defending against attack—whereas the approach of most advocates of what is variously called nonoffensive, nonprovocative, or defensive defense stresses the defensive character of the use of force, that is, its means of defending against attack. Advocates of defensive defense generally assume that the only legitimate, socially accepted role or purpose of military forces will be defense, and that the main issue is the defensive or offensive nature of the means of defense. My approach, stressing strict limits on the use of force (only as a last resort and then only the minimum needed to stop aggression and restore the status quo ante), is strengthened by defensively structured defenses, which would help communicate peaceful intentions to potential opponents, hinder illegitimate, aggressive uses of force, and increase the public's awareness of the goal of limiting the role of the military to defense. Undoubtedly, the origin of the differences in emphasis between the two approaches lies in the geopolitical context in which they were developed : the approach stressing the role of force originated in the United States, which plays an active military role in other parts of the world, while the approach stressing the character of the force used for defense originated in Europe (particularly in Germany, the Netherlands, and Scandinavia), where the role of force has been limited strictly and narrowly to defense for decades or longer.

17. See Forsberg (1992b), Kaufmann and Steinbruner (1991), and Carter et al. (1992).

18. Conflict early warning has received steadily increasing attention over the past 20 years as a result of several factors: the growing number of unstable new states in the UN system; the new, computerized technologies of global information gathering and processing; and, following the end of the Cold War, the increase in international attention to border wars, civil wars, and subnational and transnational ethnic conflicts, which lend themselves more readily than do major international wars to prevention through early warning and international political intervention.

19. The actual and potential institutions and techniques for nonviolent conflict resolution range from the creation of a world government at one end of the spectrum to individual acts of civil disobedience at the other. Among other major options are diplomacy and economic sanctions under the auspices of the United Nations, regional organizations, individual states, or nongovernmental organizations; and special courts or empowered boards which provide for mediation, arbitration, or judicial rulings.

20. Awareness of the historical examples and potential future use of organized non-military (civilian) resistance as a means of opposing oppression and aggression has also grown substantially over the past two decades, in large part as a result of Gene Sharp's major publications (1973, 1980, 1985, and 1990 with Jenkins); Sharp's efforts in establishing major research programs on the topic at Harvard's Center for International Affairs (Program on Nonviolent Sanctions) and at the independent Albert Einstein Institution in Cambridge, Massachusetts (directed by Chris Kruegler); and his extensive consulting with governmental and nongovernmental organizations interested in this approach. Building on Sharp's theory, Ackerman and Kruegler (1994) reviewed in some detail six cases of nonviolent resistance from various parts of the world over the course of the twentieth century. See also the forthcoming *Encyclopedia of Nonviolent Action*, edited by Kruegler [published as Powers, et al., 1997]. A brief theoretically oriented introduction to the topic is given in Freund (1987), which also contains a useful bibliography. Other theorists of nonmilitary defense are Galtung and Næss (1969) and Adam Roberts (1986).

21. Two (among many) recent books which look at the potential for the United Nations to play a more active and effective role in peacekeeping and peace enforcement following the end of the Cold War are those by Evans (1993) and Rochester (1993). The use of the United Nations as an institution to end war was proposed most fully in Clark and Sohn (1966) [see also Clark and Sohn (1973) and Clark (1950)]. Starke (1968, pp 194ff) lists nine plans published between 1300 and 1700 for securing peace through the creation of a world government, a federation or council of states, or a collective security system, including proposals by Dante (1960/1317) and William Penn (1693).

22. See, for example, Hart (1961), Bonkovsky (1980), Gong (1984), Kratochwil (1987, 1989), Bok (1989), and Onuf (1989).

23. In addition to Buchanan (1991), see Kratochwil et al. (1985) and Walker and Mendlovitz (1990) for interesting discussions of the nature of sovereignty and the potential for changing it by nonviolent means. The literature on revolution is also relevant here; see, for example, Moore (1978).

24. See Deutsch et al. (1957).

25. Spiritual (religious and philosophical) and political support for the pacifist approach to peace goes back for millennia. The commitment of the Quakers and other peace churches over the past several centuries is well known. See, for example, Brock (1990) on the history of Quaker pacifism, and Kohn (1987) on the history of pacifist (mainly religious-based) opposition to the draft in the United States. In this century, public interest in pacifism probably reached a peak in the period immediately before and after World War I.

Much of the post-1945 thought and literature on pacifism builds on the life and publications of Gandhi, particularly his *An Autobiography: The Story of My Experiments with Truth* (1957/1929) and other writings on *Non-violent Resistance (Satyagraha)* (1961), originally published primarily in the journal *Young India* in the 1920s and early 1930s. Among prominent civic and intellectual leaders who have studied and built on Gandhi's theory of nonviolent resistance to oppression and injustice are Chester Bowles (1955), Erik Erikson (1969), Gene Sharp (1973), Johan Galtung (Galtung and Næss 1969), and Martin Luther King, Jr.

Stassen (1992) and Lakey (1987) take the pacifist approach in new directions, the former by offering an alternative to the religious tradition of just war thinking, the latter by incorporating a pacifist commitment to nonviolence in a comprehensive alternative lifestyle and view of society.

26. Samuel Huntington's 1993 article in *Foreign Affairs*, "The Clash of Civilizations?" popularized the idea of a zone around the northern hemisphere, comprising industrialized

mainly Christian countries, in which peace might endure indefinitely while war continues in the Third World.

27. The only near-term risk of a major war in which the United States might partici-pate involves the possibility of an attack by North Korea on South Korea; but even this is considered unlikely. See United States Department of Defense (1994, 1995, and 1996).

28. See, for example, "A Structural Theory of Aggression," (Galtung 1975—, Vol. 3), and "A Structural Theory of Imperialism" (1975—, Vol. 4).

29. This school of thought is represented by a very large body of literature, which has roots in ancient and classical strategic theory, ranging from the Sun Tsu to Machiavelli, Hobbes, and Clausewitz. Modern theorists include Waltz (1959), Howard (1984), and Mearsheimer (1990).

30. Prominent among many liberal scholars who appear not to relish power balancing, but to see it as the least among evils and as strengthened by various forms of international cooperation on security matters, are the French scholar Raymond Aron (1955, 1973), Stanley Hoffmann (1965), the Australian Hedley Bull (et al., 1992), and the American Bernard Brodie (1973).

## CHAPTER 3

1. While supported by the biological and psychological studies discussed in this chap-ter, the distinction between socially sanctioned and nonsanctioned forms of individual and group violence and the rules (generalizations) about the motivational structures asso-ciated with each represent an original theoretical contribution.

2. Moyer, who wrote the first comprehensive overview of the psychobiology of aggres-sion (1976, p xvi), describes his own attempt to master the subject in the early 1970s as covering the following 18 fields (plus another 12 specialties which combine two fields): anatomy, anthropology, biochemistry, biology, ecology, electroencephalography, endocri-nology, ethology, general medicine, genetics, neurology, pharmacology, physiology, pri-matology, psychiatry, psychology, sociology, and zoology.

3. Book-length sources for this section which survey and summarize recent research on the genetic, neurobiological and biosocial nature and sources of aggressiveness are Ren-frew (1997), Stoff and Cairns (1996), Hollander and Stein (1995), Shoham et al. (1995), Huesmann (1994), Glick and Roose (1993), and Geen (1990). Baron and Richardson (1994), updating Baron's earlier survey work (1977), delineate competing approaches and schools of thought without attempting to reconcile differences or take a position on con-troversial issues. Earlier survey works which, though dated, remain useful are Ramirez et al. (1987), Blanchard and Blanchard (1984, 1986), Moyer (1987), Donnerstein and Geen (1983), Brain and Benton (1981), and Krames et al. (1978). Moyer's seminal study (1976), mentioned earlier, is still useful in providing a comprehensive framework for integrat-ing research findings concerning the diverse genetic, biological, neurological, and social sources of aggressiveness in humans.

Useful recent survey works on aggressiveness in nonhuman primates and other ani-mals, and the implications for aggressiveness in humans, are Silverberg and Gray (1992) and McGuinness (1987).

4. Adapted from Moyer (1976, 1987).

5. Crime statistics and the findings of criminologists have begun to be integrated into the biological and social scientific study of violence. Recent works of criminology which are particularly useful for this purpose and are the sources for the discussion of criminal violence are those of Johnson and Monkkonen (1996), Pallone and Hennessy (1996), Wei-tekamp and Kerner (1994), Harvey and Gow (1994), Reidel (1993), Baenninger (1991), and Flowers (1989). See also Archer and Gartner (1984, 1988) and Gatrell et al. (1980).

6. Psychoanalytic accounts of aggressiveness are discussed below.

7. See the sources cited above.

8. The account of early childhood development (or lack of development) of inhibitions against violent behavior draws heavily on Landy and Peters (1992), a survey article the purpose of which is "to review research findings that have addressed the etiology of early aggressive conduct problems," and to suggest a "developmental paradigm" for normal and abnormal development in this area. Additional sources on "social learning" as a source of violent or nonviolent behavior, most of which refer to some aspects of childhood development, are given in note 51.

9. The discussion of socialization processes in older children and teenagers draws on Archer (1994), Feshbach and Fraczek (1979), Feshbach and Zagrodzka (1997), Fraczek and Zumkley (1992), Peters et al. (1992), Potegal and Knutson (1994), Tedeschi and Felson (1994), and Wolfgang and Ferracuti (1982).

10. This phrase is the title of a groundbreaking work by Wolfgang and Ferracuti (1982).

11. The symbolic and physiological means by which the ability to control expression of affect is internalized in normal, healthy children are not well understood and, in the case of the symbolic aspect, have received surprisingly little study. Freud first wrote about the rechanneling of energy associated with affect that cannot be expressed directly and immediately in a socially acceptable form as a healthy process of "sublimation," not to be confused with the unhealthy process of repression. But Freud associated sublimation mainly if not exclusively with the channeling of sexual impulses into creative forms of work and expression. He did not do much to explore the sublimation of aggressive impulses, nor the sublimation that is inherent in the conduct of everyday life, apart from establishing the grand psychoanalytic scheme of the id (the raw impulses), the superego (the incorporation of society's norms and demands), and the ego (the reconciliation of the two in the ability to exercise a healthy form of sublimation, rather than repression or acting out).

Among subsequent psychoanalytic theorists, one has explored sublimation "in the round," that is, linking the process involved in specific acts of rechanneling affective or impulse energy to the more general process of ego formation and personality development: Hans Loewald, in *Sublimation: Inquiries into Theoretical Psychoanalysis* (1988). Laplanche (1980) and Porret (1994) have devoted book-length works in French to the subject (Laplanche in the form of a series of public lectures, without notes or sources). Unfortunately, there is no cross-referencing between Loewald and Porret, and almost no cross-referencing of the English and French sources each cites, since most of the works cited by each have not been translated. Useful insights are also offered by Sandler et al. (1991), Bergler (1989) and Sterba and Daldin (1987/1930).

Norbert Elias, in *The Civilizing Process* (1978/1939), explored theoretically in greater detail and empirically in concrete cases (over the course of medieval and renaissance France) the relationship between growing social scale and complexity, and the increasing distance of behavior from immediate affect and impulse. His empirical work focused on the elaboration of social manners and concealment of bodily functions in court society, and the development of bourgeois society, as levers of political power in a society with a lengthening chain of stages of economic dependence and hierarchically structured power. A number of European sociologists and social theorists have built on Elias' work, including Honneth and Joas (1988), Mennell (1989), and Johnson and Monkkonen (1996).

Other approaches to the relationship between successively more complex forms of social organization, human nature (that is, genetically endowed capabilities and tendencies), and social learning are offered by Glantz and Peace (1989), Maryanski and Turner (1992), and Stevens (1993). These works argue, respectively, that the biological endowment of contemporary *homo sapiens sapiens* was shaped primarily by the lifestyles of the earliest hunter-gatherers, who lived from around 40,000 BC to around 7000 BC, or by the last prehuman anthropoids, over a period of several hundred thousand years, or by the entire period of evolution from ape to human, over a period of two million years.

Older views of the relationship between civilization and human nature, less influenced by Freud or by contemporary applications of the theory of natural selection, are offered by Rousseau (1988/1755), Ferguson and Forbes (1966/1767), Condocet (1955/1795), Whitehead (1933), Schweitzer (1949), and Toynbee and Fowler (1950), as well as the 19th century philosophers Hegel, Comte, and Spencer. On the related organizing idea of "progress," see Bury (1987/1932) for a study of the historical roots of the 19th and early 20th century view, and Lasch (1991) for a contemporary view, supplemented by an excellent bibliographical essay.

12. I have not found any social psychological studies which attempt, directly, to differentiate between socially sanctioned and nonsanctioned forms of violence, with respect to the motives for participation. There is, however, a small body of literature on "crimes of obedience," that is, acts of violence which are not morally sanctioned by the society at large, but which are sanctioned and even seemingly, socially or legally required within an aberrant subgoup of society at large. (In the case of Nazi Germany, society at large must be seen as either the international community, or Germany taken over a longer period of time.) Two important recent works on the sociology and social psychology of counternorm obedience are Crelinsten and Schmid (1994) and Kelman and Hamilton (1989). See also the collection of articles bu Sabini and Silver, Lifton, Kelman and Hamilton, and Fairbank under the rubric of "Political Psychology of Destructive Obedience and Genocide," in Kressel (1993). Studies of this topic do not, however, explore the sociology or social psychology of acts of violence which are neither criminal nor "counter-norm" with respect to the larger society, but, on the contrary, condoned or required by society. Several of the collected articles in *The Psychology of War*, edited by Betty Glad (1990), touch on the subject, but only glancingly. Most relevant is that by Kellett (1990), which shows that the motivation of soldiers on the battlefield is rooted more in honor, duty, and the desire for approval and respect from colleagues than in aggressive feelings. Kellett points out, however, that the leadership of crackerjack soldiers and airmen has a decisive impact on the morale and ftlineperformance of entire units; and he speculates that such leaders may be significantly more aggressive than the average soldier.

## CHAPTER 4

1. See Chapter 2 for comments on structural violence.

2. See Davies (1981) and Hogg (1966), two general surveys which document practices of human sacrifice in a large number of countries (or prestate cultures) on all continents.

3. See Patnaik (1989), Boal (1982), Gohain (1977), Stutchbury (1982), and Basham (1954).

4. For Greece and Rome, see Green (1975), Bonfante (1984), Hughes (1991), Halm-Tisserant (1993), Schwenn (1915), Detienne (1979), and Durand (1986). For Carthage, see Brown (1991), Heider (1985), Moscati (1987), and Ribichini (1987). For Israel, Syria, and Persia, see Green (1975); for Israel, see also note 61 below.

5. Studies of human sacrifice among the Mayans and Aztecs include Agrinier (1978), Berenson (1984), Duverger (1979), Fournier (1985), González Torres (1985), Hassig (1988), Hassler (1992), McGee (1983), Nájera (1987), and Serrano Sanchez (1993).

6. Beatty (1915) gives an unusually well-documented account of the practices of the "Human Leopard Society" of Sierra Leone, based on trial transcripts; and Ross (1989) and Schöppl von Sonnwalden (1992) give an equally well-documented account of human sacrifice among the Pawnee Indians.

7. Comparative analyses of the forms and purposes of human sacrifice are given in Bloch (1992), Lewis (1986), Scot (1899), Trumbull (1898), James (1933), Loeb (1923), and

Bourdillon and Fortes (1980). See also the works of Rene Girard, particularly *Violence and the Sacred* (1977) and *Violent Origins* (Burkert et al. 1987).

8. Patnaik (1989), pp 163–164.

9. Davies (1981).

10. See Smith et al. (1939), James (1933), Hillers (1983), Lasine (1991), and Visotzky (1983).

11. Green (1975), p 201.

12. Green (1975), citing C. L. Wooley, *Ur Excavations: The Royal Cemetery*, Vol II, Oxford (Oxford University Press), 1934.

13. Davies (1981), p 40.

14. Patnaik (1989).

15. See Watson (1980), Miller (1985), Sawyer (1986), and Steinfeld (1991) for global overviews of the practice of slavery. See also Dandamaev (1984/1974) for a remarkably detailed and well-documented study of slavery in Babylonia in 656–331 BC.

16. Virtually all of the sources on cannibalism in the Americas mention this practice. See, for example, Abler and Logan (1988), Abler (1992), Albert (1988), Balée (1984), Bernal Andrade (1993), Carneiro (1990), Combès (1987, 1992), Forsyth (1985), Jamieson (1983), Pedersen (1987), Ross (1989), Schöppl von Sonnwalden (1992), Sicoli and Tartabini (1994), Sjørslev (1987), Steward (1946–1959), Castro (1984, 1992), Walens (1981), Whiffen (1915), Whitehead (1984, 1990).

17. In *The Invention of Free Labor: The Employment Relation in English and American Law 1350–1870*, Steinfeld (1991) argues that until the last century, the presumption for the majority of workers was not that labor was free, but that it was bound in various ways.

18. Hoch (1986).

19. See Emmons (1970), Hellie (1982), Hoch (1986), Holstein and Montefiore (1906), and Zaïonchkovskiĭ (1978).

20. For Britain see Keen (1990) and Stenton (1951); for continental Europe, see Bloch (1975), Wright (1966), Bonnassie (1991), and Freedman (1991); for Scandinavia, see Karras (1988).

21. Ellis (1833) gives an "abstract" of the population recorded in the Domesday book of 1086, which was enumerated by county: Ellis compiled the figures from each county for each class.

22. The Russian population estimates are provided in a remarkable document: an analysis of the results of the Russian 10th National Census (conducted in 1857) by Troĭnitskiĭ (1982/1861), who was the chief of statistics, a man sympathetic to the impending emancipation of the serfs (which the census was meant to facilitate), and later the Minister of the Interior charged with implementing this reform.

23. See Kemble (1841a).

24. See Kemble (1841b).

25. The lengthening of the average life span over the course of development of more complex societies is discussed in Chapter 6.

26. See Curtis (1988) for a brief overview and Mallory (1989) for a more thorough, scholarly overview of the theory of the origins and expansion of the proto-Indo-Europeans. *The Chalice and the Blade*, covering much of the same material, argues that the Indo-European expansion replaced more developed societies which had a female primary goddess and peace-oriented cultures with a more crude culture, prone to wandering and plundering, with a male primary god who represented and rewarded success in warfare.

27. See Wolfram (1988/1979) for a history of the successive Gothic invasions that occurred between 291 and 582.

28. Morgan (1986) reports that at the apogee of the Mongol empire, the Mongol culture supported a violently destructive form of aggression in which most adult males

participated: not only did they make a career of attacking others and seizing their wealth, in addition, in response to the unprovoked execution of their diplomatic negotiators by Persian leaders, they decimated Persian cities, killing hundreds of thousands of civilians and destroying the property they could not carry off.

29. A third, related explanation for the apparent aggressiveness of the Indo-Europeans, typical of the "ethological" analysis of culture, is that men who were genetically more aggressive may have fared better in the nomadic, pastoral lifestyle, leading over a period of centuries to a greater proclivity for aggression among peoples with this lifestyle than is typical in an agricultural setting, in which the traits of patience, industry, and placidity would be rewarded with material and social success.

## CHAPTER 5

1. The sample is drawn from the circa 1,000 contemporary and historical cultures covered in Murdock's *Ethnographic Atlas* (1967) and Murdock and White's "Standard Cross-Cultural Sample" (2006/1969) of the world, discussed further below.

2. *Divine Hunger* (Sanday, 1986).

3. Eli Sagan, a psychiatrist who lectures at the New School, wrote a thoughtful, widely cited work on the forms of and reasons for cannibalism, *Cannibalism: Human Aggression and Cultural Form* (1974). He makes a persuasive argument that both exocannibalism and endocannibalism, which he refers to as "aggressive" and "affectionate cannibalism," have roots in the desire of the nursing infant to meet all needs by actual eating up and becoming one with the source of all nourishment and security (oral incorporation), and the infant's frustration at not being able to do so (oral aggression). Sanday does not make explicit exactly why one might expect the likelihood of cannibalism to increase as a function of the length of the postpartum sexual taboo. In cross-cultural studies, other anthropologists have shown that this factor does tend to be associated with a greater incidence of socially sanctioned aggression on the part of adult males.

4. Schöppl von Sonnwalden adds to this list (p. 19) a case that involves the mingling of blood by two leaders who were uniting their tribes in a binding treaty. But this example is out of place: it merely underscores the importance of orality in the concept of cannibalism as practiced by simple societies, and in the revulsion to cannibalism experienced in the modern world. Blood transfusions and organ transplants represent the literal integration of parts of one person into another; but because in these practices the alimentary canal is bypassed and the procedure is antiseptic, the wholesale incorporation of a physical part of one person into another is not revolting to the modern mind, and does not entail the same sense of violation of dignity of another human being.

5. See note 86.

6. It is likely that Volhard and Sagan, following early travelers' accounts, mistakenly interpreted the cannibal rituals that follow war as victory celebrations, when in reality, as indicated by 20th century ethnographies and by recent reviews of the early sources, these rituals were the main or sole war objectives: that is, the purpose of war was to transfer the soul stuff, courage, and fertility possessed by other tribes to oneself and one's own tribe.

7. See Gordon-Grube (1993).

## CHAPTER 6

1. On this point see Habermas (1979) and Honneth and Joas (1988/1980).

2. This idea, in some form, is found in nearly all anthropological studies of the origins and significance of ritual cannibalism, and is illustrated the titles of the following book-length works: *The Mouth of Heaven: An Introduction to Kwakiutl Religious Thought* (Goldman 1981); *Cannibalisme et Immortalite: L'Enfant dans le Chaudron en Grece*

*Ancienne (Cannibalism and Immortality: The Child in the Cauldron in Ancient Greece)* (Halm-Tisserant 1993); *Vital Souls: Bororo Cosmology, Natural Symbolism, and Shamanism* (Crocker 1985); and *Divine Hunger: Cannibalism as a Cultural System* (Sanday 1986). *Death and the Regeneration of Life* is the title of a collection of essays edited by Bloch and Parry (1982) which includes articles about ritual cannibalism and other mortuary rituals.

3. Not surprisingly, the number of victims in burial sacrifice was inversely proportional to the wealth and power of the deceased: at one end of the spectrum, kings and emperors were buried with a huge retinue; at the other end, a wealthy farmer might be accompanied to the grave (or, in modern India, funeral pyre) by his wife.

4. See, for example, Mueller (1989), Luard (1986), and Keegan (1993).

5. In addition to Julian Steward (1955, 1977), this section draws on several general works on the theory of cultural evolution, that is, the theory of the features and causes of the development of successively larger and more complex societies over the course of human history. Approaching the subject from the perspectives of different schools of thought and different disciplines, these are: Boyd and Richerson (1985), Kroeber (1963), Lesser (1985), Bradie (1994), and Ingold (1988a, 1988b).

6. The discussion in this section of the differences between simple hunter-gatherer cultures and early agricultural states is based on three groups of scholarly sources: first, those which give overviews of prehistoric societies and modern-day hunter-gatherer societies, such as Clark (1969, 1970, 1977), Ingold et al. (1988a, 1988b), Leakey and Lewin (1977, 1979), Rouse (1972), and Wenke (1980); second, studies which review the factors involved in the rise of early states and the development of increasingly complex societies, notably Adams (1966), Fried (1967), Polgar (1975), Friedman and Rowlands (1978), Boserup (1981), Haas (1982), Sandars (1985), Haas et al. (1987), Johnson and Earle (1987), Cohen and Toland (1988), Kraus (1990), Upham (1990), and Lewellen (1992); and third, the ethnologies and histories of individual cultures and groups of cultures used as sources for Chapters 4 and 5 and the Appendix.

7. Ester Boserup's seminal study *Population and Technological Change* (1981) makes a carefully argued case for the "population push" origin of larger and more complex societies. In a recent article, Netting (1990), while building on Boserup's analysis, suggests that the rise of the early city states was less a product of the "intensification" of food production per worker through technological innovation than of the absolute size of the surrounding agricultural population in a given area. Like Boserup, Service stressed the benefits of early states as causes of their formation, including "increased production, a structure of redistribution which alleviates local disparities in resources. . ., and the rise of an . . . administrative structure which . . . would enhance and support the role of the chief, the court, and the priesthood, and ultimately would benefit the citizenry to a certain extent" (Yengoyan 1991).

8. Elman Service was a principal theorist of the characteristics of successively more complex forms of social organization, which he identified as band, tribe (a cluster of bands), chiefdom (a cluster of tribes), and primitive state (1971b). Many anthropologists have avoided the topic of the evolution of organizational scale and complexity on the grounds that it is hard to identify a set of well-defined features that are associated with any given form of organization between the small egalitarian band, with no hierarchically structured authority of any kind, and the complex early city-state. For the same reason, Service himself (1971a, p 157) later settled on just three groupings, which he called egalitarian society, hierarchical society and archaic civilization or classical empire.

9. On this point, two caveats must be added: First, the forms of institutionalized violence that arose in conjunction with new forms of organization in the past seem to have been located at weak points in the structure of society or the fabric of social thought, where sources of support were vulnerable to natural failure or human exploitation. Conceivably,

new forms of institutionalized violence could arise in future in areas where the benefits of the new global interpenetration of finance, communications, and trade are susceptible to failure or interruption. Such a development would not necessarily negate the existence of a more general, longer-term trend toward the abolition of all forms of socially sanctioned violence; it could merely stretch out the period over which the decline in tolerance for institutionalized violence takes place.

Second, there are signs that the overarching project of the modern age—to make every family in every country healthy, wealthy, and wise, enfranchised, and violence-free—has not merely stalled but gone into reverse. The regressive trends include not merely a steadily rising rate of violent crime and a new surge of ethnic conflict, but also increased use of drugs; the rise of new global criminal networks for the acquisition and sale of drugs; the rise of unprotected early sex leading to growing rates of teenage pregnancy, venereal disease, and AIDS; declining national products and high unemployment rates in both rich and poor countries; and the conditions of anarchy or near-anarchy in many parts of the world.

The perspective presented in this essay does suggest that war could end in the foreseeable future despite these trends. The key point is that the likelihood of war is a function not of turmoil and fear, but of beliefs about the acceptability of war as a means of resolving problems, and the actual utility of war as a means of addressing the issues at hand. Apart from local failures of government, which invite local wars, none of the conditions described above is amenable to amelioration by resort to warfare. Going to war will not, for example, reduce teenage pregnancy, AIDS, or drug use, nor even restore employment and economic growth over the longer term.

## APPENDIX

1. In quoting from book reviews, the author did not provide page numbers, but the full citations to the reviews are listed in the Bibliography.

2. Three book reviews—Barrett (1991), Guzman (1992), and Overmyer (1994)—make clear that Chong's work is, to date, the only systematic study of the roughly 50 written Chinese primary sources (the corpus of official and unofficial histories of China by emperor and dynasty) on the subject.

3. Indicative of the remaining strength of the language barrier, and of a partially offsetting trend toward English as the *lingua franca* of science, are the relatively rapid publication in English translation of a major, book-length Brazilian study (Castro 1992) and the publication of virtually simultaneous articles announcing major new findings by the same authors in prominent scientific journals in France and the United States (Villa, Bouville et al., 1986; Villa, Courtin et al. 1986).

4. See, for example, Nicolaïdis and Nicolaïdis, "Incorporation, pédophile, inceste" (1993), and the David Spain et al. roundtable in the *Journal of Psychohistory* (incorporating the *Journal of Psychoanalytic Anthropology*), "Incest Theory: Are There Three Aversions?" (1988). See also related works by M. Masud Khan (1973) and Jacques André (1988).

5. Works of psychological (or psychoanalytic) theory focusing on failed ego development associated with infantile oral-cannibalistic neuroses include Erich Fromm's *The Anatomy of Human Destructiveness* (1973) and related recent articles, such as Giorgio Zanocco, "Reflections on a Theme: A Revision of the Concept of Psychopathic Personality" (1973); Carl Goldberg, "The Daimonic Development of the Malevolent Personality" (1995); and James O. Koretz, "Passivity and Destructiveness: The Re-integration of Aggression into Object Relations Theory" (1986). See also M. Benezech et al., "Cannibalism and Vampirism in Paranoid Schizophrenia" (1981).

6. In some cases, anthropological works about cannibalism employ psychoanalytic theory. See, for example, Peggy Reeves Sanday, *Divine Hunger: Cannibalism as a Cultural*

*System* (1986); Jonathan Friedman, "Consuming Desires: Strategies of Selfhood and Appropriation" (1991); Jadran Mimica, "The Incest Passions: An Outline of the Logic of the Iqwaya Social Organization" (1991); and Jay Mechling, "High Kybo Floater: Food and Feces in the Speech Play at a Boy Scout Camp" (1984). In other cases, psychologists comment on culture in works of psychoanalytic theory, for example, Jean-Claude Arfouilloux, "Laios cannibale" (1993); Steven L. Ablon, "Play: 'Time to Murder and Create'" (1993); Jacques André, "Le privilege: Les deux theories freudiennes de l'originaire social" (1988); and Gail Carr Feldman, "Satanic Ritual Abuse: A Chapter in the History of Human Cruelty" (1995). Occasionally, a work is situated equally in the two fields; psychologist Eli Sagan provides one such study in *Cannibalism: Human Aggression and Cultural Form* (1974).

7. The extent of literary and artistic allusions to cannibalism is brought home in a profusely illustrated German work entitled *Menschenfresser in der Kunst und Literatur, in fernen Ländern, Mythen, Märchen und Satiren, in Dramen, Liedern, Epen und Romanen: eine kannibalische Text-Bild-Dokumentation mit 123 Abbilddungen* [Cannibalism in Art and Literature, in Foreign Lands, Myths, Fairy Tales and Satire, in Theater, Song, Epic and Fiction: A Word-Picture Documentation of Cannibalism with 123 Illustrations] (Thomsen 1983).

8. The passage continues that the most tender man "will act so meanly toward his brother, the wife of his bosom, and the remaining children that may be left to him, that he will not give any of them any of the flesh of his children he has to eat, since there is nothing else left to him in the stress of the siege. . . . " Similarly, the most tender women "will act meanly toward the husband of her bosom, her son, and her daughter, both in case of the after birth that may come from her womb and the children that she may bear; for she shall secretly eat these for want of everything in the stress of the siege." (28: 54–57) (see Visotzky 1983).

9. Hymn of the Primeval Man, *Rig Veda* X:90, translation in Basham (1954) as cited by Tannahill (1975, pp 22–23).

10. See, for example, Green (1975), Hughes (1991), Schwenn (1915), Halm-Tisserant (1993), Detienne (1979), and Durand (1986).

11. Fenton comments that "anyone familiar with the Psalms will know that people are for ever being eaten by their enemies and foes; they are consumed and swallowed up by those who hate them. There are at least twenty-eight instances of the vocabulary of ingestion in the Psalter, where the thing being eaten is human . . . One can see how, in the Old Testament eating people expresses hostility by noting the *subjects* of the eating verbs: enemies and foes do it; the abyss does it; evildoers do it; lions, fire and the sword do it. You have to be against people, to eat them; eating people in the Old Testament is never a friendly or amiable activity. Moreover, there is no sense that the eater of people is nourished by it; all the emphasis is on the destruction of the victim, none on the benefit that accrues to the consumer" (Fenton 1991, p 420, emphasis added). In other words, the symbolic consumption of Jesus' body and blood was intended to be not a ritual act linking man and god, but a reminder, given to the disciples in advance of their betrayal of him, of the sinfulness of man—of the expectation of man's betrayal and general weakness—which was the proximate cause of Jesus' death and from which he sought to redeem humankind.

This plausible interpretation of Jesus' instructions at the Last Supper is totally at odds with the 2000-year practice of the Eucharist as a ritual conferring grace or forgiveness of sins. In 1215, ending a many-centuries-long dispute over whether the communion ritual represented a reminder of Christ's sacrifice or a form of participation in it, Pope Innocent III decreed that the wafer and wine, once consecrated, did not merely symbolize but actually became the body and blood of Christ (Davies 1981). Nonetheless, a Protestant theologian, rejecting both the version of the Eucharist endorsed by the Catholic Church, with its parallel to cannibal rituals, and the Fenton interpretation, which would invalidate centuries of Christian practice, offered a third interpretation in a response to Fenton's article. Robert Morgan, lecturer in New Testament Studies at Oxford and Priest-in-Charge of Sandford-on-Thames, argues in the response (Morgan, 1991) that a careful comparative reading of the Gospels shows that at the Last Supper, Jesus meant nothing more than literally "breaking *bread* which *represents* his body, and eating the bread and drinking the cup" (p. 425, emphasis in the original)—that is, a reminder of his coming sacrifice. Though less consistent with Old and New Testament allusions to eating than Fenton's view, this interpretation is, like Fenton's, more consistent with the Jewish traditions of Jesus' era than is the cannibal-like Roman Catholic interpretation.

Both Fenton and Morgan ignore the presence in the Old Testament of older Jewish traditions involving God's demand for sacrifices of the first of everything, including the firstborn child; God's command to Abraham to spare Isaac's life, marking the start of an era when animal sacrifice replaced human sacrifice; and the subsequent ritual consumption by priests of symbolic portions of sacrificed animals, with specific instructions concerning the parts to be consumed and the timing of the consumption.

Given the rapid identification by some early Christians of the Eucharist as conferring personal participation in Jesus' sacrifice through the consumption of his "body and blood," it is hard to avoid the conclusion that even if it was not the intention of Jesus at the Last Supper, nor of his New Testament chroniclers, the Christian practice of communion was quickly confounded with ancient sacrifice-cum-consumption religious rituals. Moreover, the Church's medieval insistence that communicants actually consume the body and blood of Christ makes the Christian practice of communion parallel perfectly, in symbolic form, other earlier religious practices of sacrifice and cannibalism.

12. Another sign of the "coming of age" of animal cannibalism studies in 1992 was the presence of a panel on "Cannibalism and Infanticide" at the annual meeting of the American Zoological Society (Anon. 1992).

# Bibliography

Abler, Thomas S. 1980. "Iroquois Cannibalism: Fact Not Fiction?" *Ethnohistory* 27, No 4 (Autumn): 309–316.

Abler, Thomas S. 1988. "A Mythical Myth: Comments on Sanday's Explanation of Iroquoian Cannibalism," *American Anthropologist* 90, No 4 (December): 967–969.

Abler, Thomas S. 1992. "Scalping, Torture, Cannibalism and Rape: An Ethnohistorical Analysis of Conflicting Cultural Values in War," *Anthropologica* 34, No 1: 3–20.

Abler, Thomas S. and Michael H. Logan. 1988. "The Florescence and Demise of Iroquoian Cannibalism: Human Sacrifice and Malinowski's Hypothesis," *Man in the Northeast* No 35 (Spring), pp 1–26.

Ablon, Steven L. 1993. "Play: 'Time to Murder and Create'," in Albert J. Solnit, Donald J. Cohen, and Peter B. Neubauer, eds., *The Many Meanings of Play: A Psychoanalytic Perspective.* New Haven, CT: Yale University Press, pp 297–314.

Ackerman, Peter and Christopher Kruegler. 1994. *Stratetic Nonviolent Conflict: The Dynamics of People Power in the Twentieth Century.* Westport, CT: Praeger.

Adams, Robert McCormick. 1966. *The Evolution of Urban Society: Early Mesopotamia and Prehispanic Mexico.* New York: Aldine Pub. Co.

Addams, Jane. 1960 [1922]. *Peace and Bread in Time of War.* Boston: G. K. Hall & Co.

Agrinier, Pierre. 1978. *A Sacrificial Mass Burial at Miramar, Chiapas, Mexico.* Provo, UT: New World Archaeological Foundation, Brigham Young University.

Aiken, Lillian Woodworth. 1963. *Bertrand Russell's Philosophy of Morals.* New York: Humanities Press.

Albert, Bruce. 1988. "La Fumée du métal: Histoire et représentations du contact chez les Yanomami (Brésil)," *L'Homme* 28, Nos. 106–107: 87–119.

Alder, William Fisher. 1922. *The Isle of Vanishing Men: A Narrative of Adventure in Cannibal-Land.* London: L. Parsons.

Alker, Hayward R, Jr. 1993. *The Return of Practical Reason.* Canberra: Australian National University Department of International Relations.

Allsebrook, Mary. 1986. *Prototypes of Peacemaking: The First Forty Years of the United Nations.* Harlow, Essex, UK: Longman.

Alpers, Michael P. 1992. "Kuru," in Robert D. Attenborough and Michael P. Alpers, eds., *Human Biology in Papua New Guinea: The Small Cosmos.* Oxford, New York: Clarendon Press, pp 313–334.

Alpers, Michael and D. Carleton Gajdusek. 1965. "Changing Patterns of Kuru: Epidemiological Changes in the Period of Increasing Contact of the Fore people with Western Civilization," *The American Journal of Tropical Medicine and Hygiene* 14, no 5 (September): 852–879.

American Peace Society. 1899. *The Hague Convention for the Pacific Settlement of International Disputes.* Boston: American Peace Society.

André, Jacques. 1988. "Le privilege: Les deux theories freudiennes de l'originaire social," *Psychanalyse à l'Université* 13, No 49: 59–85.

Anon. 1916. *The reports to the Hague Conferences of 1899 and 1907: being the official explanatory and interpretative commentary accompanying the draft conventions and declarations submitted to the conferences by the several commissions charged with preparing them.* Oxford, New York: Clarendon Press.

Anon. 1918. *The Hague conventions and declarations of 1899 and 1907 accompanied by tables of signatures, ratifications and adhesions of the various powers and texts of reservations.* New York: Oxford University Press.

Anon. 1992. American Society of Zoologists (with five other societies) Annual Meeting. "Abstracts—Symposia: Cannibalism and Infanticide," *American Zoologist* 32, No 5 (November): 169A–171A.

Anon. 1995a. "Arachnophilia," *Discover* 16, No 11 (November): 32, 34.

Anon. 1995b. "Of Sex, Somersaults, and Death," *Discover* 16, No 11 (November): 34.

Archer, Dane and Rosemary Gartner. 1984. *Violence and Crime in a Cross-National Perspective.* New Haven: Yale University Press.

Archer, Dane, Rosemary Gartner, Criminal Justice Archive and Information Network, and Inter-university Consortium for Political and Social Research. 1988. *Violence and Crime in Cross-National Perspective, 1900–1972* [Computer File]. Ann Arbor, MI: Inter-university Consortium for Political and Social Research [distributor].

Archer, John. 1994. *Male Violence.* London, New York: Routledge.

Ardrey, Robert, 1967, 1961. *African Genesis: A Personal Investigation Into the Animal Origins and Nature of Man.* New York: Dell Publishing.

Ardrey, Robert. 1967. *The Territorial Imperative: A Personal Inquiry Into the Animal Origins of Property and Nations.* New York: Atheneum.

Arendt, Hannah. 1982. *Lectures on Kant's Political Philosophy* (delivered at the New School for Social Research fall 1970). Chicago: University of Chicago Press.

Arens, W. 1979a. "Cannibalism, An Exchange, with reply by Marshall Sahlins" *New York Review of Books* (March 22).

Arens, W. 1979b. *The Man-Eating Myth: Anthropology & Anthropophagy.* Oxford, New York: Oxford University Press.

Arfouilloux, Jean-Claude. 1993. "Laïos cannibale," *Revue Française de Psychanalyse* 57, No 2 (April-June): 495–506.

Arjava, Antti. 1996. *Women and Law in Late Antiquity.* Oxford, New York: Oxford University Press.

Armand, Jorge. 1985. *La Maneta: Informe Sobre Los Vestigios Esqueléticos de un Niño del Siglo XVII Con Marcas de Posible Antropofagia, Descubiertos en el Páramo el Aguila, Estado Mérida, Venezuela.* Mérida, Venezuela: Universidad de los Andes, Consejo de Desarrollo Cientifico, Humanistico y Tecnológico, Consejo de Publicaciones.

Aron, Raymond. 1955. *The Century of Total War.* Boston: Beacon Press.

Aron, Raymond. 1973. *Peace and War: A Theory of International Relations*, trans. Richard Howard and Annette Baker Fox, abr. Rémy Inglis Hall. Garden City, NY: Anchor Books.

Askenasy, Hans. 1994. *Cannibalism: From Sacrifice to Survival.* Amherst, NY: Prometheus Books.

Attenborough, Frederick Levi and Great Britain. 1922. *The Laws of the Earliest English Kings.* Cambridge: Cambridge University Press.

Aucapitaine, Henri. 1857. *Les Yem-Yem: Tribu Anthropophage de l'Afrique Centrale.* Paris: A. Bertrand.

Austen Riggs Center for the Study and Treatment of the Neuroses, Stockbridge, MA. 1954. *Psychoanalytic Psychiatry and Psychology: Clinical and Theoretical Papers*, ed. Robert P. Knight. New York: International Universities Press.

Badcock, C. R. 1990. *Oedipus in Evolution: A New Theory of Sex*. Oxford, Cambridge, MA: Blackwell.

Baenninger, Ronald. 1991. *Targets of Violence and Aggression*. Amsterdam, NY: North-Holland; New York: Elsevier Science Pub. Co. (distributors in USA and Canada).

Bahn, Paul G. 1990. "Eating people is wrong," *Nature* 348, No 6300 (November 29): 395.

Bahn, Paul G. 1991. "Cannibalism in the Neolithic (reply by Bahn)," *Nature* 351, No 6328 (June 20): 613–614.

Bahn, Paul G. 1992. "Ancestral cannibalism gives us food for thought: Review of Tim D. White, *Prehistoric Cannibalism*," *New Scientist* 134, No 1816 (April 11): 40–41.

Bailyn, Bernard. 1967. *The Ideological Origins of the American Revolution*. Cambridge, MA: Harvard University Press.

Balée, William. 1984. "The Ecology of Ancient Tupi Warfare," in R. Brian Ferguson, ed., *Warfare, Culture, and Environment*. Orlando, FL: Academic Press, pp 241–265.

Barber, Ian. 1992. "Archaeology, ethnography and the record of Maori cannibalism before 1815: A critical review," *Journal of the Polynesian Society* 101, No 3 (September): 241–292.

Barnaby, Frank and Egbert Boeker. 1982. *Defence without Offence: Non-Nuclear Defence for Europe*. London: Housmans.

Baron, Robert A. 1977. *Human Aggression*. New York: Plenum Press.

Baron, Robert A. and Deborah R. Richardson. 1994. *Human Aggression*, 2nd ed. New York: Plenum Press.

Barrett, T. H. 1991. "Review of Key Ray Chong, *Cannibalism in China*," *China Quarterly* No 128 (December): 836–837.

Basham, A. L. (Arthur Llewellyn). 1954. *The Wonder That Was India: A Survey of the Culture of the Indian Sub-Continent Before the Coming of the Muslims*. London: Sidgwick and Jackson.

Basso, Ellen B. 1990. "The Last Cannibal," in *Native Latin American Cultures Through their Discourse*, Special Publications of the Folklore Institute No. 1. Bloomington, IN: Folklore Institute, Indiana University, pp 133–173.

Baur, Bruno. 1994. "Inter-population differences in propensity for egg cannibalism in hatchlings of the land snail *Arianta arbustorum*," *Animal Behaviour* 48, No 4 (October): 851–860.

Beaton, Leonard. 1966. *The Struggle for Peace*. New York: F. A. Praeger.

Beatty, Sir Kenneth James and Sierra Leone Special Commission Court. 1915. *Human Leopards: An Account of the Trials of Human Leopards Before the Special Commission Court: with a note on Sierre Leone, past and present*. London: H. Rees.

Beau, B. 1914. *A Defense of Cannibalism*, trans. Preston William Slosson. New York: American Association for International Conciliation, 1914.

Beck, Sanderson. 1986. *The Way to Peace: Great Peacemakers, Philosophers of Peace and Efforts Toward World Peace*. Farmingdale, NY: Coleman Publishing.

Beer, Francis A. 1981. *Peace Against War: The Ecology of International Violence*. San Francisco: W. H. Freeman.

Benezech, M., M. Bourgeois, D. Boukhabza, and J. Yesavage. 1981. "Cannibalism and Vampirism in Paranoid Schizophrenia," *Journal of Clinical Psychiatry* 42, No 7: 290.

Bennike, Pia and Klaus Ebbesen. 1986. "Bog find from Sigersdal: Human Sacrifice in the Early Neolithic," *Journal of Danish Archaeology* 5, No 1: 85–115.

Benoit, Kenneth. 1994. *Reexamining democracy and war involvement: democracies really are more pacific.* Cambridge, MA: Center for International Affairs, Harvard University.

Benoit, Kenneth. 1996. "Democracies Really Are More Pacific (in General): Reexamining Regime Type and War Involvement," *Journal of Conflict Resolution* 40, No 4 (December): 636–657.

Benton, Michael. 1991. "The myth of the Mesozoic cannibals," *New Scientist* 132, No 1790 (October 12): 40–44.

Berenson, Elisabeth. 1984. *Ritual Human Sacrifice in Mesoamerica: A Conference at Dumbarton Oaks, October 13th and 14th, 1979.* Washington, DC: Dumbarton Oaks Research Library and Collection.

Bergler, Edmund. [1989] 1952. *The Superego: Unconscious Conscience—The Key to the Theory and Therapy of Neurosis.* Madison, CT: International Universities Press.

Bernal Andrade, Leovigildo. 1993. *Los Heróicos Pijaos y el Chaparral de Los Reyes.* [n.p.] [Santafe de Bogota, Colombia: Litho Imagen].

Bernheim, Pierre-Antoine and Guy Stavridès. 1992. *Cannibales!* Paris: Plon.

Berreman, Gerald D. 1979. "Stratification, Pluralism and Interaction: A Comparative Analysis of Caste," in Gerald D. Berreman, ed., *Caste and Other Inequities: Essays on Inequity.* Meerut, India: Folklore Institute, pp 71–95.

Birkhead, Tim and Susan Lawrence. 1988. "Life and loves of a sexual cannibal," *New Scientist* 118, No 1617 (June 16): 63–66.

Blackwell, Kenneth. 1985. *The Spinozistic Ethics of Bertrand Russell.* London, Boston: Allen and Unwin.

Blackwood, Caroline. 1985. *On the Perimeter: A vivid personal report from the front line of the anti-nuclear movement.* New York: Penguin Books.

Blanchard, Robert J. and D. Caroline Blanchard, eds. 1984. *Advances in the Study of Aggression,* Vol 1. Orlando, FL: Academic Press.

Blanchard, Robert J. and D. Caroline Blanchard, eds. 1986. *Advances in the Study of Aggression,* Vol 2. Orlando, FL: Academic Press.

Bloch, Marc Leopold Benjamin. 1975. *Slavery and Serfdom in the Middle Ages: Selected Essays,* trans. William R. Beer. Berkeley: University of California Press.

Bloch, Maurice. 1992. *Prey Into Hunter: The Politics of Religious Experience.* Cambridge, New York: Cambridge University Press.

Bloch, Maurice and Jonathan Parry. 1982. *Death and the Regeneration of Life.* Cambridge, New York: Cambridge University Press.

Bloom, Allan, et al. 1989. "Responses to Fukuyama by Allan Bloom, Pierre Hassner, Gertrude Himmelfarb, Irving Kristol, Daniel Patrick Moynihan, and Stephen Sestanovich," *National Interest* No 16 (Summer): 19–35.

Boal, Barbara M. 1982. *The Konds: Human Sacrifice and Religious Change.* Warminster, Wilts [England]: Aris & Phillips; Atlantic Highlands, NJ: Humanities Press (distributors in USA and Canada).

Boal, Clint W. and John E. Bacorn. 1994. "Siblicide and Cannibalism at Northern Goshawk Nests," *Auk* 111, No 3 (July): 748–750.

Boidin, Paul. 1908. *Les lois de la guerre et les deux Conférences de la Haye (1899–1907).* Paris: A. Pedone.

Bok, Sissela. 1989. *A Strategy for Peace: Human Values and the Threat of War.* New York: Pantheon Books.

Bok, Sissela. 1990. "Early Advocates of Lasting World Peace: Utopians or Realists?" *Ethics and International Affairs* 4, No 1: 145–162.

Bonfante, Larissa. 1984. "Human Sacrifice on an Etruscan Funerary Urn," *American Journal of Archaeology* 88, No 4 (October): 531–539.

Bonkovsky, Frederick O. 1980. *International Norms and National Policy*. Grand Rapids, MI: Eerdmans.

Bonnassie, Pierre. 1991. *From Slavery to Feudalism in South-Western Europe*. Cambridge, New York: Cambridge University Press; Paris: Editions de la Maison des sciences de l'homme.

Boothby, Richard. 1991. *Death and Desire: Psychoanalytic Theory in Lacan's Return to Freud*. New York: Routledge.

Boserup, Ester. 1981. *Population and Technological Change: A Study of Long-Term Trends*. Chicago: University of Chicago Press.

Bottomley, A. Keith and Kenneth Pease. 1986. *Crime and Punishment: Interpreting the Data*. Milton Keynes, Philadelphia: Open University Press.

Boulding, Kenneth. 1978. *Stable Peace*. Austin: University of Texas Press.

Bourdillon, M. F. C. and Meyer Fortes. 1980. *Sacrifice*. London: Academic Press for the Royal Anthropological Institute of Great Britain and Ireland.

Bourgeois, Léon. 1910. *Pour la Société des Nations*. Paris: E. Fasquelle.

Bowden, Ross. 1984. "Maori Cannibalism: An Interpretation," *Oceania* 55, No 2 (December): 81–99.

Bowles, Chester. 1955. *The New Dimensions of Peace*. New York: Harper & Bros.

Boxer, Sarah, ed. 1987. "Now here's a case of you eat what you are," *Discover* 8, No 6 (June): 10.

Boyd, Robert and Peter J. Richerson. 1985. *Culture and the Evolutionary Process*. Chicago: University of Chicago Press.

Bradie, Michael. 1994. *The Secret Chain: Evolution and Ethics*. Albany: State University of New York Press.

Brady, Ivan. 1982. "Review, *The Man-eating Myth*," *American Anthropologist* 84, No 3 (September): 595–611.

Brain, Paul F. and David Benton. 1981. *Multidisciplinary Approaches to Aggression Research*. Amsterdam, New York: Elsevier/North-Holland Biomedical Press.

Breden, Felix and Michael J. Wade. 1989. "Selection Within and between Kin Groups of the Imported Willow Leaf Beetle," *American Naturalist* 134, No 1 (July): 35–50.

Bregman, Ahron. 1995. "Review of *Democracy, War and Peace in the Middle East* by David Garnham and Mark Tessler," *International Affairs* 71, No 4 (October): 899–900.

Brink, Andrew. 1989. *Bertrand Russell: A psychobiography of a moralist*. Atlantic Highlands NJ: Humanities Press International.

Brock, Peter. 1990. *The Quaker Peace Testimony 1660 to 1914*. York: Sessions Book Trust; Syracuse University Press (distributor in USA).

Brodie, Bernard. 1973. *War and Politics*. New York: Macmillan.

Brown, Norman Oliver. 1985, 1959. *Life Against Death: The Psychoanalytical Meaning of History*. Middletown, CT: Wesleyan University Press.

Brown, Paula and Donald F. Tuzin, eds. 1983. *The Ethnography of Cannibalism*. Washington, DC: Society for Psychological Anthropology.

Brown, Susanna Shelby. 1991. *Late Carthaginian Child Sacrifice and Sacrificial Monuments in Their Mediterranean Context*. Sheffield [England]: published by JSOT Press for the American Schools of Oriental Research.

Brown, Vinson, ed. 1983. *Prevent Doomsday: An Anti Nuclear Anthology*. Brookline Village, MA: Branden Press.

Brundage, Burr Cartwright. 1963. *Empire of the Inca*. Norman, OK: University of Oklahoma Press.

Buchanan, Allen E. 1991. *Secession: The Morality of Political Divorce from Fort Sumter to Lithuania and Quebec*. Boulder, CO: Westview Press.

Bueno de Mesquita, Bruce and David Lalman. 1992. *War and Reason: Domestic and International Imperatives*. New Haven: Yale University Press.

Bull, Hedley, Benedict Kingsbury, and Adam Roberts. 1992. *Hugo Grotius and International Relations*. Oxford: Clarendon Press; New York: Oxford University Press.

Bullock, Peter Y. 1991. "Reappraisal of Anasazi Cannibalism," *Kiva* 57, No 1: 5–16.

Bullock, Peter Y. 1992. "Return to the Question of Cannibalism," *Kiva* 58, No 2: 203–205.

Burkert, Walter, René Girard, Jonathan Z. Smith, and Robert. Hamerton-Kelly, eds. 1987. *Violent Origins*. Stanford: Stanford University Press.

Burrows, Guy and Edgar Canisius. 1903. *The Curse of Central Africa*. London: R.A. Everett & Co.

Bury, J. B. 1987/1932. *The Idea of Progress: An Inquiry into its Origin and Growth*. New York: Dover Publications.

Buskirk, Josh Van. 1989. "Density-Dependent Cannibalism in Larval Dragonflies," *Ecology* 70, No 5 (October): 1442–1449.

Campbell, Lyle and Marianne Mithun. 1979. *The Languages of Native America: Historical and Comparative Assessment*. Austin: University of Texas Press.

Cantor, Norman F. 1967. *The English*. New York: Simon and Schuster.

Carneiro, Robert. 1990. "Chiefdom-level warfare as exemplified in Fiji and he Cauca Valley," in Jonathan Haas, ed., *The Anthropology of War*. Cambridge, New York: Cambridge University Press, pp 190–211.

Carter, Ashton B., William James Perry, and John D. Steinbruner. 1992. *A New Concept of Cooperative Security*. Washington, DC: Brookings Institute.

Carver, Michael. 1982. *A Policy for Peace*. London: Faber and Faber.

Castro, Eduardo B. Viveiros de. 1984–1985. "Os Deuses Canibais: A Morte e o Destino da Alma Entre os Arawetê," *Revista de Antropologia* 27–28: 55–90.

Castro, Eduardo Batalha Viveiros de. 1992. *From the Enemy's Point of View: Humanity and Divinity in an Amazonian Society*, trans. Catherine V. Howard. Chicago: University of Chicago Press.

Cavell, Marcia. 1993. *The Psychoanalytic Mind: From Freud to Philosophy*. Cambridge: Harvard University Press.

Chan, Steve. 1984. "Mirror, Mirror on the Wall . . . Are the Freer Countries More Pacific?" *Journal of Conflict Resolution* 28, No 4 (December): 617–648.

Chaumeil, Jean-Pierre. 1992. "La Légende d'Iquitos," *Bulletin de l'Institut français d'études andines* 21, No 1: 311–325.

Choate, Joseph Hodges. 1913. *The Two Hague Conferences*. Princeton, NJ: Princeton University Press.

Chong, Key Ray. 1990. *Cannibalism in China*. Wakefield, NH: Longwood Academic.

Clark, Grahame. 1969. *World Prehistory: A New Outline*. London: Cambridge University Press.

Clark, Grahame. 1970. *Aspects of Prehistory*. Berkeley: University of California Press.

Clark, Grahame. 1977. *World Prehistory in New Perspective*. Cambridge, New York: Cambridge University Press.

Clark, Grenville. 1950. *A Plan for Peace*. New York: Harper & Brothers.

Clark, Grenville and Louis B. Sohn. 1966. *World Peace through World Law: Two Alternative Plans*, 3rd ed. Cambridge: Harvard University Press.

Clark, Grenville and Louis B. Sohn (as revised by Louis Sohn). 1973. *Introduction to World Peace through World Law*. Chicago: World Without War Publications.

Clastres, Pierre. 1974. *Chronique des indiens Guayaki: ce que savent les Aché, chasseurs nomades du Paraguay*. [Paris]: Plon.

Clausewitz, Carl von. 1968. *On War*, trans. J. J. Graham, Anatol Rapoport, ed. Harmondsworth: Penguin Books.

Clottes, Jean, Jean Courtin, and Paul G. Bahn. 1993. "Stone Age Gallery-by-the-Sea," *Archaeology* 46, No 3 (May/June): 37–43.

Clunie, Fergus. 1987. "Rokotui Dreketi's human skull: yaqona cup?" *Domodomo: Fiji Museum Quarterly* 5, No 1&2: 50–52.

Cohen, Jack. 1989. *The Privileged Ape: Cultural Capital in the Making of Man*. Carnforth [England]: Parthenon.

Cohen, Ronald. 1984. "Warfare and State Formation: Wars make states and states make wars," in R. Brian Ferguson, ed., *Warfare, Culture, and Environment*. Orlando, FL: Academic Press, pp 1–81.

Cohen, Ronald and Judith D. Toland, eds. 1988. *State Formation and Political Legitimacy*. New Brunswick, NJ: Transaction Books.

Coles, Robert. 1987, 1970. *Erik H. Erikson: The Growth of His Work*. New York: Da Capo Press.

Combès, Isabelle. 1987. "'Dicen que por ser Ligero': Cannibales, Guerriers et Prophètes Chez les Anciens Tupi-Guarani," *Journal de la Société des Américanistes* 73: 93–106.

Combès, Isabelle. 1992. *La Tragédie Cannibale Chez Les Anciens Tupi-Guarani*. Paris: Presses Universitaires de France.

Condorcet, Jean-Antoine-Nicolas de Caritat. 1955. *Sketch for a Historical Picture of the Progress of the Human Mind*, trans. June Barraclough. New York: Noonday Press.

Conklin, Beth A. 1995. "'Thus Are Our Bodies, Thus Was Our Custom': Mortuary Cannibalism in an Amazonian Society," *American Ethnologist* 22, No 1 (February): 75–101.

Cornes, Tristan O. 1986. "The Freud/Jung Conflict: Yahweh and the Great Goddess," *American Imago* 43, No 1 (Spring): 7–21.

Craige, John Houston. 1934. *Cannibal Cousins*. New York: Minton, Balch & Company.

Crapanzano, Vincent. 1979. "We're What We Eat?: Cannibal" *New York Times Sunday Book Review* (July 29): 6, 19.

Crelinsten, Ronald D. and Alex Peter Schmid, eds. 1994. *The Politics of Pain: Torturers and Their Masters*. Boulder, CO: Westview Press.

Crocker, Jon Christopher. 1985. *Vital Souls: Bororo Cosmology, Natural Symbolism, and Shamanism*. Tucson: University of Arizona Press.

Crowley, Philip H. and Kevin R. Hopper. 1994. "How to Behave Around Cannibals: A Density-Dependent Dynamic Game," *American Naturalist* 143, No 1 (January): 117–154.

Crump, Martha L. 1991. "You Eat What You Are," *Natural History* 100, No 2 (February): 46–51.

Curtis, V. R. 1988. *Indo-European Origins*. New York: P. Lang.

Czempiel, Ernst Otto. 1995. *Are Democracies Peaceful? Not Quite Yet*. Frankfurt/Main: Peace Research Institute Frankfurt.

Dandamaev, Muhammad A. 1984. *Slavery in Babylonia: From Nabopolassar to Alexander the Great (626–331 B.C.)*, trans. Victoria A. Powell, Marvin A. Powell and David B. Weisberg, eds. DeKalb, IL: Northern Illinois University Press.

Dante, Alighieri. 1960 [1317]. *On World-Government; or, De Monarchia*. New York: Liberal Arts Press.

Darby, W. Evans. 1899. *The Peace Conference at the Hague: Its history, work, and results*. London: Peace Society.

Darling, Charles W. (Charles William). 1886. *Anthropophagy*. Utica, NY: T. J. Griffiths, printer.

Davies, Nigel. 1981. *Human Sacrifice, In History and Today*. New York: Morrow.

Davis, Calvin DeArmond. 1975. *The United States and the Second Hague Peace Conference: American Diplomacy and International Organization 1899–1914*. Durham NC: Duke University Press.

Davis, Garry. 1984. *World Government, Ready or Not!* Sorrento, ME: Juniper Ledge Publishing Co.

Day, John. 1989. *Molech: A God of Human Sacrifice in the Old Testament*. Cambridge, New York: Cambridge University Press.

de Castro e Almeida, Maria Emília, and Maria Cristina Santos Neto. 1985–86. "Brève note sur un crâne africain mutilé," *Garcia de Orta Série de Antropobiologia* 4, No 1–2: 1–6.

Detienne, Marcel. 1979. *Dionysos Slain*, trans. Mireille Muellner and Leonard Muellner. Baltimore: Johns Hopkins University Press.

Deutsch, Karl W. et al. 1957. *Political Community and the North Atlantic Area*. Princeton, NJ: Princeton University Press.

Diamond, Larry Jay and Marc F. Plattner. 1994. *Nationalism, Ethnic Conflict, and Democracy*. Baltimore: Johns Hopkins University Press.

Díaz del Castillo, Bernal. 1877. *Histoire Véridique de la Conquête de la Nouvelle-Espagne*, trans. Denis Jourdanet. Paris: G. Masson, 1877.

Dixon, William J. 1993. "Democracy and the Management of International Conflict," *Journal of Conflict Resolution* 37, No 1 (March): 42–68.

Dixon, William J. 1994. "Democracy and the Peaceful Settlement of International Conflict," *American Political Science Review* 88, No 1 (March): pp 14–32.

diZerega, Gus. 1995. "Democracies and Peace: The Self-Organizing Foundation for the Democratic Peace," *Review of Politics* 57, No 2 (Spring): 279–308.

Dobash, R. Emerson and Russell Dobash. 1979. *Violence Against Wives: A Case Against the Patriarchy*. New York: Free Press.

Dockès, Pierre. 1982. *Medieval Slavery and Liberation*, trans. Arthur Goldhammer. London: Methuen.

Docteur en Droit [anonymous]. 1908. *La Belgique et l'Arbitrage Obligatoire a la Deuxieme Conference de la Paix*. Bruxelles: A. Dewit.

Dole, Gertrude E. 1974. "Types of Amahuaca Pottery and Techniques of its Construction." *Festschrift Otto Zerries*. Ethnologische Zeitschrift Zürich, pp 145–159.

Donnerstein, Edward I. and Russell G. Green. 1983. *Aggression: Theoretical and Empirical Reviews*. New York: Academic Press.

Doyle, Michael. 1983a. "Kant, Liberal Legacies, and Foreign Affairs," *Philosophy and Public Affairs* 12, No 3 (Summer): 205–235.

Doyle, Michael. 1983b. "Kant, Liberal Legacies, and Foreign Affairs, Part 2," *Philosophy and Public Affairs* 12, No 4 (Autumn): 323–353.

Doyle, Michael W. 1986. "Liberalism and World Politics," *American Political Science Review* 80, No 4 (December): 1151–1169.

Driver, Harold Edson. 1969. *Indians of North America*, 2nd ed. Chicago: University of Chicago Press.

Duffett, John, ed. 1968. *Against the Crime of Silence: Proceedings of the Russell International War Crimes Tribunal, Stockholm, Copenhagen* (with Introduction by Bertrand Russell and Foreword by Ralph Schoenman). New York: Bertrand Russell Peace Foundation.

Dülffer, Jost. 1981. *Regeln gegen den Krieg? die Haager Friedenskonferenzen von 1899 und 1907 in der internationalen Politik*. Frankfurt am Main, Berlin, Wien: Ullstein.

Dumézil, Georges. 1935. *Flamen-brahman*. Paris: P. Geuthner.

Durand, Jean-Louis. 1986. *Sacrifice et labour en Grèce Ancienne: Essai d'anthropologie religieuse*. Paris: Découverte; Rome: Ecole française de Rome.

Duverger, Christian. 1979. *La fleur létale: économie du sacrifice aztèque*. Paris: Éditions du Seuil.

Eckhardt, William. 1992. *Civilizations, Empires and Wars: A Quantitative History of War*. Jefferson, NC: McFarland.

Eggert, Anne-Katrin and Scott K. Sakaluk. 1994. "Sexual cannibalism and its relation to male mating success in sagebrush crickets, *Cyphoderris strepitans* (Haglidae: Orthoptera)," *Animal Behaviour* 47, No 5 (May): 1171–1177.

Eichelberger, Clark Mell. 1965. *UN: The First Twenty Years*. New York: Harper & Row.

Eisler, Riane. 1988. *The Chalice and the Blade: Our History, Our Future*. San Francisco: Harper & Row.

Elgar, Mark A. 1991. "Sexual Cannibalism, Size Dimorphism, and Courtship Behavior in Orb-Weaving Spiders (Araneidae)," *Evolution* 45, No 2 (March): 444–448.

Elgar, Mark A. and Bernard J. Crespi. 1992. *Cannibalism: Ecology and Evolution Among Diverse Taxa*. Oxford, New York: Oxford University Press.

Elgar, Mark A. and David R. Nash. 1988. "Sexual cannibalism in the garden spider *Araneus diadematus*," *Animal Behaviour* 36, No 5 (September-October): 1511–1517.

Elias, Norbert. 1978. *The Civilizing Process, Vol 1: History of Manners*, trans. Edmund Jephcott. New York: Pantheon Books.

Elias, Norbert. 1982. *The Civilizing Process, Vol 2: Power and Civility*, trans. Edmund Jephcott. New York: Pantheon Books.

Ellis, Sir Henry and Great Britain Record Commission. 1833. *A General Introduction to Domesday Book: Accompanied By Indexes of the Tenants-In-Chief and Under-Tenants at the Time of the Survey: As Well As of the Holders of Lands Mentioned in Domesday Anterior to the Formation of That Record: With an abstract of the population of England at the close of the reign of William the Conqueror, so far as the same is actually entered: illustrated by numerous notes and comments*. London: Printed by command of His Majesty King William IV, under the direction of the Commissioners on the Public Records of the Kingdom. London: G. Eyre & A. Spottiswoode. [Microform]

Emmons, Terence, comp. 1970. *Emancipation of the Russian Serfs*. Hinsdale, IL: Dryden Press.

Erikson, Erik H. 1969. *Gandhi's Truth: On the Origins of Militant Nonviolence*. New York: W. W. Norton.

Erikson, Philippe. 1986. "Altérité, Tatouage et Anthropophagie Chez les Pano: La Belliqueuse Quête du Soi," *Journal de la Société des Américanistes* 72: 185–210.

Ehrlich, Paul R., Anne H. Ehrlich, and John P. Holdren. 1977. *Ecoscience: Population, Resources, Environment*. San Francisco: W. H. Freeman.

Ernandes, M. 1992. "Serotonin Deficiency Hypothesis Explaining the Aztec Human Sacrifice/Cannibalism Complex," *Antropologia Contemporanea* 15, No 2: 65–73.

Esainko, Peter. 1986. "Delinquent Ladies: Cannibal attributions toward women as protest masculinity," in *Women in Anthropology: Symposium Papers 1981, 1982, 1986* (Publication No 17). Sacramento, CA: Sacramento Anthropological Society, pp 35–52.

Estournelles de Constant, Paul-Henri-Benjamin Balluet, baron d', and David Jayne Hill. 1907. *The Results of the Second Hague Conference*. New York: American Branch of the Association for International Conciliation.

Etzioni, Amitai. 1962. *The Hard Way to Peace: A New Strategy.* New York: Collier Books.

Evans, Gareth. 1993. *Cooperating for Peace: The Global Agenda for the 1990's and Beyond.* St. Leonards, NSW, Australia: Allen & Unwin.

Eves, Richard. 1995. "Shamanism, Sorcery and Cannibalism: The Incorporation of Power in the Magical Cult of Buai," *Oceania* 65, No 3 (March): 212–233.

Fagan, Brian. 1994. "Timelines: A Case for Cannibalism," *Archaeology* 47, No 1 (January/February): 11, 13–14, 16.

Fagan, William F. and Garrett M. Odell. 1996. "Size-Dependent Cannibalism in Praying Mantids: Using Biomass Flux to Model Size-Structured Populations," *American Naturalist* 147, No 2 (February): 230–268.

Farber, Henry S. and Joanne Gowa. 1995. "Polities and Peace," *International Security* 20, No 2 (Fall): 123–246.

Feldman, Gail Carr. 1995. "Satanic Ritual Abuse: A Chapter in the History of Human Cruelty," *Journal of Psychohistory* 22, No 3 (Winter): 340–357.

Fenton, John. 1991. "Eating People," *Theology* 94, No 762 (November): 414–423.

Ferencz, Benjamin B. 1985. *A Common Sense Guide to World Peace.* New York: Oceana.

Ferguson, Adam and Duncan Forbes. 1966. *An Essay on the History of Civil Society.* Edinburgh: Edinburgh University Press.

Ferguson, Jan Helenus. 1899. *The International Conference of the Hague: A plea for peace in social evolution.* The Hague: M. Nijhoff.

Ferguson, R. Brian, ed. 1984a. *Warfare, Culture, and Environment.* Orlando, FL: Academic Press.

Ferguson, R. Brian. 1984b. "Introduction: Studying War," in R. Brian Ferguson, ed., *Warfare, Culture, and Environment.* Orlando, FL: Academic Press, pp 1–81.

Ferguson, R. Brian. 1984c. "A Re-examination of the Causes of Northwest Coast Warfare," in R. Brian Ferguson, ed., *Warfare, Culture, and Environment.* Orlando, FL: Academic Press, pp 267–328.

Ferguson, R. Brian. 1990. "Explaining War," in Jonathan Haas, ed. *The Anthropology of War.* Cambridge, New York: Cambridge University Press, pp 26–55.

Ferguson, R. Brian, Leslie E. Farragher, and Harry Frank Guggenheim Foundation. 1988. *The Anthropology of War: A Bibliography.* New York: Harry Frank Guggenheim Foundation.

Feshbach, Seymour and Adam Fraczek. 1979. *Aggression and Behavior Change: Biological and Social Processes.* New York: Praeger.

Feshbach, Seymour and Jolanta Zagrodzka. 1997. *Aggression: Biological, Developmental, and Social Perspectives.* New York: Plenum Press.

Fischer, Dietrich. 1982. "Invulnerability Without Threat: The Swiss Concept of General Defense," *Journal of Peace Research* 19, No 3: 205–225.

Fischer, Dietrich, Wilhelm Nolte, and Jan Øberg. 1989. *Winning Peace: Strategies and Ethics for a Nuclear-free World.* New York: Crane, Russak.

Fleischer, Helmut. 1973. *Marxism and History.* New York: Harper & Row.

Flesher, Paul Virgil McCracken. 1988. *Oxen, Women, or Citizens? Slaves in the System of the Mishnah.* Atlanta, GA: Scholars Press.

Flowers, R. Barri. 1989. *Demographics and Criminality: The Characteristics of Crime in America.* New York: Greenwood Press.

Fonagy, Peter, George S. Moran, and Mary Target. 1993. "Aggression and the Psychological Self," *International Journal of Psycho-Analysis* 74, No 3 (June): 471–485.

Forrester, John. 1980. *Language and the Origins of Psychoanalysis.* New York: Columbia University Press.

Forsberg, Randall. 1984. "Confining the Military to Defense as a Route to Disarmament," *World Policy Journal* 1, No 2 (Winter): 285–318.

Forsberg, Randall. 1992a. "Defense Cuts and Cooperative Security in the Post-Cold War World," *Boston Review* 17, Nos 3–4 (May-July): 5–9.

Forsberg, Randall. 1992b. "Creating a Cooperative Security System," *Boston Review* 17, No 6 (November-December): 7–10.

Forsyth, Donald W. 1985. "Three Cheers for Hans Staden: The Case for Brazilian Cannibalism," *Ethnohistory* 32, No 1 (Winter): 17–36.

Foster, Catherine. 1989. *Women for All Seasons: The Story of the Women's International League for Peace and Freedom*. Athens: University of Georgia Press.

Foster, John Watson. 1904. *Arbitration and the Hague Court*. Boston, New York: Houghton, Mifflin and Co.

Foster, Susan A. and Ernest Cooper. 1990. "Courting Disaster in Cannibal Territory: For the Threespine Stickleback, Mating Can Be a Risky Business," *Natural History* 99, No 11 (November): 52–61.

Foucault, Michel. 1979. *Discipline and Punish: The Birth of the Prison*, trans. Alan Sheridan. New York: Vintage Books.

Fournier, Dominique. 1985. "Le sacrifice humain ches les Aztèques: question de technologie?" *Techniques & culture* No 5: 49–72.

Foy, J. D., ed. 1992. *Domesday Book: Index of Subjects*. Chichester [England]: Phillimore.

Frączek, Adam and Horst Zumkley, eds. 1992. *Socialization and Aggression*. Berlin, New York: Springer-Verlag.

Frank, Erwin H. 1987. *"Y se lo comen": kritische Studie der Schriftquellen zum Kannibalismus der panosprachigen Indianer Ost-Perus und Brasiliens*. Bonn: Holos.

Frazer, Sir James George. 1980. *The Golden Bough: A Study in Magic and Religion*, 3rd ed. London: Macmillan.

Freedman, Paul H. 1991. *The Origins of Peasant Servitude in Medieval Catalonia*. Cambridge, New York: Cambridge University Press.

Frei, Daniel. 1980. *Evolving a Conceptual Framework of Inter-Systems Relations: Elements for a Common Theoretical Approach to Cooperative Transactions in East-West Relationships*. New York: United Nations Institute for Training and Research.

Freud, Sigmund. 1961, 1930. *Civilization and Its Discontents*, trans. James Strachey. New York: W. W. Norton.

Freud, Sigmund. 1953–74. *The Standard Edition of the Complete Psychological Works of Sigmund Freud*, trans. James Strachey. London: Hogarth Press and Institute of Psycho-analysis.

Freund, Norman C. 1987. *Nonviolent National Defense: A Philosophical Inquiry Into Applied Nonviolence*. Lanham, MD: University Press of America.

Fried, Morton H. 1967. *The Evolution of Political Society: An Essay in Political Anthropology*. New York: Random House.

Friedman, J., M. J. Rowlands, and the London University Research Seminar in Archaeology and Related Subjects. 1978. *The Evolution of Social Systems: Proceedings of a Meeting of the Research Seminar in Archaeology and Related Subjects, Held at the Institute of Archaeology, London University*. Pittsburgh: University of Pittsburgh Press.

Friedman, Jonathan. 1991. "Consuming Desires: Strategies of Selfhood and Appropriation," *Cultural Anthropology* 6, No 2 (May): 154–163.

Fromm, Erich. 1973. *The Anatomy of Human Destructiveness*. New York: Holt, Rinehart and Winston.

Fukuyama, Francis. 1989a. "The End of History?" *National Interest* No 16 (Summer): 3–18.

Fukuyama, Francis. 1989b. "A Reply to My Critics," *National Interest* No 18 (Winter): 21–28.

Fuller, Timothy et al. 1989. "More Responses to Fukuyama by Timothy Fuller, David Satter, David Stove and Frederick L. Will," *National Interest* No 17 (Fall): 93–100.

Galston, William A. 1975. *Kant and the Problem of History*. Chicago: University of Chicago Press.

Galtung, Johan. 1975-. *Essays in Peace Research* (5 vols.) Copenhagen: Ejlers, 1975–1980; Atlantic Highlands, NJ: Humanities Press.

Galtung, Johan. 1980. *The True Worlds: A Transnational Perspective*. New York: Free Press.

Galtung, Johan. 1984. *There are Alternatives!: Four Roads to Peace and Security*. Nottingham: Spokesman.

Galtung, Johan and Arne Næss. 1969. *Gandhis politiske etikk [Gandhi's Political Ethic]*. Oslo: Pax Forlag.

Gandhi, Mohandas K. 1929. *An Autobiography: The Story of My Experiments with Truth*, trans. Mahadev Desai. Boston: Beacon Press.

Gandhi, Mohandas K. 1957. *Gandhi, An Autobiography: The Story of My Experiments With Truth*, trans. Mahadev Desai. Boston: Beacon Press.

Gandhi, Mohandas K. 1961, 1951. *Non-violent Resistance (Satyagraha)*. New York: Schocken Books.

Gatrell, V. A. C., Bruce Lenman, and Geoffrey Parker. 1980. *Crime and the Law: The Social History of Crime in Western Europe since 1500*. London: Europa Publications.

Gay, Volney P. 1992. *Freud on Sublimation: Reconsiderations*. Albany: State University of New York Press.

Geen, Russell G. 1990. *Human Aggression*. Milton Keynes: Open University Press.

Gernet, Jacques. 1982. *A History of Chinese Civilization*. Cambridge, New York: Cambridge University Press.

Gillison, Gillian. 1983. "Cannibalism Among Women in the Eastern Highlands of Papua New Guinea," in Paula Brown and Conald Tuzin, eds., *The Ethnography of Cannibalism*. Washington, DC: Society for Psychological Anthropology, pp 33–50.

Gilpin, Robert. 1981. *War and Change in World Politics*. Cambridge: Cambridge University Press.

Giovacchini, Peter L. 1987. *A Narrative Textbook of Psychoanalysis*. Northvale, NJ: Aronson.

Girard, René. 1977. *Violence and the Sacred*, trans. Patrick Gregory. Baltimore: Johns Hopkins University Press.

Girard, René. 1987. *Job, the Victim of His People*, trans. Yvonne Freccero. Stanford: Stanford University Press.

Glad, Betty, ed. 1990. *Psychological Dimensions of War*. Newbury Park, CA: Sage Publications.

Glantz, Kalman and John K. Pearce. 1989. *Exiles From Eden: Psychotherapy From an Evolutionary Perspective*. New York: Norton.

Glass, D. V. (David Victor) and David Edward Charles Eversley, eds. 1965. *Population in History: Essays in Historical Demography*. Chicago: Aldine Pub. Co.

Gleditsch, Nils Petter. 1992. "Democracy and Peace," *Journal of Peace Research* 29, No 4 (November): 369–376.

Glick, Robert A. and Steven P. Roose. 1993. *Rage, Power, and Aggression*. New Haven: Yale University Press.

Glossop, Ronald J. 1987. *Confronting War: An Examination of Humanity's Most Pressing Problem*. Jefferson, NC: McFarland & Co.

Glotz, Gustave. 1904. *L'ordalie dans la Grèce primitive; étude de droit et de mythologie*. Paris: Fontemoing.

Gochman, Charles S., Henry S. Farber, and Joanne Gowa. 1996. "Correspondence: Democracy and Peace," *International Security* 21, No 3 (Winter): 177–187.

Goff, Peter W. and Lori Stevens. 1995. "A test of Hamilton's rule: cannibalism and relatedness in beetles," *Animal Behaviour* 49, No 2 (February): 545–547.

Gohain, B. C. 1977. *Human Sacrifice and Head-Hunting in North-Eastern India*. Gauhati: Lawyer's Book Stall.

Goldberg, Carl. 1995. "The Daimonic Development of the Malevolent Personality," *Journal of Humanistic Psychology* 35, No 3 (Summer): 7–36.

Goldman, George David and Donald S. Milman. 1978. *Psychoanalytic Perspectives on Aggression*. Dubuque, IA: Kendall/Hunt Pub. Co.

Goldman, Irving. 1981. *The Mouth of Heaven: An Introduction to Kwakiutl Religious Thought*. Huntington, NY: R. E. Krieger Pub. Co.

Goldman, Ralph M. 1990. *From Warfare to Party Politics: The Critical Transition to Civilian Control*. Syracuse: Syracuse University Press.

Goldstein, Joshua S. 1988. *Long Cycles: Prosperity and War in the Modern Age*. New Haven: Yale University Press.

Gong, Gerrit W. 1984. *The Standard of "Civilization" in International Society*. Oxford: Clarendon Press.

González Torres, Yolotl. 1985. *El Sacrificio Humano Entre los Mexicas*. México: Instituto Nacional de Antropología e Historia: Fondo de Cultura Economica.

Gordon, R. L., ed. and Marcel Detienne. 1981. *Myth, Religion, and Society: Structuralist Essays*. Cambridge, New York: Cambridge University Press.

Gordon-Grube, Karen. 1993. "Evidence of Medicinal Cannibalism in Puritan New England: 'Mummy' and Related Remedies in Edward Taylor's 'Dispensatory'," *Early American Literature* 28, No 3: 185–221.

Grant, Lindsey. 1996. *Juggernaut: Growth on A Finite Planet*. Santa Ana, CA: Seven Locks Press.

Great Britain Foreign Office. 1899. "Correspondence respecting the Peace conference held at the Hague in 1899 [in continuation of 'Russia No 1 (1899)'']," Presented to both houses of Parliament by command of Her Majesty October 1899. London: Harrison and Sons for H.M.S.O.

Green, Alberto Ravinell Whitney. 1975. *Human Sacrifice in the Ancient Near East*. Missoula, MT: Published by Scholars Press for the American Schools of Oriental Research.

Grimshaw, Beatrice. 1907. *From Fiji to the Cannibal Islands*. London: Eveleigh Nash.

Grindstaff, Carl F. 1981. *Population and Society: A Sociological Perspective*. West Hanover, MA: Christopher Pub. House.

Groebel, Jo and Robert A. Hinde, eds. 1989. *Aggression and War: Their Biological and Social Bases*. Cambridge, New York: Cambridge University Press.

Groupe parlementaire français de l'arbitrage international. 1907. *La Deuxième conférence de La Haye: Discours prononcés à la séance de rentrée du Groupe de l'arbitrage*. Paris: Delagrave.

Guha, Biraja Sankar. 1931. *A Report on the Human Relics Recovered by the Naga Hills (Burma) Expedition for the Abolition of Human Sacrifice During 1926–1927*. Calcutta: Published by the Director, Zoological Survey of India.

Guzman, Gregory G. 1992. "Review of Key Ray Chong, *Cannibalism in China*," *Journal of Asian History* 26, No 1 (Spring): 96–97.

Haas, Jonathan. 1982. *The Evolution of the Prehistoric State*. New York: Columbia University Press.

Haas, Jonathan, ed. 1990a. *The Anthropology of War*. Cambridge, New York: Cambridge University Press.

Haas, Jonathan. 1990b. "Warfare and the Evolution of Tribal Polities in the Prehistoric Southwest," in Jonathan Haas, ed., *The Anthropology of War*. Cambridge, New York: Cambridge University Press, pp 171–189.

Haas, Jonathan, Shelia Griffis Pozorski, and Thomas George Pozorski. 1987. *The Origins and Development of the Andean State*. Cambridge, New York: Cambridge University Press.

Habermas, Jürgen. 1979. *Communication and the Evolution of Society*. Boston: Beacon Press.

Hagan, Joe D. 1994. "Domestic Political Systems and War Proneness," *Mershon International Studies Review* 38, No 2 (October): 183–207.

Hallpike, C.R. 1977. *Bloodshed and Vengeance in the Papuan Mountains: The Generation of Conflict in Tauade Society*. Oxford: Clarendon Press.

Halm-Tisserant, Monique. 1993. *Cannibalisme et immortalité: l'enfant dans le chaudron en Grèce ancienne*. Paris: Les belles lettres.

Halpert-Berlin, David. 1899. *Männer der wissenschaft über die friedenskonferenz*. Berlin: P. Stankiewicz.

Halverson, John, Levon H. Abrahamian, Kathleen M. Adams, Paul G. Bahn, Lydia T. Black, Whitney Davis, Robin Frost, Robert Layton, David Lewis-Williams, Ana Maria Llamazares, Patrick Maynard, and David Stenhouse. 1987. "Art for Art's Sake in the Paleolithic [and comments and reply]," *Current Anthropology* 28, No 1 (February): 63–89.

Hamai, Miya, Toshisada Nishida, Hiroyuki Takasaki, and Linda A. Turner. 1992. "New Records of Within-Group Infanticide and Cannabalism in Wild Chimpanzees," *Primates* 33, No 2 (April): 151–162.

Harper, William, James Henry Hammond, William Gilmore Simms, and Thomas Roderick Dew. 1852. *The Pro-Slavery Argument: As Maintained By the Most Distinguished Writers of the Southern States*. Charleston: Walker, Richards & Co.

Hart, H. L. A. 1961. *The Concept of Law*. Oxford: Clarendon Press.

Harvey, Penelope and Peter Gow, eds. 1994. *Sex and Violence: Issues in Representation and Experience*. London, New York: Routledge.

Hassig, Ross. 1988. *Aztec Warfare: Imperial Expansion and Political Control*. Norman: University of Oklahoma Press.

Hassler, Peter. 1992. *Menschenopfer bei den Azteken?: eine quellen- und ideologiekritische Studie*. Bern, New York: P. Lang.

Hatch, Elvin. 1973. *Theories of Man and Culture*. New York: Columbia University Press.

Haynal, André. 1993. *Psychoanalysis and the Sciences: Epistemology–History*, trans. Elizabeth Holder. London: Karnac.

Heider, George C. 1985. *Cult of Molek: A Reassessment*. Sheffield: JSOT Press, Dept. of Biblical Studies, The University of Sheffield.

Heimer, Mel. 1988. *The Cannibal*. London: Xanadu.

Heizer, Robert Fleming and Mary Anne Whipple, eds. 1971. *The California Indians: A Source Book*, 2nd ed. Berkeley: University of California Press.

Hellie, Richard. 1982. *Slavery in Russia, 1450–1725*. Chicago: University of Chicago Press.

Hermann, Margaret G. and Charles W. Kegley, Jr. 1995. "Rethinking Democracy and International Peace: Perspectives From Political Psychology," *International Studies Quarterly* 39, No 4 (December): 511–533.

Hermann, Margaret G, and Kegley, Charles W, Jr. 1996. "Ballots, a Barrier Against the Use of Bullets and Bombs: Democratization and Military Intervention," *Journal of Conflict Resolution* 40, No 3 (September): 436–459.

Herrmann, Bernd, Rolf Sprandel, and Ulf Dirlmeier. 1987. *Determinanten der Bevölkerungsentwicklung im Mittelalter*. Weinheim: VCH.

Hillers, Delbert R. 1983. "History and Poetry in *Lamentations*," *Currents in Theology and Mission* 10 (June): 155–161.

Hobbes, Thomas. 1985. *Leviathan*. New York: Penguin.

Hoch, Steven L. 1986. *Serfdom and Social Control in Russia: Petrovskoe, a Village in Tambov*. Chicago: University of Chicago Press.

Hoffmann, Stanley. 1965. *The State of War: Essays on the Theory and Practice of International Relations*. New York: Frederick A Praeger.

Hoffmann, Stanley. 1987. "The Rules of the Game," *Ethics and International Affairs* 1, No 1 (March): 37–51.

Hoffmann, Stanley, Robert O. Keohane, and John J. Mearsheimer. 1990. "Correspondence: Back to the Future, Part II: International Relations Theory and Post-Cold War Europe," *International Security* 15, No 2 (Fall): 191–199.

Hogg, Garry. 1966, 1958. *Cannibalism and Human Sacrifice*. New York: Citadel Press.

Holdsworth, Sir William Searle. 1956. *A History of English Law*, Vol 1. London: Methuen.

Hollander, Eric and Dan J. Stein, eds. 1995. *Impulsivity and Aggression*. New York: Wiley & Sons.

Hollingsworth, T. H. 1969. *Historical Demography*. Ithaca, NY: Cornell University Press.

Hollins, Elizabeth Jay, ed. 1966. *Peace is Possible: A Reader for Laymen*. New York: Grossman.

Hollins, Harry B., Averill L. Powers, and Mark Sommer. 1989. *The Conquest of War: Alternative Strategies for Global Security*. Boulder, CO: Westview Press.

Holls, Frederick W. 1900. *The Peace Conference at the Hague and its Bearings on International Law and Policy*. New York: Macmillan Co.

Holstein, Alexandra and Dora B. Montefiore. 1906. *Serf Life in Russia: The Childhood of a Russian Grandmother*. London: Heinemann.

Honneth, Axel and Hans Joas. 1988. *Social Action and Human Nature*, trans. Raymond Meyer. Cambridge, New York: Cambridge University Press.

Hopper, Kevin R., Philip H. Crowley, and Donna Kielman. 1996. "Density Dependence, Hatching Synchrony, and Within-Cohort Cannibalism in Young Dragonfly Larvae," *Ecology* 77, No 1 (January): 191–200.

Howard, Alan. 1986. "Cannibal Chiefs and the Charter for Rebellion in Rotuman Myth," *Pacific Studies* 10, No 1 (November): 1–27.

Howard, Michael. 1984. *The Causes of Wars and Other Essays*, 2nd ed. Cambridge, MA: Harvard University Press.

Howard, Michael. 1993. "To the Ruthless Belong the Spoils: Review of *A History of Warfare* by John Keegan," *New York Times Book Review*, November 14, p 10.

Hubert, Henri and Marcel Mauss. 1964. *Sacrifice: Its Nature and Function*, trans. W. D. Hall. Chicago: University of Chicago Press.

Huesmann, L. Rowell. 1994. *Aggressive Behavior: Current Perspectives*. New York: Plenum Press.

Hughes, Dennis D. 1991. *Human Sacrifice in Ancient Greece*. London, New York: Routledge.

Hull, William Isaac. 1908. *The Two Hague Conferences and Their Contributions to International Law*. Boston: Ginn and Co. for the International School of Peace.

Hunter, Anne E., Catherine M. Flamenbaum, and Suzanne R. Sunday, eds. 1991. *On Peace, War, and Gender: A Challenge to Genetic Explanations*. New York: Feminist Press at the City University of New York.

Huntington, Samuel P. 1989. "No Exit: The Errors of Endism," *National Interest* No 17 (Fall): 3–11.

Huntington, Samuel P. 1993. "The Clash of Civilizations?" *Foreign Affairs* 72, No 3 (Summer): 22–49.

Idoyaga Molina, Anatilde. 1985. "The Myth of NesóGe: Hermeneutic Analysis of a Pilagà Relation," *Latin American Indian Literatures Journal* 1, No 1 (Spring): 1–12.

Illouz, Charles. 1985. "Les constantes symboliques et leur fonction dans la mythologie de Maré," *Journal de la Société des Océanistes* 41, No 81: 185–191.

Ingold, Tim, David Riches, and James Woodburn, eds. 1988a. *Hunters and Gatherers 1: History, Evolution and Social Change*. Oxford, New York: Berg; New York: distributed by St. Martin's Press.

Ingold, Tim, David Riches, and James Woodburn, eds. 1988b. *Hunters and Gatherers 2: Property, Power and Ideology*. Oxford, New York: Berg; New York: distributed by St. Martin's Press.

Jackson, Robert R. 1992. "Eight-legged Tricksters: Spiders That Specialize in Catching Other Spiders," *BioScience* 42, No 8 (September): 590–598.

James, E. O. [Edwin Oliver]. 1933. *Origins of Sacrifice: A Study in Comparative Religion*. London: John Murray.

Jamieson, James B. 1983. "An Examination of Prisoner-Sacrifice and Cannibalism at the St. Lawrence Iroquoian Roebuck Site," *Canadian Journal of Archeology* 7, No 2: 159–175.

Jenness, Eileen. 1933. *The Indian Tribes of Canada*. Toronto: Ryerson Press.

Jessor, Richard, ed. 1991. *Perspectives on Behavioral Science: The Colorado Lectures*. Boulder, CO: Westview Press.

Johansen, Robert C. 1991. "World Security, Democracy, and Military Force," *Report*, Joan B Kroc Institute for International Peace Studies, No 1. South Bend, IN: University of Notre Dame.

Johnson, A. H. (Allison Heartz). 1958. *Whitehead's Philosophy of Civilization*. Boston: Beacon Press.

Johnson, Allen W. and Timothy Earle. 1987. *The Evolution of Human Societies: From Foraging Group to Agrarian State*. Stanford: Stanford University Press.

Johnson, Eric A. and Eric H. Monkkonen, eds. 1996. *The Civilization of Crime: Violence in Town and Country Since the Middle Ages*. Urbana: University of Illinois Press.

Joseph, Betty. 1989. *Psychic Equilibrium and Psychic Change: Selected Papers of Betty Joseph*, ed. Michael Feldman and Elizabeth Bott Spillius. London, New York: Tavistock/Routledge.

Joyce, James Avery. 1975–1976. *World Population: Basic Documents*. Dobbs Ferry, NY: Oceana Publications.

Kalmbacher, Carol. 1983. "Came, Female Cannibal Culture Hero," International Museum of Cultures, *Publications in Ethnography* 17: 25–41.

Kant, Immanuel. 1963. *On History*, ed. Lewis White Beck, trans. Lewis White Beck, Robert E. Anchor, and Emil L. Fackenheim. Indianapolis: Bobbs-Merrill.

Karras, Ruth Mazo. 1988. *Slavery and Society in Medieval Scandinavia*. New Haven: Yale University Press.

Kaufmann, William W. and John D. Steinbruner. 1991. *Decisions for Defense: Prospects for a New Order*. Washington, DC: Brookings Institution.

Keegan, John. 1993. *A History of Warfare*. New York: A. A. Knopf.

Keen, Maurice Hugh. 1990. *English Society in the Later Middle Ages, 1348–1500*. London: Penguin Books.

Kegley, Charles W, Jr. 1993. "The Neoidealist Moment in International Studies? Realist Myths and the New International Realities," *International Studies Quarterly* 37, No 2 (June): 131–146.

Kegley, Charles W., Jr. and Margaret G. Hermann. 1996. "How Democracies Use Intervention: A Neglected Dimension in Studies of the Democratic Peace," *Journal of Peace Research* 33, No 3 (August): 309–322.

Kehoe, Alice Beck. 1981. *North American Indians: A Comprehensive Account.* Englewood Cliffs, NJ: Prentice-Hall.

Kellett, Anthony. 1990. "The Soldier in Battle: Motivational and Behavioral Aspects of the Combat Experience," in Betty Glad, ed., *Psychological Dimensions of War.* Newbury Park, CA: Sage Publications, pp 215–235.

Kelman, Herbert C. and V. Lee Hamilton. 1989. *Crimes of Obedience: Toward a Social Psychology of Authority and Responsibility.* New Haven: Yale University Press.

Kemble, John Mitchell. 1841a. "The Laws of King Æthelbirht," *Anglo-Saxon Laws and Institutes: Incunabula Juri Anglicani.* London: R. and J. E. Taylor.

Kemble, John Mitchell. 1841b. "The Laws of King Alfred," *Anglo-Saxon Laws and Institutes: Incunabula Juri Anglicani.* London: R. and J. E. Taylor.

Khan, M. Masud R. 1973. "The Role of Illusion in the Analytic Space and Process," *Annual of Psychoanalysis* 1: 231–246.

Kilgour, Maggie. 1990. *From Communion to Cannibalism: An Anatomy of Metaphors of Incorporation.* Princeton, NJ: Princeton University Press.

Kilman, Edward W. 1959. *Cannibal Coast.* San Antonio: Naylor Co.

Klingemann, Hans-Dieter. 1994. *Parties, Policies, and Democracy.* Boulder, CO: Westview.

Kohn, Stephen M. 1987. *Jailed for Peace: The History of American Draft Law Violators 1658–1985.* New York: Praeger.

Kooijmans, L. P. Louwe, Yuri Smirnov, Ralph S. Solecki, Paola Villa, Thomas Weber, and Robert H. Gargett. 1989. "On the Evidence for Neandertal Burial," *Current Anthropology* 30, No 3 (June): 322–230.

Kool, Vinod K., ed. 1993. *Nonviolence: Social and Psychological Issues.* Lanham, MD: University Press of America.

Koretz, James O. 1986. "Passivity and Destructiveness: The Re-integration of Aggression into Object Relations Theory" PhD diss., University of Tennessee, Knoxville.

Krames, Lester, Patricia Pliner, and Thomas Alloway, eds. 1978. *Aggression, Dominance, and Individual Spacing. Proceedings of the Sixth Annual Symposium on Communication and Affect, held at Erindale College, University of Toronto April 1–3, 1976.* New York: Plenum Press.

Kratochwil, Friedrich V. 1987. "Norms and Values: Rethinking the Domestic Analogy," *Ethics and International Affairs* 1, No 1: 135–159.

Kratochwil, Friedrich V. 1989. *Rules, Norms, and Decisions: On the Conditions of Practical and Legal Reasoning in International Relations and Domestic Affairs.* Cambridge: Cambridge University Press.

Kratochwil, Friedrich, Paul Rohrlich, and Harpreet Mahajan. 1985. *Peace and Disputed Sovereignty: Reflections on Conflict over Territory.* New York: University Press of America.

Kraus, Gerhard. 1990. *Human Origins and Development From An African Ancestry: A Review of Cultural Theory From the Beginning.* London: Karnak House.

Kreeger, Karen Young. 1993. "Consuming passion for distant relatives," *New Scientist* 139, No 1881 (July 10): 15.

Kressel, Neil J., ed. 1993. *Political Psychology: Classic and Contemporary Readings.* New York: Paragon House.

Kroeber, A. L. (Alfred Louis). 1963. *An Anthropologist Looks at History.* Berkeley: University of California Press.

Kytle, Calvin. 1982. *Gandhi, Soldier of Nonviolence: An Introduction.* Cabin John, MD: Seven Locks Press.

Lakey, George. 1987. *Powerful Peacemaking: A Strategy for a Living Revolution.* Philadelphia: New Society Publishers.

Landar, Herbert Jay. 1973. *The Tribes and Languages of North America: A Checklist.* [The Hague]: Mouton.

Landy, Sarah and Ray DeV. Peters. 1992. "Toward an Understanding of a Developmental Paradigm for Aggressive Conduct Problems During the Preschool Years," in Ray DeV. Peters, Robert J. McMahon, and Vernon L. Quinsey, eds., *Aggression and Violence Throughout the Life Span.* Newbury Park, CA: Sage Publications, pp 1–30.

Langer, Erick D. 1990. "Andean Rituals of Revolt: The Chayanta Rebellion of 1927," *Ethnohistory* 37, No 3 (Summer): 227–253.

Langmore, Diane, 1985. "'Exchanging Earth for Heaven': Death in the Papuan Missionfields," *Journal of Religious History* 13, No 4 (December): 383–392.

Laplanche, Jean. 1980. *La Sublimation.* Paris: Presses universitaires de France.

Lasch, Christopher. 1991. *The True and Only Heaven: Progress and Its Critics.* New York: W. W. Norton.

Lasine, Stuart. 1991. "Jehoram and the Cannibal Mothers (2 Kings 6.24–33): Solomon's Judgment in an Inverted World," *Journal for the Study of the Old Testament* 50 (June): 27–53.

Lātūkefu, Sione. 1988. "Noble Traditions and Christian Principles as National Ideology in Papua New Guinea: Do Their Philosophies Complement or Contradict Each Other?" *Pacific Studies* 11, No 2 (March): 83–96.

Lawrence, S. E. 1992. "Sexual Cannibalism in the Praying Mantid, *Mantis religiosa*: A Field Study," *Animal Behaviour* 43, No 4 (April): 569–583.

Lazzaretto, Ivana and Benedetto Salvato. 1992. "Cannibalistic Behaviour of the Harpacticoid Copepod *Tigriopus fulvus*," *Marine Biology* 113, No 4 (August): 579–582.

Le Bras, Hervé. 1985. *Population.* Paris: Hachette.

Le Mort, Françoise. 1985. "Un exemple de modification intentionnelle: La dent humaine perforée de Saint-Germain-la-Rivière," *Bulletin de la Société préhistorique française* 82, No 6: 190–192.

Le Mort, Françoise. 1988. "Cannibalisme ou rite funéraire?" [Cannibalism or Burial Rite?], *Histoire et archéologie* No 124: 46–49, 98.

Le Mort, Françoise. 1989. "Traces de décharnement sur les ossements néandertaliens de Combe-Grenal (Dordogne)," *Bulletin de la Société préhistorique française* 86, No 3: 79–87.

Leacock, Eleanor and Richard Lee, eds. 1982. *Politics and History in Band Societies.* Cambridge: Cambridge University Press.

Leakey, Richard E. and Roger Lewin. 1977. *Origins: What New Discoveries Reveal About the Emergence of Our Species and Its Possible Future.* New York: E. P. Dutton.

Leakey, Richard E. and Roger Lewin. 1979. *People of the Lake: Mankind and Its Beginnings.* New York: Doubleday & Co.

Lee, Harry B. 1939. *A Critique of the Theory of Sublimation.* [n.p.].

Leertouwer, L. 1971. "Cannibalism of the Batak," trans. G. van Baaren-Pape, *Nederlands Theologisch Tijdschrift* 25 (June): 241–260.

Lemonick, Michael D. 1996. "Sex as Suicide: Why Self-Sacrifice Makes Perfect Sense for Spiders," *Time* 147, No 3 (January 15): p 60.

Leonardsson, Kjell. 1991. "Effects of Cannibalism and Alternative Prey on Population Dynamics of *Saduria entomon* (Isopoda)," *Ecology* 72, No 4 (August): 1273–1285.

Lesser, Alexander. 1985. *History, Evolution, and the Concept of Culture: Selected Papers by Alexander Lesser*, ed. Sidney W. Mintz. Cambridge, New York: Cambridge University Press.

Lester, David. 1987. *Suicide as a Learned Behavior*. Springfield, IL: Thomas.

Levy, Jack S. 1988. "Domestic Politics and War," *Journal of Interdisciplinary History* 18, No 4 (Spring): 653–673.

Levy, Jack S. 1989. "The Causes of War: A Review of Theories and Evidence," in Philip E. Tetlock, et al., eds., *Behavior, Society, and Nuclear War*, Vol. I. Oxford: Oxford University Press, pp 209–333.

Lewellen, Ted C. 1992. *Political Anthropology: An Introduction*, 2nd ed. Westport, CT: Bergin & Garvey.

Lewis, I. M. 1986. *Religion in Context: Cults and Charisma*. Cambridge, New York: Cambridge University Press.

Liep, John. 1987. "Kannibaler og Kulier: Antropofagiske Scener fra en Sydhavso," *Stofskifte* No 15: 25–37.

Loeb, Edwin M. (Edwin Meyer). 1923. *The Blood Sacrifice Complex*. Menasha, WI: American Anthropological Association.

Loewald, Hans W. 1988. *Sublimation: Inquiries Into Theoretical Psychoanalysis*. New Haven: Yale University Press.

London Committee of the International Peace Crusade. 1899. A *scheme for the establishment of international courts or tribunals for settling disputes between states by arbitration and mediation submitted to the representatives of the powers at the Hague Peace Conference May 1899*. London: [n.p.].

Lorenz, Eckehart. 1984. *Peace: What Can We Do? International Lutheran Contributions to Peace Ethics*. Geneva: Lutheran World Federation, Department of Studies.

Lorenz, Konrad. 1967. *On Aggression*, trans. Marjorie Kerr Wilson. New York: Bantam.

Luard, Evan. 1968. *Conflict and Peace in the Modern International System*. Boston: Little, Brown.

Luard, Evan. 1982. *A History of the United Nations*. New York: St. Martin's Press.

Luard, Evan. 1986. *War in International Society: A Study in International Sociology*. New Haven: Yale University Press.

Lyman, R. Lee and Pat Shipman. 1987. "Hunting for Evidence of Plio-Pleistocene Hominid Scavengers," *American Anthropologist* 89, No 3 (September): 710–715.

Lynch, Cecelia. 1994. "Kant, the Republican Peace, and Moral Guidance in International Law," *Ethics and International Affairs* 8, No 1: 39–58.

MacAloon, John J. 1981. *This Great Symbol: Pierre de Coubertin and the Origins of the Modern Olympic Games*. Chicago: University of Chicago Press.

Maccoby, Hyam. 1982. *The Sacred Executioner: Human Sacrifice and the Legacy of Guilt*. New York: Thames and Hudson.

MacCormack, Carol P. 1983. "Human Leopards and Crocodiles: Political Meanings of Categorical Anomalies," in Paula Brown and Donald Tuzin, eds., *The Ethnography of Cannibalism*. Washington, DC: Society for Psychological Anthropology, pp 51–60.

MacMillan, John. 1998. *On Liberal Peace: Democracy, War and the International Order*. London: Tauris Academic Studies.

Macpherson, E. and A. Gordoa. 1994. "Effect of Prey Densities on Cannibalism in Cape Hake (*Merluccius capensis*) off Namibia," *Marine Biology* 119, No 1 (April): 145–149.

Maenchen, Anna. 1984. "The Handling of Overt Aggression in Child Analysis," *The Psychoanalytic Study of the Child* 39: 393–405.

Mallory, J. P. 1989. *In Search of the Indo-Europeans: Language, Archaeology and Myth*. London: Thames and Hudson.

Malville, Nancy J. 1989. "Two Fragmented Human Bone Assemblages from Yellow Jacket, Southwestern Colorado," *Kiva* 55, No 1: 3–22.

Mandell, Richard D. 1976. *The First Modern Olympics*. Berkeley: University of California Press.

Mansfield, Edward D. and Jack Snyder. 1995a. "Democratization and War," *Foreign Affairs* 74, No 3 (May–June): 79–97.

Mansfield, Edward D. and Jack Snyder. 1995b. "Democratization and the Danger of War," *International Security* 20, No 1 (Summer): 5–38.

Maoz, Zeev and Nasrin Abdolali. 1989. "Regime Types and International Conflict, 1816–1976," *Journal of Conflict Resolution* 33, No 1 (March): 3–35.

Maoz, Zeev and Bruce Russett. 1993. "Normative and Structural Causes of Democratic Peace, 1946–1986," *American Political Science Review* 87, No 3 (September): 624–638.

Marriner, Brian. 1992. *Cannibalism: The Last Taboo*. London: Arrow.

Maryanski, Alexandra and Jonathan H. Turner. 1992. *The Social Cage: Human Nature and the Evolution of Society*. Stanford: Stanford University Press, 1992.

Mattson, David J., Richard R. Knight, and Bonnie M. Blanchard. 1992. "Cannibalism and Predation on Black Bears by Grizzly Bears in the Yellowstone Ecosystem, 1975–1990," *Journal of Mammalogy* 73, No 2 (May): 422–425.

McAllister, Pam, ed. 1982. *Reweaving the Web of Life: Feminism and Nonviolence*. Philadelphia: New Society Publishers.

McGee, R. Jon. 1983. "Introduction and Appendix," in R. Jon McGee, *Sacrifice and Cannibalism: An Analysis of Myth and Ritual among the Lacandon Maya of Chiapas Mexico*, PhD Diss., Rice University.

McGuinness, Diane. 1987. *Dominance, Aggression, and War*. New York: Paragon House.

McManis, J. Allen. 1946. *"Flesh of My Brother": Or, "Kia Kia" (Flesh Eaters)*. Culver City, CA: Murray & Gee.

McNeill, William H. 1963. *The Rise of the West: A History of the Human Community*. Chicago: University of Chicago Press.

McNeill, William H. 1976. *Plagues and Peoples*. Garden City, NY: Anchor Press.

McNeill, William H. 1980. *The Human Condition: An Ecological and Historical View*. Princeton, NJ: Princeton University Press.

McNeill, William H. 1982. *The Pursuit of Power: Technology, Armed Force, and Society Since A.D. 1000*. Chicago: University of Chicago Press.

McPhee, John. 1984. *La Place de la Concorde Suisse*. New York: Farrar, Straus, Giroux.

Mearsheimer, John J. 1990. "Back to the Future: Instability in Europe after the Cold War," *International Security* 15, No 1 (Summer): 5–56

Mechling, Jay. 1984. "High Kybo Floater: Food and Feces in the Speech Play at a Boy Scout Camp," *Journal of Psychoanalytic Anthropology* 7, No 3 (Summer): 256–268.

Melbye, Jerry and Scott I. Fairgrieve. 1994. "Massacre and Possible Cannibalism in the Canadian Arctic: New Evidence from the Saunaktuk Site (NgTn-1)," *Arctic Anthropology* 31, No 2: 57–77.

Melko, Matthew. 1990. *Peace in Our Time*. New York: Paragon House.

Mennell, Stephen. 1989. *Norbert Elias: Civilization and the Human Self-Image*. Oxford: Basil Blackwell.

Menninger, Annerose. 1995. *Die Macht der Augenzeugen: Neue Welt und Kannibalen Mythos, 1492–1600*. Stuttgart: F. Steiner.

Messner, Steven F., Marvin D. Krohn, and Allen E. Liska. 1989. *Theoretical Integration in the Study of Deviance and Crime: Problems and Prospects*. Albany: State University of New York Press.

Miller, Benjamin. 1995. *When Opponents Cooperate: Great Power Conflict and Collaboration in World Politics*. Ann Arbor: University of Michigan Press.

Miller, Joseph Calder. 1985. *Slavery: A Worldwide Bibliography, 1900–1982*. White Plains, NY: Kraus International.

Millis, Walter, Reinhold Niebuhr, Harrison Brown, James Real, and William O Douglas. 1961. *A World Without War*. New York: Washington Square Press [A reprint of material originally published by the Center for the Study of Democratic Institutions].

Mimica, Jadran. 1991. "The Incest Passions: An Outline of the Logic of the Iqwaya Social Organization," *Oceania* 62, No 2 (December): 81–113.

Mock, Douglas. 1992. "Dining Respectably: Review of *Cannibalism: Ecology and Evolution among Diverse Taxa*, Mark A. Elgar and Bernard J. Crespi, eds." *Science* 258, No 5090 (December 18): 1969–1970.

Molet, Louis. 1956. *Le Bain Royal à Madagascar: Explication De La Fête Malgache Du Fandroana Par La Coutume Disparue De La Manducation Des Morts*. Tananarive: Impr. luthérienne.

Møller, Bjørn. 1987–. *Non-offensive Defense [irregular series]*. Copenhagen: Institute for Peace Research.

Montaigne, Michel de. 1931. *Essays*, trans. John Florio, ed. J. I. M. Stewart. London: Nonesuch Press.

Moore, Barrington. 1978. *Injustice: The Social Bases of Obedience and Revolt*. Armonk, NY: M. E. Sharpe.

Morgan, David. 1986. *The Mongols*. Oxford: Basil Blackwell.

Morgan, Robert. 1991. "A Response to John Fenton," *Theology* 94, No 762 (November): 423–425.

Morren, George B., Jr. 1984. "Warfare on the Highland Fringe of New Guinea, or the Case of the Mountain Ok," in R. Brian Ferguson, ed., *Warfare, Culture, and Environment*. Orlando, FL: Academic Press, pp 169–207.

Morris, Desmond. 1991. "A Taste for Their Own Kind," *National Wildlife* 29, No 4 (June–July): 14–16.

Morris, John, ed. and trans. 1975. *Domesday Book*. Chichester: Phillimore.

Moscati, Sabatino. 1987. *Il Sacrificio Punico dei Fanciulli, Realtà o Invenzione? Relazione Svolta Nella Seduta del 14 Febbraio 1987*. Rome: Accademia nazionale dei Lincei.

Moyer, Kenneth E. 1976. *The Psychobiology of Aggression*. New York: Harper & Row.

Moyer, Kenneth E. 1987. *Violence and Aggression: A Physiological Perspective*. New York: Paragon House.

Mueller, John E. 1989. *Retreat from Doomsday: The Obsolescence of Major War*. New York: Basic Books.

Munroe, Robert L. and Ruth H. Munroe. 1977. *Cross-Cultural Human Development*. New York: J. Aronson.

Murdock, George Peter. 1967. *Ethnographic Atlas*. Pittsburgh: University of Pittsburgh Press.

Murdock, George Peter. 1981. *Atlas of World Cultures*. Pittsburgh: University of Pittsburgh Press.

Murdock, George Peter and Douglas R. White. 1969. "Standard Cross-Cultural Sample." *Ethnology* 9, no 4 (October): 329–369 (2006 on-line edition at http://repositories.cdlib.org/imbs/socdyn/wp/Standard_Cross-Cultural_Sample).

Myers, A. R. (Alec Reginald). 1975. *Parliaments and Estates in Europe to 1789.* London: Thames and Hudson.

Nájera, Martha Ilia. 1987. *El Don de la Sangre en el Equilibrio Cósmico: El Sacrificio y el Autosacrificio Sangriento Entre los Antiguos Mayas.* México, D.F.: Universidad Nacional Autónoma de México, Instituto de Investigaciones Filológicas, Centro de Estudios Mayas.

Nam, Charles B., ed. 1968. *Population and Society: A Textbook of Readings.* Boston: Houghton Mifflin.

National Conference of Catholic Bishops. 1983. *The Challenge of Peace: God's Promise and our Response: A Pastoral Letter on War and Peace: May 3, 1983.* Washington, DC: Office of Publishing Services, United States Catholic Conference.

Neary, Ian. 1989. *Political Protest and Social Control in Pre-War Japan: The Origins of Buraku Liberation.* Atlantic Highlands, NJ: Humanities Press International.

Netting, Robert McC. 1990. "Population, Permanent Agriculture, and Polities: Unpacking the Evolutionary Portmanteau," in Steadman Upham, ed., *The Evolution of Political Systems: Sociopolitics in Small-Scale Sedentary Societies.* Cambridge, New York: Cambridge University Press, pp 21–61.

Newman, Jonathan A. and Mark A. Elgar. 1991. "Sexual Cannibalism in Orb-Weaving Spiders: An Economic Model," *American Naturalist* 138, No 6 (December): 1372–1395.

Nichols, Bruce. 1987. "Rubberband Humanitarianism," *Ethics and International Affairs* 1, No 1: 191–210.

Nicolaïdis, Graziella and Nicos Nicolaïdis. 1993. "Incorporation, pédophilie, inceste," *Revue Française de Psychanalyse* 57, No 2 (April–June): 507–514.

Nishida, Toshisada and Kenji Kawanaka. 1985. "Within-Group Cannibalism by Adult Male Chimpanzees," *Primates* 26, No 3 (July): 274–284.

Noel-Baker, Philip. 1958. *The Arms Race: A Programme for World Disarmament.* London: J. Calder; New York: Oceana Publications.

Noel-Baker, Philip. 1979. *The First World Disarmament Conference 1932–1933 and Why It Failed.* New York: Pergamon Press.

Nolte, Hans-Heinrich and Wilhelm Nolte. 1984. *Ziviler Widerstand und autonome Abwehr* [Civilian Resistance and Autonomous Defense]. Baden-Baden: Nomos.

Oates, Stephen B. 1982. *Let the Trumpet Sound: The Life of Martin Luther King, Jr.* New York: Harper & Row.

Obeyesekere, Gananath. 1992. "'British Cannibals': Contemplation of an Event in the Death and Resurrection of James Cook, Explorer," *Critical Inquiry* 18, No 4 (Summer): 630–654.

Omnes, J. 1989. "Traces de décarnisation sur rachis humains, au Chalcolithique, dans la grotte d'Artigaou a Esparros (Hautes-Pyrénées)," *Bulletin de la Société préhistorique française* 86, No 2: 35–36.

Onuf, Nicholas Greenwood. 1989. *World of Our Making: Rules and Rule in Social Theory and International Relations.* Columbia, SC: University of South Carolina Press.

Orr, Bruce K., William W. Murdoch, and James R. Bence. 1990. "Population Regulation, Convergence, and Cannibalism in *Notonecta* (Hemiptera)," *Ecology* 71, No 1 (February): 68–82.

Overbeek, Johannes. 1976. *The Population Challenge: A Handbook for Nonspecialists.* Westport, CT: Greenwood Press.

Overing, Joanna. 1986. "Images of Cannibalism, Death and Domination in a Non-violent Society," in David Riches, ed., *The Anthropology of Violence*. Oxford, New York: Blackwell.

Overmyer, Daniel L. 1994. "Review *Cannibalism in China* by Key Ray Chong," *Pacific Affairs* 67, No 3 (Autumn): 483.

Palencia-Roth, Michael. 1993. "Cannibal Law of 1503," in Jerry M. Williams and Robert E. Lewis, eds., *Early Images of the Americas: Transfer and Invention*. Tucson: University of Arizona Press, pp 21–63.

Pallone, Nathaniel J. and James Hennessy. 1996. *Tinder-Box Criminal Aggression: Neuropsychology, Demography, Phenomenology*. New Brunswick, NJ: Transaction Publishers.

Patnaik, Nihar Ranjan. 1989. *Social History of 19th Century Orissa*. Allahabad: Vohra Pub. and Distributors.

Pauling, Linus. 1958. *No More War!* New York: Dodd, Mead.

Pedersen, Kennet. 1987. "Ist der Mensch was er ißt? En historisk moralitet, der ogsa er en moralsk historie, med udgangspunkt i Jean de Lerys. En rejse gjort til Brasiliens land fra 1578," *Stofskifte* No 15: 87–120.

Penn, William. 1693. *Essay towards the Present and Future Peace of Europe*.

Perrigault, Jean. 1932. *L'Enfer des Noirs: Cannibalisme et fétichisme fans la Brousse*. Paris: Nouvelle librairie francaise.

Peter-Rocher, Heidi. 1994. *Kannibalismus in der prähistorischen Forschung: studien zu einer paradigmatischen Deutung und ihren Grundlagen*. Bonn: in Kommission bei Dr. Rudolf Habelt.

Peters, Ray DeV., Robert J. McMahon, and Vernon L. Quinsey. 1992. *Aggression and Violence Throughout the Life Span*. Newbury Park, CA: Sage Publications.

Petersen, Christopher W. and Karen Marchetti. 1989. "Filial Cannibalism in the Cortez Damselfish *Stegastes rectifraenum*," *Evolution* 43, No 1 (January): 158–168.

Petranka, James W. and Daphne A. G. Thomas. 1995. "Explosive breeding reduces egg and tadpole cannibalism in wood frog, *Rana sylvatica*," *Animal Behaviour* 50, No 3 (September): 731–739.

Pfennig, David W. and James P. Collins. 1993. "Kinship affects morphogenesis in cannibalistic salamanders," *Nature* 362, No 6423 (April 29): 836–838.

Pfennig, David W., Hudson K. Reeve, and Paul W. Sherman. 1993. "Kin recognition and cannibalism in spadefoot toad tadpoles," *Animal Behaviour* 46, No 1 (July): 87–94.

Piaget, Jean. 1965. *The Moral Judgment of the Child*, trans. Marjorie Gabain. New York: MacMillan Free Press.

Piaget, Jean and Bärbel Inhelder. 1969. *The Psychology of the Child*, trans. Helen Weaver. New York: Basic Books.

Pickering, Michael P. 1988. "Food for Thought: An Alternative to 'Cannibalism in the Neolithic'," *Artefact* 12, 1987–1988, pp 17–24.

Pilette, Marie-Laure. 1990. "Des cannibales accoucheurs à l'oncle qui voulait manger en copulant: Petite histoire de famille sénéca," *Culture* 10, No 2: 25–37.

Pilette, Marie-Laure. 1993. "Oeuvre de chair: la petite histoire du pie mangeur d'hommes," *Anthropologica* 35, No 1: 39–57.

Pineda Camacho, Roberto. 1987. "Malocas de terror y jaguares españoles: aspectos de la resistencia indígena del Cauca ante la invasión española en el siglo XVI," *Revista de Antropologia*, Universidad de los Andes 3, No 2: 83–114.

Plucknett, Theodore F. T. 1960. *Taswell-Langmead's English Constitutional History: From the Teutonic Conquest to the Present Time*. London: Sweet & Maxwell.

Polgar, Steven, ed. 1975. *Population, Ecology, and Social Evolution*. The Hague: Mouton.

Pomerance, Michla. 1973. *The Advisory Function of the International Court in the League and U.N. Eras*. Baltimore: Johns Hopkins University Press.

Poole, Austin Lane. 1955. *From Domesday Book to Magna Carta, 1087–1216*, 2nd ed. Oxford: Clarendon Press.

Poole, Fitzjohn Porter. 1983. "Cannibals, Tricksters, and Witches: Anthropophagic Images among Bimin-Kuskusmin," in Paula Brown and Donald Tuzin, eds., *The Ethnography of Cannibalism*. Washington, DC: Society for Psychological Anthropology, pp 6–32.

Porret, Jean-Michel. 1994. *La consignation du sublimable: les deux théories freudiennes du processus de sublimation et sotions limitrophes*. Paris: Presses universitaires de France.

Potegal, Michael and John F. Knutson, eds. 1994. *The Dynamics of Aggression: Biological and Social Processes in Dyads and Groups*. Hillsdale, NJ: L. Erlbaum.

Powers, Roger S., William B. Vogele, eds. Christopher Kruegler and Ronald M. McCarthy, assoc. ed. 1997. *Protest, Power, and Change: An Encyclopedia of Nonviolent Action From ACT-UP to Women's Suffrage*. New York: Garland.

Quigley, Carroll. 1979. *The Evolution of Civilizations: An Introduction to Historical Analysis*, 2nd ed. Indianapolis: Liberty Press.

Ramírez, Jesús Martín, Robert A. Hinde, and Jo Groebel. 1987. *Essays on Violence*. Sevilla [Spain]: Publicaciones de la Universidad de Sevilla.

Ray, James Lee. 1995. *Democracy and International Conflict: An Evaluation of the Democratic Peace Proposition*. Columbia, SC: University of South Carolina Press.

Redfield, Robert. 1953. *The Primitive World and Its Transformations*. Ithaca, NY: Cornell University Press.

Reid, Escott. 1983. *On Duty: A Canadian at the Making of the United Nations 1945–1946*. Kent, OH: Kent State University Press.

Reischauer, Edwin O. 1981a. *The Japanese*. Cambridge MA: Belknap/Harvard University Press.

Reischauer, Edwin O. 1981b. *Japan: The Story of a Nation*, 3rd ed. New York: Knopf.

Renfrew, John W. 1997. *Aggression and Its Causes: A Biopsychosocial Approach*. Oxford, New York: Oxford University Press.

Ribichini, Sergio. 1987. *Il Tofet e il Sacrificio dei Fanciulli*. Sassari: Chiarella.

Riches, David. 1986. "The Phenomenon of Violence," in David Riches, ed., *The Anthropology of Violence*. Oxford, New York: Blackwell.

Riedel, Marc. 1993. *Stranger Violence: A Theoretical Inquiry*. New York: Garland Pub.

Rightmire, G. Philip. 1991. "The Dispersal of *Homo erectus* from Africa and the Emergence of More Modem Humans," *Journal of Anthropological Research* 47, No 2 (Summer): 177–191.

Rightmire, G. Philip. 1993. "Variation Among Early *Homo* Crania from Olduvai Gorge and the Koobi Fora Region," *American Journal of Physical Anthropology* 90, No 1 (January): 1–33.

Rivière, P. G. 1980. "Review of W. Arens, *The Man-eating Myth*," *Man* 15, No 1 (March): 203–205.

Roberts, Adam. 1986. *Nations in Arms: The Theory and Practice of Territorial Defence*, 2nd (rev. and enl.) ed. New York: St. Martin's Press.

Robinson, Conway. 1882. *History of the High Court of Chancery and Other Institutions of England, From the Time of Caius Julius Caesar Until the Accession of William and Mary (in 1688–9)*. Richmond, VA: J. W. Randolph & English.

Rochester, J. Martin. 1993. *Waiting for the Millennium: The United Nations and the Future of World Order*. Columbia, SC: University of South Carolina Press.

Rockman, Jane, ed. 1979. *Peace in Search of Makers: Riverside Church Reverse the Arms Race Convocation (4–5 December 1978)*. Valley Forge, PA: Judson Press.

Róheim, Géza. 1948. *Psychoanalysis and Anthropology: Culture, Personality and the Unconscious*. New York: International Universities Press (2nd printing, 1968).

Ross, Sonja Brigitte. 1989. *Das Menschenopfer der Skidi-Pawnee*. Bonn: In Kommission bei Holos.

Rossi, Ino. 1974. *The Unconscious in Culture: The Structuralism of Claude Lévi-Strauss in Perspective*. New York: Dutton.

Rotberg, Robert I. and Theodore K. Rabb, eds. 1989. *The Origin and Prevention of Major Wars*. Cambridge: Cambridge University Press.

Rothstein, Arnold. 1991. *The Moscow Lectures on Psychoanalysis*. Madison, CT: International Universities Press.

Rouse, Irving. 1972. *Introduction to Prehistory: A Systematic Approach*. New York: McGraw-Hill.

Rousseau, Jean-Jacques. 1987. *The Basic Political Writings*, ed. and trans. Donald A. Cress. Indianapolis: Hackett Publishing.

Rousseau, Jean-Jacques. 1988. *Rousseau's Political Writings: Discourse on Inequality, Discourse on Political Economy, On Social Contract*, ed. Alan Ritter and Julia Conaway Bondanella, trans. Julia Conaway Bondanella. New York: W. W. Norton.

Rummel, R. J. 1983. "Libertarianism and International Violence," *Journal of Conflict Resolution* 27, No 1 (March): 27–71.

Russell, Bertrand. 1967–69. *The Autobiography of Bertrand Russell*. New York: Simon and Schuster.

Russell, Mary D. 1987a. "Bone Breakage in the Krapina Hominid Collection," *American Journal of Physical Anthropology* 72, No 3 (March): 373–379.

Russell, Mary D. 1987b. "Mortuary Practices at the Krapina Neandertal Site," *American Journal of Physical Anthropology* 72, No 3 (March): 381–397.

Russell, Ruth B. 1958. *A History of the United Nations Charter: The Role of the United States 1940–1945*. Washington, DC: Brookings Institution.

Russett, Bruce. 1990a. "Politics and Alternative Security: Toward a More Democratic, Therefore More Peaceful, World," in Burns H. Weston, ed., *Alternative Security: Living Without Nuclear Deterrence*. Boulder, CO: Westview Press, pp 107–136.

Russett, Bruce. 1990b. *Controlling the Sword: The Democratic Governance of National Security*. Cambridge, MA: Harvard University Press.

Russett, Bruce. 1995, 1993. *Grasping the Democratic Peace: Principles for a Post-Cold War World*. Princeton, NJ: Princeton University Press.

Russett, Bruce and William Antholis. 1992. "Do Democracies Fight Each Other? Evidence from the Pelopeonnesian War," *Journal of Peace Research* 29, No 4 (November): 415–434.

Russett, Bruce, Christopher Layne, David E. Spiro, and Michael W. Doyle. 1995. "Correspondence: The Democratic Peace," *International Security* 19, No 4 (Spring): 164–184.

Ryan, Alan. 1988. *Bertrand Russell: A Political Life*. New York: Hill and Wang.

Sagan, Eli. 1974. *Cannibalism: Human Aggression and Cultural Form*. New York: Harper & Row.

Sahlins, Marshall David. 1978. "Culture as Protein and Profit," review of *Cannibals and Kings* by Marvin Harris, *New York Review of Books* 25, No 18 (November 23): 45–52.

Sahlins, Marshall David, Elman Rogers Service, and Thomas G. Harding. 1960. *Evolution and Culture*. Ann Arbor: University of Michigan Press.

Saignes, Thierry. 1985. "La Guerre Contre l'Histoire," *Journal de la Société des Américanistes* 71: 175–190.

Sandars, N. K. 1985. *The Sea Peoples: Warriors of the Ancient Mediterranean 1250–1150 BC.* New York: Thames & Hudson.

Sanday, Peggy Reeves. 1981. *Female Power and Male Dominance: On the Origins of Sexual Inequality.* Cambridge, New York: Cambridge University Press.

Sanday, Peggy Reeves. 1986. *Divine Hunger: Cannibalism as a Cultural System.* Cambridge, New York: Cambridge University Press.

Sanday, Peggy Reeves. 1988a. "Response to Abler," *American Anthropologist* 90, No 4 (December): 969–970.

Sanday, Peggy Reeves. 1988b. "Toward Thick Comparison and a Theory of Self-Awareness," *Behavior Science Research* 22, No 1–4 (February): 82–96.

Sandler, Joseph, Ethel Spector Person, and Peter Fonagy, eds. 1991. *Freud's "On Narcissism: An Introduction."* New Haven: Yale University Press.

Sapir, Edward, William Bright, and Victor Golla. 1900–1991. *American Indian Languages.* Berlin, New York: Mouton de Gruyter.

Sartore, Richard L. 1994. *Humans Eating Humans: The Dark Shadow of Cannibalism.* Notre Dame, IN: Cross Cultural Publications.

Sasaki, Takeshi and Osamu Iwahashi. 1995. "Sexual cannibalism in an orb-weaving spider *Argiope aemula*," *Animal Behaviour* 49, No 4 (April): 1119–1121.

Sawyer, Roger. 1986. *Slavery in the Twentieth Century.* London, New York: Routledge & Kegan Paul.

Schell, Jonathan. 1982. *The Fate of the Earth.* New York: Alfred A. Knopf.

Schell, Jonathan. 1984. *The Abolition.* New York: Alfred A. Knopf.

Schoch, Alfred. 1954. *Rituelle Menschentötungen in Polynesien. Ein Beitrag zur Frage der Menschenopfer unter Berücksichtigung der kulturellen, soziologischen und wirtschftlichen Struktur dieser unter dem ethnologischen Sammelbegriff "polynesische Kultur" zusammengefassten Bevölkerungsgruppe auf den Inseln der Südsee.* Ulm (Donau): [n.p.].

Schoenly, Kenneth, R. A. Beaver, and T. A. Heurnier. 1991. "On the Trophic Relations of Insects: A Food-Web Approach," *American Naturalist* 137, No 5 (May): 597–638.

Schöppl von Sonnwalden, Herman. 1992. *Kannibalismus bei den nordamerikanischen Indianern und Eskimo* [Cannibalism Among the North American Indians and Eskimos]. Wyk auf Föhr: Verlag für Amerikanistik.

Schücking, Walther. 1912–1917. *Das Werk vom Haag.* Munich: Duncker & Humblot.

Schweitzer, Albert. 1899. *Die Religionsphilosophie Kants von der Kritik der reinen Vernunft bis zur Religion innerhalb der Grenzen der blossen Vernunft.* Freiburg: J. C. B. Mohr.

Schweitzer, Albert. 1923. *The Decay and Restoration of Civilization* [Verfall und Wiederaufbau der Kultur] [and] *Civilization and Ethics* [Kultur und Ethik]. London: A & C Black and Munich: Beck.

Schweitzer, Albert. 1949. *The Philosophy of Civilization*, trans. Charles T. Campion. New York: Macmillan Co.

Schwenn, Friedrich. 1915. *Die Menschenopfer bei den Griechen und Romern.* Giessen: A. Töpelmann.

Scot, A. F. [pseud. for Alexander H. Japp]. 1899. *Offering and Sacrifice: An Essay in Comparative Customs and Religious Development.* London: Thomas Burleigh.

Scott, James Brown, ed. 1908. *Texts of the peace conferences at the Hague, 1899 and 1907, with English translation and appendix of related documents.* Boston, London: Ginn & Co., published for the International School of Peace.

Scott, James Brown. 1909. *The Hague Peace Conferences of 1899 and 1907: A series of lectures delivered before the Johns Hopkins University in the year of 1908.* Baltimore: Johns Hopkins Press.

Sebeok, Thomas Albert, ed. 1976. *Native Languages of the Americas.* New York: Plenum Press.

Seibt, Uta and Wolfgang Wickler. 1987. "Gerontophagy versus cannibalism in the social spiders *Stegodyphus mimosarum* Pavesi and *Stegodyphus dumicola* Pocock," *Animal Behaviour* 35, No 6 (December): 1903–1905.

Serrano Sanchez, Carlos. 1994. "Funerary Practices and Human Sacrifice in Teothihuacan Burials," in Kathleen Berrin, Esther Pasztory, and Fine Arts Museums of San Francisco, *Teotihuacan: Art from the City of the Gods.* New York: Thames and Hudson, pp 108–115.

Service, Elman R. 1971a. *Cultural Evolutionism: Theory in Practice.* New York: Holt, Rinehart and Winston.

Service, Elman R. 1971b. *Primitive Social Organization: An Evolutionary Perspective,* 2nd ed. New York: Random House.

Service, Elman R. 1971c. *Profiles in Ethnology,* rev. ed. New York: Harper & Row.

Sharp, Gene. 1973. *The Politics of Nonviolent Action* (3 vols). Boston: Porter Sargent.

Sharp, Gene. 1979. *Gandhi as a Political Strategist, with Essays on Ethics and Politics.* Boston: Porter Sargent.

Sharp, Gene. 1980. *Social Power and Political Freedom.* Boston: Porter Sargent.

Sharp, Gene. 1985. *Making Europe Unconquerable: The Potential of Civilian-Based Deterrence and Defense.* Cambridge, MA: Ballinger Publishing Co.

Sharp, Gene and Bruce Jenkins. 1990. *Civilian-Based Defense: A Post-Military Weapons System.* Princeton, NJ: Princeton University Press.

Sherratt, Thomas N. and Stuart C. Church. 1994. "Ovipositional preferences and larval cannibalism in the Neotropical mosquito *Trichoprosopon digitatum*," *Animal Behaviour* 48, No 3 (September): 645–652.

Sherzer, Joel. 1976. *An Areal-Typological Study of American Indian Languages North of Mexico.* Amsterdam: North-Holland Pub. Co.; New York: American Elsevier Pub. Co. (distributors in USA and Canada).

Shipman, Pat. 1994. "Review of *Prehistoric Cannibalism at Mancos 5MTUMR-2346* by Tim D. White," *American Scientist* 82, No 4 (July–August): 387.

Shoham, S. Giora, J. J. M. Ashkenasy, G. Rahav, F. Chard, A. Addi, and M. Addad. 1995. *Violence: An Integrated Multivariate Study of Human Aggression.* Aldershot [England], Brookfield, VT: Dartmouth Pub.

Sicoli, F. M. and A. Tartabini. 1994. "Amerindian Cannibalism: Practice and Discursive Strategy," *Human Evolution* 9, No 3 (January): 249–255.

Sikkel, Paul C. 1994. "Filial cannibalism in a paternal-caring marine fish: the influence of egg developmental stage and position in the nest," *Animal Behaviour* 47, No 5 (May): 1149–1158.

Silverberg, James and J. Patrick Gray, eds. 1992. *Aggression and Peacefulness in Humans and Other Primates.* Oxford, New York: Oxford University Press.

Siran, Jean-Louis. 1989. "Pourquoi les filles mangent-elles leur mère?" *L'Homme,* 29 no 111–112 (July–December): 237–244.

Sjørslev, Inger. 1987. "At aede eller blive aedt: kannibalismemetaforer og Brasiliens karakterlose helt," *Stofskifte* No 15: 7–23.

Small, Melvin and J. David Singer. 1976. "The War-Proneness of Democratic Regimes 1816–1965," *Jerusalem Journal of International Relations* 1, No 4 (Summer): 50–69.

Smith, J. M. Powis, Edgar J. Goodspeed, and Theophile James Meek. 1939. *The Complete Bible: An American Translation.* Chicago: University of Chicago Press.

Smith, Tony. 1994. "Winning the Peace: Postwar Thinking and the Defeated Confederacy," *World Policy Journal* 11, No 2 (Summer): 92–102.

Smoke, Richard. A. 1990. *Theory of Mutual Security*. Providence, RI: Brown University Center for Foreign Policy Development.

Smoke, Richard, and Willis W. Harman. 1987. *Paths to Peace: Exploring the Feasibility of Sustainable Peace*. Boulder, CO: Westview Press.

Sørensen, Georg. 1992. "Kant and Processes of Democratization: Consequences for Neorealist Thought," *Journal of Peace Research* 29, No 4 (November): 397–414.

Spain, David H., et al. 1988. "Incest Theory: Are There Three Aversions?" *Journal of Psychohistory* (incorporating the *Journal of Psychoanalytic Anthropology*) 15, No 3 (Winter): 235–280.

Spennemann, Dirk H. R. 1987. "Cannibalism in Fiji: The Analysis of Butchering Marks on Human Bones and the Historical Record with an Appendix on Experimental Butchering with Bamboo Blades," *Domodomo: Fiji Museum Quarterly* 5, Nos 1&2: 29–46.

Spiegelman, Mortimer. 1968. *Introduction to Demography*. Cambridge, MA: Harvard University Press.

Spiro, David E. 1994. "The Insignificance of the Liberal Peace," *International Security* 19, No 2 (Fall): 50–86.

Springer, James W. 1980. "Review of *The Man-eating Myth: Anthropology and Anthropophagy* by William E. Arens," *Anthropological Quarterly* 53, No 2 (April): 148–150.

Sprod, Dan. 1977. *Alexander Pearce of Macquarie Harbour: Convict—Bushranger—Cannibal*. Hobart: Cat & Fiddle Press.

Starke, J. G. 1968. *An Introduction to the Science of Peace (Irenology)*. Leyden: A. W. Sijthoff.

Starr, Harvey. 1992. "Democracy and War: Choice, Learning and Security Communities," *Journal of Peace Research* 29, No 2 (May): 207–213.

Stassen, Glen H. 1992. *Just Peacemaking: Transforming Initiatives for Justice and Peace*. Louisville, KY: Westminster/John Knox Press.

Stead, W. T. 1899. *The United States of Europe on the Eve of the Parliament of Peace*. New York: Doubleday & McClure Co.

Steadman, Lyle and Charles F. Merbs. 1982. "Review: Kuru and Cannibalism?" *American Anthropologist* 84, No 3 (September): 611–627.

Steinfeld, Robert J. 1991. *The Invention of Free Labor: The Employment Relation in English and American Law and Culture, 1350–1870*. Chapel Hill: University of North Carolina Press.

Stenton, Lady Doris Mary Parsons. 1951. *English Society in the Early Middle Ages, 1066–1307*. Harmondsworth [England]: Penguin Books.

Sterba, Richard F. and Herman Daldin. 1987. *Richard Sterba: The Collected Papers*. Croton-on-Hudson, NY: North River Press.

Stevens, Anthony. 1993. *The Two Million-Year-Old Self*. College Station: Texas A&M University Press.

Steward, Julian Haynes, ed. 1946–1959. *Handbook of South American Indians. Prepared in Cooperation With the U.S. Department of State as a Project of the Interdepartmental Committee on Cultural and Scientific Cooperation*. Washington, DC: US Government Printing Office.

Steward, Julian Haynes. 1955. *Theory of Culture Change: The Methodology of Multilinear Evolution*. Urbana: University of Illinois Press.

Steward, Julian Haynes. 1977. *Evolution and Ecology: Essays on Social Transformation*. Urbana: University of Illinois Press.

Stiner, Mary C. 1991. "The Faunal Remains from Grotta Guattari: A Taphonomic Perspective," *Current Anthropology* 32, No 2 (April): 103–117.

Stockwell, Edward G. and H. Theodore Groat. 1984. *World Population: An Introduction to Demography.* New York: F. Watts.

Stoff, David M. and Robert B. Cairns, eds. 1996. *Aggression and Violence: Genetic, Neurobiological, and Biosocial Perspectives.* Mahwah, NJ: L. Erlbaum Associates.

Stone, Judith. 1992. "The days of swine and roses," *Discover* 13, No 9 (September): 102–104.

Stonier, T. T. 1976. *The Natural History of Humanity: Past, Present and Future: an inaugural lecture delivered at the University of Bradford on 17 February 1976.* Bradford, UK: University of Bradford, 17 February.

Strack, Hermann Leberecht. 1909. *The Jew and Human Sacrifice: Human Blood and Jewish Ritual, an Historical and Sociological Inquiry, trans. from the 8th edition by Henry Blanchamp with corrections and additions by the author.* London: Cope and Fenwick.

Strathern, Andrew, 1982. "Witchcraft, Greed, Cannibalism and Death: Some Related Themes from the New Guinea Highlands," in Maurice Bloch and Jonathan Parry, eds., *Death and the Regeneration of Life.* Cambridge, New York: Cambridge University Press, pp 111–133.

Studiengruppe Alternative Sicherheitspolitik. 1984. *Strukturwandel der Verteidigung: Entwürfe für eine konsequente Defensive.* Opladen: Westdeutscher Verlag.

Stutchbury, Elizabeth. 1982. *Women in India and Nepal.* Canberra: Australian National University.

Suter, Keith D. 1984. *The Australian Campaign for a Ministry for Peace.* Chatswood, NSW: United Nations Association of Australia.

Suter, Keith D. 1985. *Peaceworking: The United Nations and Disarmament.* Sydney: United Nations Association of Australia.

Sutton, Donald S. 1995. "Consuming Counterrevolution: The Ritual and Culture of Cannibalism in Wuxuan, Guangxi, China, May to July 1968," *Comparative Studies in Society and History* 37, No 1 (January): 136–172.

Swanton, John Reed. 1952. *The Indian Tribes of North America.* Washington, DC: US Government Printing Office.

Tafoya, Terry. 1981. "Dancing with Dash-Kayah: The Mask of the Cannibal Woman," *Parabola* 6, No 3 (Summer): 6–11.

Tannahill, Reay. 1975. *Flesh and Blood: A History of the Cannibal Complex.* New York: Stein and Day.

Tartabini, Angelo. 1991. "Mother-Infant Cannibalism in Thick-Tailed Bushbabies (*Galago crassicaudatus umbrosus*)," *Primates* 32, No 3 (July): 379–383.

Taswell-Langmead, Thomas Pitt and Theodore F. T. Plucknett. 1960. *English Constitutional History, From the Teutonic Conquest to the Present Time,* 11th ed. London: Sweet & Maxwell.

Taube, Baron Mikhail Aleksandrovich, Russian ambassador to the Hague Conference of 1907. N.d. Collected papers of Baron Mikhail Aleksandrovich Taube. Bakhmeteff Archive of Russian and East European History and Culture, Columbia University Library, New York, NY.

Taylor, William Sentman. 1933. *A Critique of Sublimation in Males: A Study of Forty Superior Single Men.* Worcester, MA: Clark University.

Tedeschi, James T. and Richard B. Felson. 1994. *Violence, Aggression and Coercive Actions.* Washington, DC: American Psychological Association; Hyattsville, MD.

Teicher, Morton I. and American Ethnological Society. 1960. *Windigo Psychosis: A Study of a Relationship Between Belief and Behavior Among the Indians of Northeastern Canada*. Seattle: American Ethnological Society.

ter Meulen, Jacob. 1990. "Bibliography of the Peace Movement Before 1899," in Peter Van den Dungen, ed., *From Erasmus to Tolstoy: The Peace Literature of Four Centuries: Jacob ter Meulen's Bibliographies of the Peace Movement before 1899*. New York: Greenwood Press.

Thomas, Louis V. 1980. "La Mort et ses issues," *Archives de Sciences Sociales des Religions* 25, No 49.2 (April-June):179–200.

Thompson, Kenneth. 1990. "Peace Studies: Social Movement or Intellectual Discipline?" *Ethics and International Affairs* 4, No 1, 163–174.

Thompson, William R. 1996. "Democracy and Peace: Putting the Cart Before the Horse?" *International Organization* 50, No 1 (Winter): 141–174.

Thomsen, C. W. 1983. *Menschenfresser in der Kunst und Literatur, in fernen Ländern, Mythen, Märchen und Satiren, in Dramen, Liedern, Epen und Romanen: eine kannibalische Text-Bild-Dokumentation Mit 123 Abbildungen* [Cannibalism in Art and Literature, in Foreign Lands, Myths, Fairy Tales and Satire, in Theater, Song, Epic and Fiction: A Word-Picture Documentation of Cannibalism with 123 Illustrations]. Vienna: Christian Brändstatter.

Thwaites, Reuben Gold, ed. 1896–1901. *The Jesuit Relations and Allied Documents: Travels and Explorations of the Jesuit Missionaries in New France, 1610–1791; the original French, Latin, and Italian texts, with English Translations and Notes*. Cleveland : Burrows Bros. Co.

Tickner, J Ann. 1992. *Gender in International Relations: Feminist Perspectives on Achieving Global Security*. New York: Columbia University Press.

Tierney, Patrick. 1989. *The Highest Altar: The Story of Human Sacrifice*. New York: Viking.

Timson, John. 1990. "Cannibal snails are more likely to reach maturity," *New Scientist* 128, No 1740 (October 27): 22.

Tolstoy, Leo. 1899. *Stop and Think!: also A Letter on the Peace Conference*, trans. E. J. W. Warren and Aylmer Maude, respectively. London: Brotherhood Publishing Co.

Toynbee, Arnold and Albert Vann Fowler. 1950. *War and Civilization*. New York: Oxford University Press.

Trinkaus, Erik. 1985. "Cannibalism and Burial at Krapina," *Journal of Human Evolution* 14, No 2 (February): 203–216.

Troĭnitskiĭ, A. (Aleksandr) 1982. *The Serf Population in Russia, According to the 10th National Census: A Statistical Study*, trans. Elaine Herman. Newtonville, MA: Oriental Research Partners.

Trumbull, H. Clay. 1898. *The Blood Covenant: A Primitive Rite and Its Bearing on Scripture*, 3rd ed. Philadelphia: J. D. Wattles 1898.

Tryon, James L. 1910. *The Peace Movement and the Hague*. Boston: Graduate Department of the Boston University.

Turner, Christy G., II. 1983. "Taphonomic Reconstructions of Human Violence and Cannibalism Based on Mass Burials in the American Southwest," in G. LeMoine and A. MacEachem, eds, *Carnivores, Human Scavengers and Predators: A Question of Bone Technology, Proceedings of the 15th Annual Conference, Archaeological Association of the University of Calgary*. Calgary, No 5: pp 219–240.

Turner, Christy G., II. 1989. "Teec Nos Pos: More Possible Cannibalism in Northeastern Arizona," *Kiva* 54, No 2: 147–152.

Turner, Christy G., II. 1993. "Cannibalism in Chaco Canyon: The Charnel Pit Excavated in 1926 at Small House Ruin by Frank H. H. Roberts, Jr.," *American Journal of Physical Anthropology* 91, No 4 (August): 421–439.

Turner, Christy G, II, Roger C. Green, and Jacqueline A. Turner. 1993. "Taphonomic Analysis of Anasazi Skeletal Remains from Largo-Gallina Sites in Northwestern New Mexico," *Journal of Anthropological Research* 49, No 2 (Summer): 83–110.

Turner, Christy G., II and Jacqueline A. Turner. 1992a. "The First Claim for Cannibalism in the Southwest: Walter Hough's 1901 discovery at Canyon Butte Ruin 3, Northeastern Arizona," *American Antiquity* 57, No 4 (October): 661–682.

Turner, Christy G., II and Jacqueline A. Turner. 1992b "On Peter Y. Bullock's 'A Reappraisal of Anasazi Cannibalism'," *Kiva* 58, No 2: 189–201.

Tuzin, Donald. 1983. "Cannibalism and Arapesh Cosmology: A Wartime Incident with the Japanese," in Paula Brown and Donald Tuzin, eds., *The Ethnography of Cannibalism*. Washington, DC: Society for Psychological Anthropology, pp 61–71.

Tyson, J. 1986. *World Peace and World Government: From Vision to Reality: A Bahá'í Approach*. London: G. Ronald.

United Nations Economic Commission for Latin America and the Caribbean, and United Nations Population Fund. 1993. *Population, Social Equity, and Changing Production Patterns*, 3rd ed. Santiago, Chile: United Nations Economic Commission for Latin America and the Caribbean, Latin American Demographic Centre.

United States Commission to the International Peace Conference at the Hague. 1899. *Report of the Commission of the United States of America to the International Peace Conference at The Hague*. Washington, DC.

United States Department of Defense. 1994. *Annual Report of the Secretary of Defense on the Program and Budget for Fiscal Year 1995*. Washington, DC: Government Printing Office.

United States Department of Defense. 1995. *Annual Report of the Secretary of Defense on the Program and Budget for Fiscal Year 1996*. Washington, DC: Government Printing Office.

United States Department of Defense. 1996. *Annual Report of the Secretary of Defense on the Program and Budget for Fiscal year 1997*. Washington, DC: Government Printing Office.

United States Department of State. 1899. *Instructions to the International Peace Conference at the Hague*. Washington, DC.

Upham, Steadman, ed. 1990. *The Evolution of Political Systems: Sociopolitics in Small-Scale Sedentary Societies*. Cambridge, New York: Cambridge University Press.

van Muijen, Marie-Louise. 1993. *"Better Safe than Provocative": A Policy Science Perspective on the West European Non-Provocative Defence Debate in the 1980s*. Amsterdam: VU University Press.

Vandermeersch, Bernard. 1987. "Sépulture et cannibalisme," *Histoire et archéologie* No 114: 56–69.

Vellacott, Jo. 1981. *Bertrand Russell and the Pacifists in the First World War*. New York: Martin's Press.

Vestal, Bedford M. 1991. "Infanticide and cannibalism by male thirteen-lined ground squirrels," *Animal Behaviour* 41, No 6 (June): 1103–1104.

Villa, Paola. 1991. "Middle Pleistocene Prehistory in Southwestern Europe: The State of Our Knowledge and Ignorance," *Journal of Anthropological Research* 47, No 2 (Summer): 193–217.

Villa, Paola. 1992a. "Cannibalism in Prehistoric Europe," *Evolutionary Anthropology* 1, No 3: 93–104.

Villa, Paola. 1992b. "Light on Dark Matters: Review of *Prehistoric Cannibalism at Mancos 5MTUMR-2346*, Tim D. White." *Science* 257, No 5075 (September 4): 1420–1421.

Villa, Paola, Claude Bouville, Jean Courtin, Daniel Helmer, Eric Mahieu, Pat Shipman, Giorgio Belluomini, and Marilí Branca. 1986. "Cannibalism in the Neolithic," *Science* 233, No 4762 (July 25): 431–437.

Villa, Paola, Jean Courtin, and reply by Paul G. Bahn. 1991. "Cannibalism in the Neolithic," *Nature* 351, No 6328 (June 20): 613–614.

Villa, Paola, Jean Courtin, Daniel Helmer, and Pat Shipman. 1987. "Cannibalisme dans la grotte de Fontbrégoua," *Archeologia* No 223 (April): 40–52.

Villa, Paola, Jean Courtin, Daniel Helmer, Pat Shipman, Claude Bouville, and Éric Mahieu. 1986. "Un Cas de cannibalisme au Néolithique: Boucherie et reject de restes humains et animaux dans la grotte de Fontbrégoua à Salernes (Var)," *Gallia préhistoire* 29, fasc. l: 143–171.

Villa, Paola, D. Helmer, and J. Courtin. 1988. "Cannibalism in Old World Prehistory," *Rivista di Antropolgia* 66 (Supplement): 47–64.

Villa, Paola and Eric Mahieu. 1991. "Breakage Patterns of Human Long Bones," *Journal of Human Evolution* 21, No 1 (July): 27–48.

Villeneuve, Roland. 1965. *Histoire du Cannibalisme*. [Paris]: Livre club du libraire.

Virgoe, Roger. 1989. *Private Life in the Fifteenth Century: Illustrated Letters of the Paston Family*. New York: Weidenfeld & Nicolson.

Visotzky, Burton L. 1983. "Most Tender and Fairest of Women: A Study in the Transmission of Aggada," *Harvard Theological Review* 76, No 4 (October): 403–418.

Volhard, Ewald. 1939. *Kannibalismus*. Stuttgart: Strecker und Schröder.

Wagner, James D. 1995. "Egg sac inhibits filial cannibalism in the wolf spider, *Schizocosa ocreata*," *Animal Behaviour* 50, No 2 (August): 555–557.

Wagner, Ulla. 1979. "Review of *The Man-eating Myth*, W. Arens," *Ethnos* 44, Nos. 3–4: 267–270.

Walens, Stanley. 1981. *Feasting With Cannibals: An Essay on Kwakiutl Cosmology*. Princeton, NJ: Princeton University Press.

Walker, R. B. J. and Saul H. Mendlovitz, eds. 1990. *Contending Sovereignties: Redefining Political Community*. Boulder, CO: Lynn Rienner.

Wallace, Henry A. 1948. *Toward World Peace*. New York: Reynal & Hitchcock.

Walls, Susan C. and Andrew R. Blaustein. 1995. "Larval marbled salamanders, *Ambystoma opacum*, eat their kin," *Animal Behaviour* 50, No 2 (August): 537–545.

Walsh, Martin W. 1991. "From Cannibal to Clown: Observations on the Grotesque Mask in Woodland North America," *Journal of Ritual Studies* 5. No 1 (Winter): 27–50.

Waltz, Kenneth N. 1959. *Man, the State, and War: A Theoretical Analysis*. New York: Columbia University Press.

Watson, James L, ed. 1980. *Asian and African Systems of Slavery*. Oxford: Basil Blackwell.

*Webster's Unabridged Dictionary of the English Language*. 1989. New York: Portland House.

Weede, Erich. 1984. "Democracy and War Involvement," *Journal of Conflict Resolution* 28, No 4 (December): 649–664.

Weede, Erich. 1992. "Some Simple Calculations on Democracy and War Involvement," *Journal of Peace Research* 29, No 4 (November): 377–383.

Wehberg, Hans. 1918. *The Problem of an International Court of Justice*, trans. Charles G. Fenwick. Oxford: The Clarendon Press.

Weitekamp, Elmar G. M. and Hans-Jürgen Kerner eds. 1994. *Cross-National Longitudinal Research on Human Development and Criminal Behavior*. Dordecht, Boston: Kluwer Academic Publishers.

Wendt, Astrid. 1989. *Kannibalismus in Brasilien: eine Analyse europäischer Reiseberichte und Amerika-Darstellungen für die Zeit zwischen 1500 und 1654.* Frankfurt am Main, New York: P. Lang.

Wenke, Robert J. 1980. *Patterns in Prehistory: Mankind's First Three Million Years.* Oxford, New York: Oxford University Press.

Westermarck, Edward. 1970. *Ethical Relativity.* Westport, CT: Greenwood Press.

Weston, Burns H., ed. 1990. *Alternative Security: Living Without Nuclear Deterrence.* Boulder, CO: Westview Press.

Wheeler, Valerie and P. Esainko. 1983. "Bogus Cannibal: Epithets as Social Boundaries," Women in Anthropology: Symposium Papers 1979 and 1980, No. 16. Sacramento, CA: Sacramento Anthropological Society, California State University, Sacramento, pp 94–106.

Whiffen, Thomas. 1915. *The North-West Amazons: Notes of Some Months Spent Among Cannibal Tribes.* New York: Duffield.

White, Archer M. 1895. *Outlines of Legal History.* London: S. Sonnenschein.

White, Luise. 1993. "Vampire Priests of Central Africa: African Debates about Labor and Religion in Colonial Northern Zambia," *Comparative Studies in Society and History* 35, No 4 (October): 746–772.

White, T. D. 1985. *Acheulian Man in Ethiopia's Middle Awash Valley: The Implications of Cutmarks on the Bodo Cranium.* Amsterdam: Stichting Nederlands Museum voor Anthropologie en Praehistorie.

White, Tim D. 1992. *Prehistoric Cannibalism at Mancos SMTUMR-2346.* Princeton, NJ: Princeton University Press.

White, Timothy D., Nicholas Toth, Philip G. Chase, G. A. Clark, Nicholas J. Conrad, Jill Cook, F. d'Errico, Randolph E. Donahue, Robert H. Gargett, Giacomo Giacobini, Anne Pike-Tay and Alan Turner. 1991. "The Question of Ritual Cannibalism at Grotta Guattari [and comments and replies]," *Current Anthropology* 32, No 2 (April): 118–138.

Whitehead, Alfred North. 1933. *Adventures of Ideas.* New York: The Macmillan Co.

Whitehead, Neil L. 1984. "Carib Cannibalism: The Historical Evidence," *Journal de la Société des Américanistes* 70: 69–87.

Whitehead, Neil L. 1990. "The Snake Warriors—Sons of the Tiger's Teeth: A Descriptive Analysis of Carib Warfare ca. 1500–1820," in Jonathan Haas, ed., *The Anthropology of War.* Cambridge, New York: Cambridge University Press, pp 146–170.

Whittle, Will. 1984. *How to Stop Believing in War: Religion and the Politics of War and Peace.* Los Altos, CA: New World Library.

Wickham, Harvey. 1970. *The Unrealists: James, Bergson, Santayana, Einstein, Bertrand Russell, John Dewey, Alexander and Whitehead.* Freeport, NY: Books for Libraries Press.

Wieseltier, Leon. 1989. "Spoilers at the Party," *National Interest* No 17 (Fall): 12–16.

Wilson, George Grafton, ed. 1915. *The Hague Arbitration Cases: Compromis and awards, with maps, in cases decided under the provisions of the Hague conventions of 1899 and 1907 for the pacific settlement of international disputes and texts of the conventions.* Boston, London: Ginn and Co.

Wissinger, Scott A. 1992. "Niche Overlap and the Potential for Competition and Intraguild Predation Between Size-Structured Populations," *Ecology* 73, No 4 (August): 1431–1444.

Wolf, Reinhard, Erich Weede, Andrew J. Enterline, Edward D. Mansfield, and Jack Snyder. 1996. "Correspondence: Democratization and Danger of War," *International Security* 20, No 4 (Spring): 176–207.

Wolfgang, Marvin E. and Franco Ferracuti. 1982. *The Subculture of Violence: Towards an Integrated Theory in Criminology.* Beverly Hills: Sage Publications.

Wolfram, Herwig. 1988. *History of the Goths*, rev. ed., trans. Thomas J. Dunlap. Berkeley: University of California Press.

Wolpert, Stanley A. 1982. *A New History of India*, 2nd ed. Oxford: Oxford University Press.

Wood, Alan. 1958. *Bertrand Russell: The Passionate Skeptic.* New York: Simon and Schuster.

Wright, Quincy. 1964. *A Study of War*, abr. Louise Leonard Wright. Chicago: University of Chicago Press.

Wright, William E. 1966. *Serf, Seigneur, and Sovereign: Agrarian Reform in Eighteenth-Century Bohemia.* Minneapolis: University of Minnesota Press.

Wrigley, E. A. 1969. *Population and History.* New York: McGraw-Hill.

Xanthakou, Margarita. 1988. *Cendrillon et les sœurs cannibales: de la stakhtobouta maniote (Grèce) à l'approche comparative de l'anthropophagie intraparentale imaginaire.* Paris: Editions de l'Ecole des hautes études en sciences sociales.

Yan, Guiyun, Lori Stevens, and Jos J. Schall. 1994. "Behavioral Changes in *Tribolium* Beetles Infected With a Tapeworm: Variation in Effects Between Beetle Species and Among Genetic Strains," *American Naturalist* 143, No 5 (May): 830–847.

Yengoyan, Aram A. 1991. "Evolutionary Theory in Ethnological Perspectives," in A. Terry Rambo and Kathleen Gillogly, eds., *Profiles in Cultural Evolution.* Ann Arbor: University of Michigan, pp 3–21.

Yoon, Carol Kaesuk. 1992. "In Some Species, Eating Your Own Is Good Sense: In Some Species, Cannibalism Is Good Sense," *New York Times*, September 29, C1, C8.

Young, Katharine. 1992. "Visuality and the Category of the Other: The Cannibal Tours of Dean MacCannell and Dennis O'Rourke," *Visual Anthropology Review* 8, No 1 (March): 92–96.

Zaïonchkovskiï, Petr Andreevich. 1978. *The Abolition of Serfdom in Russia*, ed. and trans. Susan Wobst. Gulf Breeze, FL: Academic International Press.

Zanjani, Sally. 1984. "Paiute Revenge: Grisly Crime Brought Threat of Massacre," *American West* 21 (July–August): 52–56.

Zanocco, G. 1973. "Reflections on a Theme: A Revision of the Concept of Psychopathic Personality," (Ital.). *Rivista di Psichiatria* 8, No 6: 633–649.

Zubrow, Ezra B. W., ed. and School of American Research (Santa Fe, NM). 1976. *Demographic Anthropology: Quantitative Approaches.* Albuquerque: University of New Mexico Press.

## About the Author

*Randall Caroline Watson Forsberg* (1943–2007) was born in Huntsville, Alabama, and educated at Barnard College in New York City, where she majored in English. She began her career as an analyst of military policy at the Stockholm International Peace Research Institute in 1968. In 1974, she moved to Cambridge, Massachusetts, to study at the Massachusetts Institute of Technology, where she would eventually receive her PhD. In 1979, she founded the Institute for Defense and Disarmament Studies and drafted the Call to Halt the Nuclear Arms Race, a manifesto that helped launch the Nuclear Weapons Freeze Campaign. In 1982, the campaign organized what was then the largest political demonstration in U.S. history in New York's Central Park. Forsberg was a MacArthur Fellow and a member of the Director's Advisory Committee of the U.S. Arms Control and Disarmament Agency. She wrote or cowrote several books and was granted honorary doctorates from the University of Notre Dame and Governors State University. At the time of her death at age sixty-four she held the Anne and Bernard Spitzer Chair in Political Science at The City College of New York.

# About the Editors

*Matthew Evangelista* is President White Professor of History and Political Science and former chair of the Department of Government at Cornell University, where he also directed the Judith Reppy Institute for Peace and Conflict Studies. As an undergraduate at Harvard he worked as a student intern at Randall Forsberg's Institute for Defense and Disarmament Studies, collecting data on Soviet military capabilities in the years after World War II. He wrote his honors thesis on that topic under Forsberg's supervision while she was a graduate student at MIT and revised it as his first academic publication for the journal *International Security*. He has since published five single-authored books, seven edited or coedited volumes, and more than one hundred articles.

*Neta C.* Crawford is Professor and Chair of the Department of Political Science at Boston University and codirector of the Costs of War Project at Brown University. As an undergraduate at Brown, she worked as an intern and then a staff member for the Institute for Defense and Disarmament Studies in the early and mid 1980s, first as a member of the Nuclear Weapons Freeze Campaign, then on the World Weapon Database project, for which she authored her first book, *Soviet Military Aircraft*, published in 1987. She contributed to the *Arms Control Reporter*, also published by IDDS, for a number of years while she was in graduate school at MIT.

# Index

Tables are indicated by a "*t*" after the page number.